THE LAST
OF MY
MANY
FRIENDSHIPS

THE LAST
OF MY
MANY
FRIENDSHIPS

Rev. Msgr. Francis A. Galles

Library of Congress Control Number: 2017913138
ISBN: Hardcover   978-1-5434-4469-8
                 Softcover   978-1-5434-4470-4
                 eBook   978-1-5434-4652-4

Print information available on the last page.

Rev. date: 09/13/2017

To order additional copies of this book, contact:
Xlibris
1-888-795-4274
www.Xlibris.com
Orders@Xlibris.com
553896

THE LAST OF MY MANY FRIENDSHIPS

Author Description

Rev. Msgr. Francis A. Galles was born in Iona, Minnesota on March 8, 1927 to Charles and Virginia (Boltz) Galles. He completed his studies at Loras College in Dubuque, Iowa; the Catholic University in Washington, D.C.; and the Gregorian University in Rome. On December 20, 1952, Monsignor Galles was ordained to the priesthood at the Basilica of St. John Lateran in Rome by His Eminence Clement Cardinal Micara. Monsignor Galles' assignments as Parochial Vicar were at St. John Nepomucene in Winona and St. Pius X in Rochester. As Pastor, he served at St, Francis Xavier in Windom, St. Augustine in Jeffers, St. Columban in Preston, St. Lawrence O'Toole in Fountain, and St. Patrick in Lanesboro, Other notable assignments include Religion Instructor at Cotter High School in Winona; Assistant Editor of The Courier; Diocesan Director for Family Life and the Spiritual Renewal Program; Spiritual Director for Immaculate Heart of Mary Seminary in Winona for three years and the North American College in Rome for nine years; Advocate and Notary for the Tribunal; Junior Clergy Examiner; Chaplain for the Sisters of St. Francis Motherhouse in Rochester; and Parochial Administrator for St. Columban in Preston, St. Lawrence O'Toole in Fountain, St. Ann in Slayton, St Mary in Lake Wilson, St. Ignatius in Spring Valley, St. Finbarr in Grand Meadow, and St. Patrick in LeRoy. In 1962 he was named Papal Chamberlain by Pope John XXIII and in 1968 he was named Domestic Prelate. On July 1, 1997, Monsignor Galles joined the rank of senior priests of the diocese, and continued to offer daily Mass several days a week at St. Columban Church, Preston, where he still lives, and also fills in at parishes throughout the Diocese on occasions.

Msgr. Francis Galles

Foreword

If Jesus had lived to my age (90 years) I think he might have written his autobiography. Unfortunately, however, he was killed by those he had come to save. Fortunately four of his disciples wrote up the story of his life, and gave us the four Gospels which are a marvelous account of his life and his teaching. We are tremendously indebted to Matthew, Mark, Luke and John who have given us an inspired account of all that Jesus did and taught. Recognizing the great value that a biography or autobiography may have, I decided to write and publish my autobiography.

From a thirty day retreat I made back in 1977 I learned that an autobiography may not only be a blessing to the readers of it, but also to the author. The healing I experienced through the 800 pages I wrote at that time and shared with my director convinced me that the writing of an autobiography can be a blessing to the author, perhaps more than to later readers. I am so convinced of the benefit the author of an autobiography may receive that I would encourage parents and teachers to teach children, perhaps, by the age of eight or ten to begin to write a diary or journal.

Very helpful to me in writing my autobiography was the practice I began about 1949 (When I was 22 years old) of keeping a journal or appointment book in which I kept a record of all the persons I met or places where I travelled, and things I saw, and reflections that seemed to be significant.

In the course of writing my autobiography I became more aware of the many people who have had a significant role in my life and development. More important, I have discovered at a deeper level how important in my life has been the friendship I have developed with Jesus. I am convinced that Jesus has had a very important part in bringing into my life the many people who have touched and transformed my life. That is why I consider Jesus the first and greatest of all my friends.

I heartily agree with St. Paul when he wrote to the Corinthians: "Brothers, you are among those called. Consider your situation. Not many of you are wise, as men account wisdom, not many are influential, and surely not many are well born. God chose those whom the world considers absurd to shame the wise; he singled out the weak of this world to shame the strong. He chose the worlds's lowborn and despised, those who count for nothing, to reduce to nothing those who were something: so that mankind can do no boasting before God. God it is who has given you life in Christ Jesus. He has made him our wisdom and also our justice, our sanctification, and our redemption. This is just as you find it written, "Let him who would boast, boast in the Lord." (I Cor. 1:26 - 31)

I) <u>Introduction</u>

The best scientific evidence today would seem to indicate that the dust, out of which I was created, originated in a cataclysmic explosion that took place in the universe over fifteen billion years ago. Whether God created an original mass of material long before this explosion took place, I do not think we presently know, but, for this story, I am content to trace my origin and history back fifteen billion years ago!

When I was ordained, over 65 years ago, it was generally thought that the human race originated about 4000 years ago and that the earth was probably created at about the same time. A homily I once gave was based on a reading from the Book of the Prophet, Daniel (Dn. 12:1-3), and a reading from the Holy Gospel according to Mark (Mk. 13:24-32). Both of these readings, in apocalyptic terms, speak of the end time of the world, as we know it. In the homily I reflected with the congregation on how greatly our knowledge has developed even in the 90 years that I have lived.

Some 90 years ago, God breathed into a tiny portion of this 15 billion year old dust. With his breath I became a living person in my mother's womb. In the homily, I reflected with the congregation about the end time of my life and of the lives of all, celebrating with me, whether the dust out of which we have been made will live forever as "an everlasting horror and disgrace," or whether we shall be like "those who lead the many to justice" and "shall be like the stars forever."

After Mass, I was invited by Mary Whalen to attend a brunch served by the American Veterans at Spring Valley. Another dear friend of mine, Arlette Kvam, who had attended the Mass at Grand Meadow the night before, came back to join me for brunch. When the brunch closed down, Arlette and I went to the indoor room of the A&W Drive Inn for a root beer and ice cream. As usual, Arlette and I had a long visit that went on until 3:30 that afternoon.

At one point in our long and interesting conversation, I mentioned that I had been thinking about writing my autobiography. I told about how I had debated for quite some time about whether I should spend my retirement years writing my autobiography. To what purpose would it be? Have I learned anything in my 90 years that would be worthwhile for anyone to spend time reading? Even if no one ever read my autobiography, would the gathering of my life experiences have sufficient value for me, personally, to spend that much time on such a project?

From an experience I had in 1977 when I made a 30-day Ignatian retreat by the ocean at Gloucester, Massachusetts, I knew well the value of reflecting on one's life experience and writing about it. I wrote 800 pages about my life. The occasion for this retreat was my 25th anniversary of ordination as a priest and my 50th year of life. The healing I went through during that retreat has convinced me of the value of writing one's life, especially if you share it with another as I did with my Director during that retreat. But I will have more to say about that retreat when the time comes.

My friend, Arlette, knew about that 30-day retreat I had made, and she also knew about many of the other experiences that have been a part of my life. When I mentioned to Arlette that I had been thinking about writing my autobiography, and about the personal reasons that gave me pause, she emphatically insisted that I take out the notebooks, which I had bought for this purpose some time ago, and, closing myself off from the telephone calls, doorbells, the computer and television, begin immediately to draw up an outline and begin anew writing the story of my life.

Arlette, who has had great struggles in her life and has suffered great and many bouts with depression, knows well the value of reflecting intensely on life experiences and sharing it with others.

My high regard for Arlette's intelligence and opinion prompted me to take my notebooks and begin my writing. Though I do not know clearly at this time why I am writing my autobiography, I expect that in the course of reflecting and writing, I will discover the purpose and find the meaning.

I know that I no longer have the good memory that I had in 1977 when I wrote about my first 50 years. But I also have available to me now many appointment books that go back to 1949 when I went to Rome as a student, and many retreat notes and other memory aids that will prove quite helpful. I also have a longer and deeper experience with life that will enable me to improve on my journal and continue and enhance my journey of reflection begun in 1977.

Another great advantage I have at this time is retirement. While I am kept quite busy in my retirement, I find that I do have considerable periods of time, which I, unfortunately, tend to waste somewhat with too much television, cooking and eating and taking catnaps.

Though I retired from active priestly ministry in 1997 (20 years ago), I do offer Mass at St. Columban Church in Preston, MN, twice a week, every Wednesday and Thursday. Many weekends, I am offering Masses in parishes, filling in where I am needed. I am also quite active in the Preston Area Art Council. We are presently engaged in trying to produce a 30-foot artistic metal trout, since Preston is considered to be the trout capital of the United States. But, in spite of these and other activities, I still have considerable time to reflect and write about the life with which God has blessed me.

II) <u>Family Background:</u>

Life could have taken many different turns depending on decisions of my forbearers and my own decisions. The background of my parents, especially my mother's side, is I think quite unusual. My mother, Virginia Boltz, born April 26, 1888, weighing six pounds at birth, was the 18th child of her parents, and a twin. Her twin brother who weighed ten pounds at birth died shortly after being born.

My grandparents on my mother's side were Henri Boltz, born December 3, 1838, in Budler, Luxembourg, dying in 1896, and Anna Marie Kolkes, born in 1846 in Waldbilling, Luxembourg, dying July 2, 1920. They were married on July 4, 1866, in Budler. My grandmother was apparently the dominant personality in the marriage. My father often spoke of his love for his mother-in-law.

When my mother was about three years old, the family, with eight children, joined a group of fifty families who emigrated from Luxembourg to Argentina and arrived March 24, 1891. They had been promised machinery, cattle, food etc. and when they arrived they found they had nothing. Conditions were so bad that my grandparents and their children soon returned to Luxembourg.

I can imagine that journey on the ocean in those days probably took about a month. Because pregnant women especially often had trouble on the ship to keep food down, grandmother asked the captain if she could go into the scullery, and she prepared what she called "Bray", a kind of custard, and this went well with the pregnant passengers. This makes me think that grandma was a dominant person.

Frank, one of my mother's brothers, had emigrated to America and settled in Nebraska. I think he may have told his family back in Luxembourg that Nebraska, especially along the Niabrara River was similar to Luxembourg. And so when my mother was about five or six years old, the family pulled up stakes again and emigrated to Nebraska. Being able to travel that much in so short a time indicated to me that the Boltz family must have had some financial resources.

My mother often told the story about the local Catholic priest who would come to Grandma and tell her of someone who was going to have a baby and there was no one else to help. Grandma would take a bottle of brandy as an anesthetic and ride in her buggy to the sod shanties where most of the people lived and would deliver the baby and take over whatever needed to be done in the household. Grandma gave my dad a scale on which she said she had weighed over one thousand babies she had delivered.

After some time, a doctor came to the little town of Verdel where my mother's family lived. The people, however, continued to call upon grandma, rather than the doctor, because she did better than the doctor did. When the doctor's next-door neighbor called for grandma rather than the doctor, it was the straw that broke the camel's back, and the doctor wanted to prosecute grandma for practicing midwifery without license. The people in the town got together and told the doctor he had 48 hours to get out of the town. Grandma was there before he came and she would be there after he left.

I must tell a story that my dad used to tell about grandma. Once, while she was in Chicago, riding a streetcar or trolley, supporting herself with her hand on the strap hanging from the ceiling, she became terribly embarrassed when she noticed that her bloomers, which were a bit too large, had slipped over her hips and fallen to the floor. Because of her long skirt, her embarrassing situation was not too evident to the other passengers. Had she bent down to draw up her bloomers it would have been very evident to everyone in the area what had happened. Being very enterprising, Grandma simply stepped out of her bloomers, and then to destroy the evidence, she gave a good swift kick to her bloomers, which went flying through the air and landed on the lap of a man sitting away at some distance. Grandma never indicated that the bloomers were hers. I can well imagine how she loved to tell the story. Wouldn't it be interesting to hear the version of this story as told by the man, who had just come into the possession of a woman's bloomers?

Now for a bit of background on my father's side: My grandfather, the son of John and Mary (Guber) Galles, was John W. Galles, who was born July 7, 1851. My grandmother was Margaret Wagner, the daughter of Mike and Mary Wagner. They were married in 1878 and had ten children, namely, John P., Joseph W., Edwin, Charles, Michael, Anna, Mary, Clara, Margaret, and Clem.

My grandfather had a strong temper and was very difficult to get along with. My dad, however, managed to get along quite well with him. Consequently, when many of the other children had already left home, my grandfather urged my dad to stay with him on the farm and promised that when he (Dad) got married he would start him out farming.

With the aid of my dad and due to certain economic developments in the country, my grandfather became quite wealthy and owned several farms and houses in Remsen, IA. When my dad did marry at the age of 29, instead of starting him out farming as his father had promised, he made a loan to him for, I think, $6000, which was a lot of money at that time. Interest accrued on this loan. My grandma felt so sorry for Dad not getting what had been promised to him that she buried a couple sacks of potatoes in a load of oats that my dad got from his father. Thus, Dad actually paid for the potatoes because they were weighed in with the oats.

Unfortunately, this betrayal by my grandfather had very unfortunate effects on my dad. In later years, when the other children persuaded grandfather to give away some of his money before he died, he would send out a check for several thousand dollars to each of the children and Dad would simply get a letter that stated that this amount was reduced on the amount of debt that he owed. For many years, my father suffered anger and bitterness because of this betrayal and even became alienated from many of his brothers and sisters.

It is very interesting to know how my mother and dad met each other. Dad was living in Remsen, IA, and mother lived in Nebraska. At one time, my grandmother and her daughter, Catherine, came to Remsen to visit some relatives. Dad was with them when they were picking potatoes and Dad saw what a good worker Catherine was. He said to grandma that he wished he could find as a wife a good worker like Catherine. Grandma said, "I have another daughter at home just as good." And so Dad married Virginia.

Mother and Dad married January 23, 1912, at St. Ludger's Church, Creighton, NE, and had ten children. The ten children in the family were: Leona, Lawrence, Eugene, Charles, the twins, Lester and Sylvester, Clara, Gerald, myself (Francis), and Rose Virginia.

My parents began farming in Nebraska, but then moved to Remsen, IA, in 1914, and farmed on the home place for five years. They then moved to Alton, IA, in1918 and farmed there until 1924.

The family moved by train to a farm one mile north of Iona, MN. There they rented 160 acres from Catherine Kilberg, who lived in Washington, DC. John Hanson from Remsen, IA, took care of the farm for her. I was not born until 1927, and so I came to know about the move only by hearing about it from dad and others. I understand that it was rather interesting to have the cattle unloaded from the boxcar of the train and herded a mile north to the farm. At that time, dad had a very vicious bull, but he was exceedingly courageous and, with a ring in the bull's nose, to which was attached a stick, he herded this mean bull all the way to the farm.

My dad was a very good farmer and took exceedingly good care of the farm and buildings. I remember how he transplanted a large number of trees from the grove that was some distance from the house and surrounded the house with these lovely trees. Though dad only went to school two years, and made four grades in two years, he was very intelligent and could do many things other farmers could not do. He was frequently asked to help neighbors dehorn cattle, castrate hogs, butcher, break in horses and do many other things that they were not able to do. It was amazing that my parents were able to support a family of ten children on 160 acres for which they paid rent. We never owned a tractor, but farmed with horses. Mother raised a large garden and chickens and helped on the farm. She was a good milker and could milk a cow by hand better than most men. She probably resented the fact that she had so many children and was a kind of slave to the house and kitchen. Before marriage, her work had been more outside. Her love was expressed by baking, sewing, scrubbing, and so forth. I could probably have used a lot more affection from her rather than all this work. Later in life, I became more reconciled that this was her nature She was very precise and because she worked slowly, she needed time to get everything in order. She probably only felt good when when she had her work under control.

I remember coming down from upstairs often at night, supposedly for a glass of water, at one or two o'clock in the morning, and I would find mother darning stockings at the dining room table. At times, she would fall asleep over her work. I probably was looking for affection. I think I used to worry about mother and feared she might die. She often made us feel guilty that she had so much work. I probably got my gift of precision and neatness from my mother.

Mother was quite rigid and probably somewhat compulsive. She was not too spontaneous. She always wanted to be ready for every occasion. It was important that we made a good appearance in public - especially in regard to being neat and clean. Often, our ears would be checked and washed with spittle as we were in the car and on the way to church. Mother did not reveal her feelings a great deal. She probably covered up a lot of anger and resentment. She carried a bit of a persecution complex. Hardly ever did mother and dad have strong words between them in the children's presence.

Dad was a much more spontaneous and fun-loving person. It was dad that encouraged so much singing in the home. He loved music. I was also very adept at singing at a very early age. My sister, Leona, would play the guitar and I would sing with her, or alone. I can remember they would often ask me to sing "That Little Boy of Mine." The gift of voice and pitch goes back to my home and principally to dad. I often wonder why I did not learn to play the guitar or some other instrument.

Dad also was with us in playing ball. I played softball, but I think I was always somewhat afraid and felt inferior to my older brothers and sisters. Often we were late in coming to supper because of a ball game we had started after work. This would make mother angry.

Most of our entertainment was at home. As a kid, I remember running around the yard with a tire or wagon hoop that we pushed with a crossed stick. We also made stilts, had a swing, and used to make merry go rounds and teeter totters. I guess we had more fun at home than I realized. We didn't have much in the way of toys bought from a store, but we were able to make things that were just as much fun.

About the only toy I had that was bought was an iron truck that dad got for me because he had promised me something if I didn't go to the county fair with the other kids. I also got a train later from my sister, Leona, and her husband, Lloyd, one Christmas. One of my favorite things was scrap wooden blocks that I could use to build things.

The birth of my twin brothers was quite interesting. Mother told dad that she was about to give birth and he ought to call the doctor. He called the doctor, but the doctor did not come, so dad did whatever was necessary to take care of the child that was born - cutting the umbilical cord and so forth. After quite some time, mother told dad that he better call the doctor again; she thought she was going to have another baby. And so she did. Dad called the doctor and told him that he better get out in a hurry because he had started something that he couldn't stop.

I was born March 8, 1927. Apparently, I nearly died when I was six months old. I had whooping cough. A number of times, I would stop breathing and my mother dropped me on the bed and said, "He's gone." Dad came and picked me up by the feet and spanked my butt and after a short time, I again began breathing.

I was very thin and fragile until about the age of ten. What the difficulty was, I don't know. I'm sure we always had plenty of food, but it may be that I did not always eat the food that was most nourishing. Consequently, there were times when I would become very faint. I remember one time standing in the closet quite incapable of moving or doing anything and, at times, at night, I would awake to feel very faint. Mother would then give me homemade bread dipped in milk and I would soon regain my strength. After those early years,

I began to gain weight. When I was only twelve years old, I weighed 145 pounds.

Some of my earliest memories seem to indicate a somewhat contemplative aspect at a very early age. I can remember sitting on the front steps that faced south, in the spring of the year, and enjoy feeling the warmth of the sun and resented when a draft of cool air would blow over me. It seems I simply appreciated the quiet and reflective situation. Or, again, I remember sitting behind and underneath the water reservoir on our cookstove in the kitchen during the winter and here again, it seemed to be the contemplative atmosphere (sacred space) that appealed to me.

As strong as the memory of these contemplative spots was the memory of being bored, that I didn't have anything to do. Maybe this was why I returned to my quiet places. Mother would often suggest work, but that was not what I wanted. I don't remember playing with Gerald and Rosie much - my older brother and sister. I did, perhaps, play house with Rosie some. Gerald seemed to have different interests. He was more bold and inventive. I seem to have been very passive. With six older brothers and two older sisters, I didn't need to organize the ball game. I only would need to fall in and play. This may account for some of my lack of leadership qualities to this day.

I seem to have had a rather fanciful imagination at an early age and did a lot of daydreaming. I think it was the result of some books that I read that I became very interested in flying and imagined myself often piloting a plane. Another rather fanciful daydream I had was running a factory, being the owner and manager. And, strangely enough, this factory was producing toilet paper. And it was very interesting to think of the wood pulp that this paper would be made from and see the rollers through which the pulp would pass and be compressed and cut into toilet paper.

At a very early age, apparently about five, I was very adept at card playing. I was able to play the game Five Hundred with the older members of the family and, apparently, compete very well with them. As a family, we often played cards a great deal. It seems that the family and guests would marvel at the way I could play. Mother, however, disliked us playing cards because there were often squabbles.

I have reflected at considerable length about each of my siblings, how they affected me and how I interacted with them. Each one of them was a very special gift to me.

Beginning with my youngest sister, Rose Virginia, I perhaps had felt love from her more than any other member of my family. I have a number of pictures of the two of us together. Even though I fought with her and was mean to her at times, I think she had a great love for me. She would often want me to play house with her out in our grove. We would make rooms by placing twine string from tree to tree. We also enjoyed playing together on our sack swing and the merry-go-round that we had made. We usually walked together the mile from our home to our school in Iona. I remember one time when I chose Rosie to be on my team for a catechism contest, because I knew she would remember well the responses to many catechism questions.

Rosie's final illness and death most stand out in my mind. Rosie was born on July 27, 1929, and she died Nov 21, 1941. Prior to her death, Rosie came home from school on a Friday, and we noticed that she was now somewhat cross-eyed and, as brothers can do, we razzed her about it, not realizing how serious her illness was. On Saturday, my parents took her to Slayton to see a doctor. The doctor apparently recognizing that her condition was quite serious wanted to put her in the hospital. Since she had not been ill, my parents didn't think that was necessary and Rosie, too, wasn't too eager to go to the hospital. However, on Sunday night, she developed a nose bleed that, in spite of all my parents' efforts, would not stop. Finally, they had to call the doctor to the farm in the middle of the night. By Monday morning, she was taken to the hospital and not expected to live. She lived for seventeen days. During that time, she went blind and was burned by a heating pad when a nurse didn't watch closely enough. I, apparently, didn't go to see her when she was in the hospital, but one evening, she asked specifically that I would come to see her. Lester came and picked me up at the farm and took me to the hospital. I was quite embarrassed to be such a center of attention when I entered her hospital room. Many years later, in a kind of fantasy, I asked Rosie what we talked about that night I came to see her. She said she really didn't remember, but she knew she was grateful that I had come.

During her stay in the hospital, Rosie received seven transfusions of blood. I was apparently considered too young to give blood at that time. It was my brothers and sisters who gave. After each transfusion, Rosie would cough up blood. Finally, my parents, in consultation with Father Paul Britz, our pastor, and the doctor, decided to discontinue transfusions. That must have been a hard decision for my parents to make.

When Rosie died on November 21st, about eleven o'clock at night, I was in her hospital room and standing at the foot of her bed. The room was filled with family and two religious sisters, Sister Mary Jane and Sister Felicia, who were good friends of the family, were leading us in praying the rosary. As I stood at the foot of the bed I could see Rosie's breast heaving as she was gasping for air. Then everything stopped, the heaving of her breast, her gasping for air, and the praying of the rosary . A nurse was called in and checked her and said that she was dead. My sister, Clara, who was standing over by the side wall gave out a bloodcurdling scream. We thought that she'd gone berserk and was very quickly taken out. At an earlier time, she had promised our Lord that, if Rosie lived, she would go into the convent and become a nun. She never remembered any of this event until many years later, when I read to her the journal I had written telling about this event. I expect the experience was so painful for her that she simply buried it in the subconscious.

An indication as to the extent to which I had learned to repress my feelings, is evidenced by the fact that I do not recall crying as I watched my sister die. Neither do I remember crying throughout the time of her funeral.

As was the custom in those days, the wake service for Rosie was held at our home. She was laid out by the undertaker in my parents' bedroom. I seem to recall that, when relatives came for the wake service, while they greeted me they apparently had little sensitivity to the feelings that I must have greatly repressed.

Father Paul Britz, the pastor, celebrated her funeral Mass. I have a written copy of the homily he gave on the occasion. His theme was that God had picked a beautiful flower from the garden of our family at a very early stage, but that she would now show forth all of her beauty in heaven.

I was fourteen years old when Rosie died and it was probably years later when I realized the full extent of the feelings of love that I had for her. I am confident that from her place in heaven, she has assisted me often with her prayers. I don't recall hearing my parents speak much of her or of her death, but I am sure it must have been a very painful event in their lives.

A very beautiful chapter in Rosie's life was her relationship with my brother, Charlie. Being considerably older, Charlie was away from home working for the Schroeder family, our neighbors. Whenever he would come home, Rosie would sit on his lap and cling to him and he to her. It was a thing of beauty to see the relationship the two of them had. But, it was equally sad when Rosie became ill and died that Charlie was now in the Navy, and due to the threat of war with Japan at the time, was unable to get a leave and come home. As painful as his absence must have been for Rosie, it must have been more painful for Charlie to know that she was ill and then to hear of her death and his not being able to be present.

I vividly recalled, many years later, my relationship with Rosie and her death. At that time, I was really moved to tears, which made me aware of the extent to which I had repressed my feelings in my younger days. In fact, when I made a thirty day retreat in 1977 and relived and wrote up my whole life (800 pages), my retreat director, when he saw how much feeling I had repressed, wondered that I hadn't become an alcoholic or a suicide.

My brother, Gerald, was born October 7, 1925. He was quite different then me and I was never very close to him. I don't recall that I ever played much with him. I used to envy the things he would acquire by swapping with kids in school. He would collect lead and sell it to Francis Hartman and, thus, made some spending money. He spent his money freely and seemed to enjoy life more than I did. I was always very saving. I remember being praised because I came back from the County Fair and still had some change left. Gerald had spent all his money in the Erie Diggers. He could risk! I was very cautious. Gerald had old second-hand bicycles and such-like things. I was too timid to weal and deal.

Camilla Galles, Fr. Francis and his mother, Gerald G. Galles, Jr.

Gerald was usually considered the black sheep of the family. Dad seemed to resent his free spirit and tried to break his spirit. Gerald was not to be broken. The more pressure that was brought to bear upon him, the more he resisted.

I felt sorry for him at times, especially when Lester was beating him up in the barn, and his head began to bleed. Dad, too, would take him out to the barn and beat him with a strap when Gerald had done something that dad thought was wrong.

It was especially unfortunate that Dad would put Gerald in competition with me knowing that I would win. At times, when we had company, Dad would have me and Gerald wrestle on the lawn. Though Gerald was stronger than me, I was quite heavy, and I could invariably wrestle Gerald down. However, I always feared that he would get the better of me. Later, when Gerald suffered psychological problems, it became evident that this competition with me in childhood was a factor in his psychological difficulty. How terrible Gerald must have felt when I would constantly overcome him, even though he was a year and a half older than me.

Underneath, I think Gerald had a lot of feeling and was very tender. The fact that children, like my niece, Christie Base, loved him, says something. Women also really loved him, even though he could be both cruel and gentle.

Gerald became very successful later in life as an electrician. My brother, Eugene, who was a Master Electrician, and had introduced Gerald to the field, admired how quickly Gerald could learn a rather complex skill and solve problems quite readily.

Eugene and Evelyn Galles (First wife)

Gerald's later years were very unfortunate, but I will have more about that later.

My sister, Clara, was born April 13, 1923. Though I had very warm feelings toward her, I apparently antagonized her a great deal. She once remarked that no one could make her quite as angry as I could. Again, I don't remember a lot of specific interaction with Clara.

Unfortunately, I think we often razzed her and made jokes about her that were very painful to her. I don't know how many times the story was told of her carrying a bottle of our homemade beer to Iona from our farm to give to Mr. Stoderl, who had done something special for her class and she wanted to show appreciation. The fact that she concealed the bottle in her bloomer and it dropped out at one point gave special poignancy to the story.

Later in life, I was the Mass server at her wedding Mass when she married Morris Crawford.

I visited Clara in her room, one time, when she was especially lonely, pregnant and waiting for Morrie to come home from the service.

I don't remember too many childhood experiences of relating to my twin bothers, Lester and Sylvester. Lester got along with me a lot better than he did with Gerald. I usually did what he told me. Lester was the dominant twin.

I felt a kind of sympathy for Sylvester. He was considered the runt, but in many ways, I think, he was the more feeling person. Lester was always considered the responsible one. He got along well with Dad because he was a hard worker. I remember especially his early rising in the morning, and the way he would get us up at five o'clock in the morning to do chores. It seemed to me there was no need to get up that early in the morning.

I think of Lester plowing a field with a two-bottom plow pulled by five or six horses. Because we didn't have enough money to buy a sufficient amount of oats for the horses, they lacked the strength and energy they might have had if they had more grain to eat. As a result, they would not pull the plow fast enough to do a good job of turning the sod over and pleasing Lester. As a result, Lester would holler and curse and swear at the horses. Like children, the horses became so immune to his shouting that they paid no attention to him.

Sylvester seemed to have more friends than Lester. His friendship with Holly Fitzgerald, a poor kid from town, was deep and beautiful - perhaps similar to my relationship with Jim Larson. I tend to think of Sylvester in relation to the part Indian horse we had that was quite wild and rambunctious, and that he used to like to ride. He was a more fun-loving person than Lester and could get things goofed up. He must have felt the favoritism that was shown to Lester.

I think Sylvester must have worked for the neighbors at a rather early age, and then, later, went into the Navy. It was later, with Lester, that I went on some of my first dates.

My brother, Charlie, was known as Butzie. In my earliest memories of him, he was away from home and working for Schroeders, our neighbors.

I remember the time he as plowing for the neighbors with a tractor, and he let me drive. I did something wrong - perhaps stepped on one brake - and the tractor swung around, went through a fence and landed in the ditch. I expected Charlie to be very angry with me, but he was very sensitive to my feelings and seemed to know how frightened and embarrassed I was.

I also remember the time when I was only five or six years old, and was helping with the milking. I milked only one cow and she had lost milk because I was not strong enough to milk her properly. I used to turn around and get some milk from the cow behind me.

This night, Charlie was home and helped with the milking. He milked the cow behind me and, thus, I was not able to supplement my supply. When it was discovered that I only had about a quart of milk, it was decided that I better wait awhile to help with the milking.

Charlie's beautiful love for Rosie inspired me. I don't think I ever felt jealous. It was just taken for granted that she was his girl, and she would always sit on his lap when he came home.

I think I felt close to Butzie. He always had a twinkle in his eye. I remember the time when he held me and had his girlfriend, Jean Murphy, kiss me. Though I was embarrassed and fought to get away, I really thought she was a beautiful girl and I could have enjoyed her kiss under other circumstances.

I was about twelve years old when Charlie went into the Navy. I remember, especially, his leave home after he had been in many battles in the South Pacific, onboard the aircraft carrier, the USS Enterprise, the most decorated ship of the Second World War. He was quite a hero in my mind when I heard him tell us some of his experiences.

The memory that most stands out in my mind in regard to my brother, Eugene, was the time in our hay loft in the barn, where he had put up a metal tube from one side of the barn to the other. He was going hand over hand on this pipe when it broke, and Eugene dropped about twenty feet into the hay. At first, we thought he had probably broken his neck. Fortunately, his injury was not too serious.

I have few memories of how Eugene touched my life in my early years. It seems that he was away from home working for Charlie Kellen, cutting wood for 25 cents a day. He stands out in my memory as the electrician. He had become an Electrical Journeyman and later a Master Electrician. That was like being educated. He could talk a good line. He seemed daring to me - something like Gerald. He had a motorcycle.

My brother, Lawrence, was the neat one. He sold Fuller brushes for a short time. I remember him as a Nash clothes salesman. Because of his precision and neatness, he could do a good job in measuring and fitting a person with a suit.

Lawrence had a Terraplane car, which he kept in immaculate condition. We had a goat on the farm, and when Lawrence would park his car in the yard and leave, this goat, like a mischievous kid, would jump up on the hood. As soon as Lawrence would come out of the house to drive him away, he would take off and then come back again as soon as Lawrence would leave.

Lawrence seemed to know something about engines and cars. This was quite interesting to me because I can remember, at a rather early age, I bought a large book about gasoline engines and was very interested and fascinated to see how they worked.

Lawrence had a girlfriend by the name of Camilla, who was very attractive to me.

I think I was in high school when I worked for Lawrence one summer. He had now gone into the chicken hatchery business, first at Worthington and then at Adrian. He was quite hard to work for. He never knew when to quit. You would never know when you were going to eat. Marcella, his wife, must have often been frustrated in waiting for him to come to meals.

My oldest sibling, Leona, had a great influence upon me throughout my life, even in my younger years. I think she always liked me, and was very good to me. She, too, would have been working away from home in my early years. She would have been about fourteen years old when I was born. I was about six years old when she got married.

Some of my earliest memories of Leona were her playing the guitar and singing. She would play for me and I would sing.

Leona influenced me most during the summers when I would go to her home at Balaton and spend a week or two. Those were the only real vacations I had in my early years.

It was during one of those vacations that I came to know and love Mulligan Stew. Mother never made Mulligan Stew at home, but in working out for other people Leona had learned how to make Mulligan Stew. Later, when I got older and did some cooking, I learned how to make Mulligan Stew and, to this day, it is still one of my favorite dishes.

Leona was the only person I remember giving me a Christmas present - a train. She was a real sister to me.

III) My First Interactions (Grade School Years)

My grade school years seem to have been very ordinary. There was not much real challenge or excitement in my life during those years. School was no great thrill, but neither was it greatly burdensome.

Sister Amata was very dear to me and a great grace in my first and second years of school. The students from both years were in the same classroom at St. Columba School in Iona, MN. As children often have, I had quite a crush on St. Amata. She was a very young teacher in those days. I was privileged to offer the Mass and officiate at her funeral when she died.

Under Sister Amata, we had a percussion band and I was the director with a baton that dad had made for me.

I remember little about preparing for First Confession and Communion, but both experiences seem to have been characterized principally by fear. The preparation would have consisted mostly in memorizing the Baltimore catechism.

How fear characterized a lot of my early religious formation is evidenced by the very powerful experience I had one time when I was alone in our grove, which was about two thousand feet from our house on the farm.

Suddenly, the thought of the end of the world came upon me. I was so frightened by the thought of being alone, should the end of the world come, that I had to go back to the house to be with someone. This, perhaps, says something about the religious formation that must have been imparted to me.

In addition to conducting our percussion band in the second grade, I also danced the Virginia Reel with Eunice McCormick. We were dressed up as George and Martha Washington. This left a strong impression on me because I was very much attracted to Eunice. She was also very adept at tap dancing.

My second grade class. I am the fourth from the left in the top row

Sister Leonard was my third and fourth grade teacher. I especially remember her being harsh with me for something I did not do. My impression is that I did not like her very much.

Miss Jilk, I think, filled in for part of the fourth grade. I liked her but felt sorry for her because she was new at teaching and she could not keep order. I, too, joined in some of the activity that, at times, made her cry. At the end of the year, when she was leaving, I felt terrible about the way we had treated her, and I wanted to go to her and thank her and apologize. For some reason or other, this didn't work out. Many years later, I did get to meet her again before she died.

It was probably about this time that Joe Disch and Francis (Fat) Hartman began bullying me. And so, bullying is not just a modern problem. Both Joe and Francis were older than my other classmates. Most of the other fellows knuckled under to them, but I would answer them back even though they would beat my upper arm till I had black and blue marks. They were too big for me to attempt to really take them on.

Jim Larson continued as a very good friend of mine. I can't remember which grade it was when his family moved away from Iona. He came back again later in high school.

Sister Jolenta was my fifth grade teacher. She was quite fat, but jovial. I remember, especially, the time when I brought our zither from home to school to be used for a play. Sister claimed that a string snapped on it while it was just sitting there. I guess I found it hard to believe that. She later left the religious life.

It was the fifth or sixth grade that Sister Vitalian (later Clara) came to teach us history. She was an excellent teacher and a fine person. She gave me a considerable appreciation of Native American culture. We would even imitate some of their art work.

I also had Sister Alena and Sister Aloyse for part of my sixth grade.

We used to have the Sisters come to our home for a dinner about once a year. This was always a big occasion.

My Dad's brother, Uncle John, and his sons, Bill and Johnny, came to our home quite often. Their visits affected me and all the family. It must have been quite a burden to feed and care for all those extra people. Sometimes, they would stay for a month, or longer, and go out to play for dances. Bill, especially, seemed to be a good fellow and, later, I liked his wife, Evelyn.

Uncle John was quite a politician and got me interested in Fr. Charles Coughlan, from Michigan, and the Townsend retirement plan. According to this plan, all senior citizens over 65 years of age would receive $200 a month from the government. However, they would then have to retire so that more jobs would be created for younger people.

Uncle John always seemed to have some plan in mind to make the world better. He was a good talker and could be quite convincing. He seemed more educated than dad because he read a lot. His housekeeper (I think her name was Teresa) was also his mistress. I guess I worried about Uncle John's salvation. He didn't seem to be a churchgoing man, but he was a good and kind person.

There was a period of time when my Dad also did not go to church. I don't know what was behind this. Could it be that he was going through some personal crisis in his life? I wish he would have shared this with us. I feared he might go to hell if he died.

Later, Dad returned to church again, and even went to daily Mass when we lived in town. I am not sure just how dad's falling away from the Church affected me. It probably made me feel more distant from dad. It was like a rebellion on his part. Dad could often be quite critical about certain of our pastors, thinking that they lived too high and wanted too much money for the parish.

My Dad's brother, Clem, and his wife, Viola, were also frequent visitors to our home. Uncle Clem was a great tenor singer and was very well liked. My dad was not angry with him as he was with most of his other brothers and sisters.

Harry Wagner, a cousin, and his wife, were occasional visitors to our home. Their daughter was Vera, who was a very close friend with my sister, Clara. Mrs. Wagner was a French woman, whom Harry married after meeting her in the first World War. She always gave us the impression that the French are quite sophisticated.

My mother's sister, Catherine, and her daughter, Lila, and her sons, Lawrence, Fred and Gilbert were also occasional visitors to our home.

IV) The Beginning of a Vocation

I received considerable amount of encouragement, and even pressure, from the Franciscan Sisters, who were my teachers through twelve grades of school, to go on to high school with the idea of becoming a priest. None of my brothers and sisters before me had gone to high school. The usual thinking, at that time, was that you did not need to go to high school, to be a farmer. I remember Sister Alvina, my eighth grade teacher, in trying to persuade me to go on for more schooling, asking: "What do you want to do? Do you want to be a farmer all your life?

My sister, Clara, seems to have been the only member of my family, who ardently wanted to go to high school, and even cried when my father refused her. Later in her life, she did go on and get a GED certificate for taking correspondence courses. Clara had a phenomenal spelling ability, which works to her advantage today in playing Scrabble, which she loves.

The Sisters frequently speaking about the religious vocation and encouraging me to become a priest did influence my decision. It was probably good that my parents never pushed me or even encouraged me in that direction.

Reading the lives of some of the saints or other holy persons affected me.

I was inspired and considerably influenced by reading the lives of St. Francis of Assisi, my patron saint, St. Bernard of Clairvaux, Brother Andre Bessette up in Canada, and Charles de Foucould. I seemed to lean toward the life of a hermit.

I had a great fear of responsibility, at this time in my life. There were occasions when I thought it would be good to have a crippling disease, or an accident that would put me in a condition where nothing would be expected of me.

However, being of Luxembourg background which is close to the German, I also felt a strong need to do something in my life that would make a difference in the world. The priesthood seemed to be a rather ideal way to make a difference, to do something worthwhile.

I am somewhat surprised, now, when I look back, that it seems a personal relationship with Jesus was not a strong factor in my decision to become a priest. Now, after 65 years of being a priest, I have a strong desire for a very personal relationship with Jesus. Would that I might have a very dramatic experience of Jesus as St. Paul did at the Damascus Gate. Ever after that experience Jesus was very real to Paul. So much so that he could say, "I live now, not I, but Christ lives within me."

One of the greatest satisfactions of my life is to have someone open up and reveal his/her life to me. While I know a great deal about Jesus' life and his love for me, I still long for signs of his presence and his love.

Perhaps the way in which I most know Jesus, personally, is through the way he has made his presence felt through the things that I have been able to do and to say that I can only attribute to Jesus being within me and working through me with His Spirit.

Hopefully, someday, that personal presence of Jesus will become so strong in my life that it will be the sole source of my motivations.

When Jesus becomes the most real person in my life, his presence will be my motivation to avoid all sin.

When the personal presence of Jesus becomes more real to me, I will become much more zealous to do good and to fulfill his will.

My family readily went along with the idea that I go to high school. I don't remember talking much about it. My sister, Rosie, would probably have gone to high school also, if she lived.

I think I liked high school a bit more than grade school. I began losing weight when I started high school. I weighed 145 pounds when I was 12 years old. I have a picture of me at that time. I loved to eat. It was probably a desire to be more popular with girls that prompted me to lose weight when I was in high school.

I went to my first public dance at Slayton, MN, with my brother, Lester. I did dance at card parties we had at the parish. Marion Ehleringer was the first person I danced with and she somewhat taught me how to dance. I was a sophomore, about 15 years old, when I went to that public dance at Slayton. I danced with Alice Scully and was bold enough to ask if I might take her home. Lester probably gave me encouragement there. She refused saying she was going home with her brother and sisters.

For days after that dance I was in a cloud—even though Dad had strong words to express his disapproval of my going to a dance so young. I had all kind of fantasies about Alice Scully. I could savor the smell of her lilac perfume. All through high school, I had a crush on her. During our dance together, I remember how she kept rubbing her finger against mine. I remember, well, a red dress she often wore. I really don't think she had much interest in me.

At this stage in my life, I now really began to become concerned about my appearance. I remember how often I combed my hair, and even tried to make it wavy. It seems that when I combed it a certain way that a bit of a kink would come into it.

All my brothers were now going into the Navy. Charlie had enlisted in 1939. Sylvester and Lester followed. Gerald was still too young to enlist, but Dad figured he could not continue farming with him, because they did not get along. I wasn't much help, because I was going to school. So Dad decided to sell out and move into town. I remember practically nothing about the farm sale, but it went well because prices were good, as a result of the war.

My brother, Charles, and myself when I was about 12 years old

Since it was during the war I was able to get a job during the summer working with an extra-gang on the Milwaukee Railroad. My friend, Hank Ehleringer heard about the job and got me in on it together with him.

This extra gang consisted of about 80 high school students. We rode about an hour on the bus each day to work. The work consisted in raising and graveling railroad ties. For the first time in my life I got a Social Security card. I got paid 64 cents an hour in the beginning and we worked ten hour days counting our travel time on the bus.

The foreman wanted the gravel to be about a half an inch from the top of the tie in the center and about an inch toward the ends of the tie. I apparently did such a good job that the foreman asked me to follow after the other crew members and clean up where the others had not done a good job.

Later in the summer an opening came so that I was able to run an electric tamper rather than gravel. This job paid four cents an hour more. The first day my hands would get so sore and stiff that I would have to slide them off the end of the tamper to open them.

I didn't think I would be able to take another day of this. Fortunately the next day it rained and we didn't have to run the tampers. When we returned to work with the tampers my hands were sufficiently healed so that I was able to carry on the job without difficulty.

Hank Ehleringer and I rented a room in Pipestone and it was a good experience for me to be living away from home and earning my own money.

Toward the end of the summer an opening came to work on a regular section gang on the same Milwaukee Railroad at Iona. Hank and I now took this job. We could now live at home and worked a regular eight-hour day.

I can remember that while working with the Section crew at Iona I though at times that might be what I would to do the rest of my life. It was nice to be able to work an eight-hour day and then come back home and have no other responsibilities. Remember as I said earlier I had a fear of responsibility. This seemed to be the easy way out. Thank God I never followed that inclination!

Dad was able to buy a big two story, 14 room house for $3,500 with four lots, a barn, and a chicken house. It was located across the street from the Catholic school and church, and so was very convenient. We did a lot of refinishing inside. The upstairs, we rented out. It was a Sears Roebuck house, which had been shipped out from Chicago. It was very elegant, and very comfortable.

After we got settled into our house in town, my life really became ideal for a student. I had my own very lovely room. I wasted a lot of time in the process, but I usually studied from 7:00 until 11:00 p.m. with no distractions or farm chores to do. Consequently, I did well in school. I excelled especially in declamatory contest in St. Columba High School and with other schools in the area.

During much of my high school years, I was very concerned about my acceptance by my peers. The Sisters, of course, thought highly of me. Some of my teachers in high school were Sisters Felicia, Mary Edward, Gonzaga, Camilla, Arthur, Mary Clare, and Gertrude Ann. I remember coming home from dances feeling very depressed and angry, often determining I would never go back to another dance. I don't know just why this was so. I was a quite good dancer. I don't know if my feelings were to girls turning me down, or my not having the courage to ask for a dance, and expecting the girls to come to me. I think many of the boys didn't care to dance, and I didn't want to be the only one to break rank.

I remember Fr. Paul Britz criticized Rusty Schoo once for dancing too close to me.

Hank Ehleringer and the Ehleringer twins, Viola and Leola, were important to me in my high school years. They just lived a couple of houses down the street from our house. We didn't have a car, but Ehleringers would often invite me along for dances or movies or other events. I used to dance a lot with the twins, and they, together with Bernetta Koob, taught me how to play tennis, and I was quite good at it and enjoyed the game for many years. I really had warm feelings for Leola, especially. She used to snuggle up so close to me when we would dance. They were about four years older than I was. I guess that is what prevented me from asking Leola for a date, but I would have liked to.

On June 1, 1944, my mother and I went to Los Angeles to see Aunt Katie. Aunt Katie had been very helpful to our family during the years when we were quite poor. She had a position in the Good Shepherd Convent where by she had contact with movie stars and wealthy people. Oftentimes, she would send us boxes of clothing and other things that were very useful for all the members of my family. Through my Aunt Katie (Sister Mary of St. Louis), in the Good Shepherd Convent in Los Angeles, a Mr. and Mrs. Milton and Genevieve Vedder, offered to pay for my education should I decide to be a priest. This had some influence on my deciding to go into the seminary.

During the month we were in Los Angeles Aunt Katie arranged for us to meet many of her friends and they enabled us to see many of the places of interest in and around Los Angeles.

A more important event happened in the middle of my senior year in high school. The Second World War was now on and five of my brothers had enlisted in the Navy. One of my brothers, Sylvester, was killed on the aircraft carrier, the U.S.S. Franklin.

If I went into the service, I would have wanted to go in to the Navy. However, you had to enlist before you were 18 years old if you wanted to choose the branch of service you preferred. Otherwise, the government could put you into the infantry or wherever they most needed recruits.

So, now I had to decide before my 18th birthday, which was in March, whether I was going to enlist in the Navy, or leave high school in the middle of my senior year, and go into a recognized seminary so that I would be deferred from the draft as a student studying for the priesthood. In the back of my mind was also the offer from Mr. and Mrs. Vedder.

I decided to speak with Sister Mary Clare about this. I respected her very much. I found she was a good counselor. She never gave answers, but she helped me to talk it out and look at all the facets.

After a long discussion, and when we were about to conclude, the pastor, Fr. Stephen Majerus, came into the school, and Sister Mary Clare asked if I would now like to talk to him about it. I don't recall that I had discussed this with anyone else, other than Sr. Mary Clare, not even my parents.

I briefly repeated for Fr. Majerus what I had discussed with Sr. Mary Clare. Fr. Majerus suggested that I go into the seminary. I could always change direction if I decided that priesthood was not my calling.

Now the wheels began to move very quickly. Fr. Majerus advised Bishop Leo Binz of my inclination. He gave me three choices as to the seminary where I could go: Loras College in Dubuque, IA, St. Mary's College in Winona, MN, or Crosier Seminary in Onamia, MN. He himself seemed to prefer that I go to Loras College. I took the leap and decided to try my vocation at Loras College.

If I were to make that decision today, it would be quite easy and I might decide after three or four days. But when you are a youth not accustomed to giving away your life, this is a serious and challenging decision.

There is a very elaborate system of journaling developed by Ira Progoff. One of the 16 or more methods of journaling that Ira proposes is to view a time in your life where you came to a fork where you could go right or left. You now write about what might have happened in your life, if you had gone the other way - the way you did not choose.

If I had gone into the Navy rather than into the seminary, I think I probably would have married too young and who knows what the consequences would have been. As a result of the way I chose I received a good education, a great deal of travel and many friendships all over the world.

It was a quite moving experience for me to leave high school in the middle of my senior year. I was to begin the second semester at Loras College in February.

I don't remember too much about talking this over with my parents. They sort of stayed in the background, in regard to my vocation, and left me free, but they must have been proud and happy. Mother had, of course, been in communication with my aunt, Sister Mary of St. Louis, who also was overjoyed.

I broke down and cried when my nephew and niece, Dale and Shirley Buse, came over to our house from school to say goodbye to me. I felt a real pain at parting and going into the unknown. I don't know why I was moved so much by their coming to say goodbye. My classmates and other high school students also came to our house to say goodbye.

While in high school I had two steady girlfriends, Delphine Voss and Sylvia Platt. I was still going steady with Sylvia Platt when I prepared to leave high school and go to college. Sylvia Platt was among the high school students who had come to say goodbye. I didn't know if I should kiss her goodbye in front of my schoolmates. I guess I didn't, but I did say a special word of goodbye to her. It had all been handled rather quietly at school. There was no big fanfare.

Mother had, of course, helped me pack my suitcase. When the time came to leave home and to board the train at Iona that would take me to Dubuque, I don't think I cried as I said goodbye to Mother. I probably tried to get the parting over with as quickly as possible because, as usual, I had all my feelings bottled up inside. It seems that, whenever I faced a parting situation, I tried to get it over with as quickly as possible, but it was unknown to me at the time that I was reluctant to let out my feelings.

Dad went along with me on the train to Dubuque. I thought this was nice of him. I wonder what he felt. Like me he was usually reluctant to show his feelings.

I had never travelled on a train other than the bit when I worked on the railroad at Pipestone one summer during high school.

When we got to Loras College, Dad had a terrible cold and Sister Leota, who did house cleaning at the College put him to bed for a couple of days. I ran into a difficulty the first week I was at Loras College. Some of my new classmates graciously invited me to go to a movie with them. After the movie, they suggested we stop for some ice cream.

When we got back to the college we had to sign in and enter the time of our return. The next morning, Monsignor Breen, the Dean of Discipline called me down to his office. He told me that he observed I had returned to the College after midnight. He asked if I knew that freshman were to be in before midnight. I told him I didn't know that and I just assumed the other fellows would know what the rules are. Msgr. Breen asked if I had a rule book and I said I did. He said that was all he needed to know and that I was campused for a month, which meant I could not leave the college campus for a month. With that he dismissed me.

I felt terrible thinking I had already gotten into trouble during my first week at college. This made me resolve that I would never break another rule. So fearful was I about breaking a rule that throughout most of the rest of my seminary life I didn't really want to have any visitors because I was afraid that through their visit I might miss a class or some appointment and thus break a rule.

Fortunately when I told my story to Sister Leota she went to Msgr. Breen and explained my situation and he removed my month long campus. Sister Leota became a very dear friend of mine and later I worked for her to help pay some of my tuition.

After about a year and a half at Loras College, Bishop Binz asked me to apply for the Theodore Basselin scholarship. Theodore Basselin had become very wealthy in the lumber business. After hearing a very poor homily given by a priest, he decided to do something to try to improve the preaching of priests. He left three quarters of a million dollars to establish the scholarship. I was accepted and had all my expenses paid at the Catholic University for three years (1946 – 1949). I was at Loras Collage only a year and half. After my first year in college, I went to the Catholic University in Washington, D.C.

Study at the University was a profound challenge. All of the textbooks were in Latin. Even some of the professors lectured in Latin. I did not have a strong foundation in Latin and consequently, this was quite difficult for me.

The first year, I carried a load of 27 credit hours. At times, I thought I would never be able to make it. But, as time went on, I began to get into the swing of things and felt much more comfortable.

During the three years at Catholic University, we lived at Theological College and went across the Michigan Avenue to classes at the University.

In the beginning, this scholarship enabled the candidates for the priesthood to get special training in speech and English. Later on, however, it was adjusted to enable the candidates, like me, to get a Master's Degree in philosophy with special courses of speech and English on the side. Every year, there was a Basselin speech contest. In 1949, I won first place in this contest and was given a special plaque.

Perhaps my most profound influence at Theological College was my relationship with Albert Giaquinto. He was just a year from ordination when I met him. He apparently perceived that I was rather shy. One of the most difficult parts of seminary life for me was the social aspect. Oftentimes, during the social time, to avoid relationships with others, I would go into the Prayer Hall where parts of the daily paper and journals were available I would spend my time there rather than recreating with fellow students. At times, Albert would find me there and ask me to go for a walk. He had been a Basselin, himself, and he knew well what I was going through. We would often discuss philosophy, which I was taking, or we would talk about prayer and spirituality. My encounters with him would give me a shot in the arm that would inspire me for a month. During Al's final year at college, I was privileged to sit at the same table with him. Although our meals were usually in silence, occasionally, we were given the privilege of a talking meal. It was during those times that he would be a tremendous inspiration to me. I remember one time we discussed the liturgy. He felt that he had not given enough explanation of what it was. When he went to his room, he typed three pages to give further explanation.

I remember so well yet when it became time for him to leave college, to go home to be ordained as a priest. He was ordained on May 28, 1948 The night before his departure, I visited with him for the last time. The next day, as he and the other deacons were leaving for ordination, we sent them off with the whole community singing Ad Multos Annos. I have the letter that he wrote to me a month after his ordination.

In June of 1949, I received a Masters Degree in philosophy. My Masters dissertation was Blaise Pascal's Concept of Man and a Thomistic Critique. Msgr John K Ryan was my advisor.

V) Painful Experiences

Every life has its painful experiences. I think that in my life I have had fewer painful experiences than most people who have lived as long as I have. I am mindful, however, of three especially painful experiences I have had and all three were associated with deaths.

I have recounted at considerable length the first painful experience which was my sister, Rosie's death at the very early age of 12.

The second painful experience of my life was the death of my brother, Sylvester on the U.S.S Franklin. Sylvester followed my brother, Charlie to the Navy. After his basic training he was assigned to the U.S.S Franklin a new 45,000 ton aircraft carrier.

He came home for a leave rather shortly before his death. He had met Emmagene Tate in Chicago and fell in love with her. Due to the pressure of service he married her after a very brief courtship. They were married by a Baptist minister.

Emmagene (Tate) Galles and daughter, Sylvia Gail

Shortly after Sylvester's return to the U.S.S. Franklin my parents received a telegram from the War Department informing them that Sylvester was missing in action. We found it quite impossible to admit that he might be dead especially since he was married outside the Catholic Church and thus was excommunicated, and as our mentality was at that time he was in danger of going to hell. We held out the hope that he might be on some island in the South Pacific.

Dad went to some place where Fr. Callaghan, the chaplain on the ship, was speaking to see if he could give any information about Sylvester. Fr. Callaghan seemed to have spoken in generalities about the goodness and the bravery of the man as a way of offering Dad some consolation. We collected the numerous pictures and newspaper articles about the U.S.S Franklin. Over 800 sailors died as a result of the destructive bombs the Japanese war planes had dropped on the ship. Many of the sailors were having breakfast on the main deck when the ship was struck. The captain of the ship was later criticized for not ordering the sailors to abandon the ship, but he was afraid if he did this many sailors in the lower decks would have perished.

When we received news from the War Department again that Sylvester was now presumed to be dead, it was like news that he had gone to hell. As I mentioned obviously according to our mentality in that day he couldn't be saved. He was outside the Church. He had been excommunicated for being married before a Baptist minister.

The whole thing about Sylvester's marriage and now his death had to be hush-hush. It was only shortly before that we received news of his marriage. In our way of thinking and believing then this was God's punishment for his sin.

Also Sylvester, in our way of thinking at the time was the first blot upon the Galles escutcheon. There would be many more in the future, but we didn't know that then. How could he have done that to us and our reputation? This probably hurt us more in our pride than the belief we had that he may have gone to hell. We had to sort of cancel him out of the family. He had gone wrong. We just couldn't understand how he could have done that "to us."

As I recall the funeral Mass at St. Columba Church in Iona in the absence of a body was a very private affair. The priest was probably afraid to offer a public Mass for him at all. I don't remember anything about it. Our relatives were probably not even informed of the Mass.

At first, there was anger toward Emmagene for having done this thing to Sylvester, and our family, for being married outside the Catholic Church.

She fabricated a story about having had their marriage straightened out by a priest. Later, when she went through her "conversion" experience, she came out and told the truth and said she did not feel she could bring her daughter, Sylvia Gail, up as a Catholic. She had been conceived by Sylvester, and born after Sylvester's death

Emmagene was a very fine person and a very good Christian in her own faith, and she took the initiative in restoring a good relationship with the family. My mother, in spite of her rigidity in regard to the faith, was probably the best in keeping the lines of communication open.

Sylvia Gail Ellsworth and sons Tim and Martyn

For years in my mind I had excluded Sylvester from the family. If he was outside the Church he was also outside the family.

When I made the 30-day retreat in 1977, I relived the whole story of Sylvester, his marriage and death and the reaction that I and our family had toward him. I begged and seemed to have received his forgiveness. He understood why we felt as we did at the time. I shed many tears during that retreat in 1977 when I relived the whole history of Sylvester. I now appreciate him as a gift in my life.

Now I can see that what Sylvester did was such a human thing. He was freer than the rest of us. He was simply seeking fulfillment of his need for affection. Emmagene gave him one of his first real experiences of love. She made him more human and more a man. I am glad he was able to have intercourse with her and beget a child even though they were together such a short time.

The third most painful event of my life was the violent death of my brother, Gerald. As soon as Gerald was old enough he enlisted in the Navy. Being trained by the Navy as a nurse he was transferred to the Marines, because the Navy does not have its own medical corp.

Gerald served in the South Pacific and apparently had many horrible experiences in the war. He married Helen Hargrove, a very lovely and talented lady from South Carolina. After Gerald completed his time in the Marine Corp under the encouragement and support of my brother, Eugene, he began learning to be an electrician, and was apparently well liked and very good in his work.

He was often away from home for long periods of time and his wife, Helen, was left alone. For a period of time she lived with my parents.

During one of her stays at Iona, Helen took instructions in the Catholic Church and became an ardent Catholic. Previously she had been a Baptist.

Gerald had strong swings in his personality. Some of this may have resulted from his experiences in the war. At times he could be very warm and kind and gentle and then again he could be very mean and violent and abusive. These strange swings in his character eventually led to separation and divorce from Helen.

In the following years Gerald had a number of relationships and marriages to a number of women. During his marriage to Helen and afterwards Gerald also began drinking excessively. This addiction compounded the other problems he had.

Gerald began dating a Native American woman who was separated from her husband, Carl Lee Morris (831 Booth Drive,

Shreveport, LA) but not yet divorced. He was a very wealthy man in the oil business in Texas. He had showered her with many gifts and some of these she shared with Gerald. Now with their divorce coming up she began giving back some of these gifts.

Gerald and Carl Lee Morris had a rather cordial relationship. On one occasion he was visiting at Gerald's home. He had some item he wanted to show to Gerald and Gerald was gullible enough to believe him. When Gerald went to his home he shot both Gerald and his wife. His wife lived for a time but eventually died. Carl Morris fabricated the story that they got into an argument and that Gerald went to his car to get his gun and so he shot him. He also said a stray bullet hit his wife.

Eugene who lived in the area suggested that our family not try to prosecute Carl Morris because he had so much money that he could hire a whole bank of lawyers and it would be impossible to try to convict him. Also Eugene feared that Carl or some hit-man he hired would kill our family members.

Lloyd and Leona Buse, Lawrence and Marcella, Lester, Clara and I drove down to Louisiana for the funeral. I offered a funeral Mass for Gerald in Eugene's home just for the immediate family, and then a public funeral was held at a Protestant Church where Gerald had been friendly with the pastor. Some of those of our family who had gone down for the funeral thought we ought not tell the whole gruesome story to mother, but I insisted she had a right to know everything that we knew, and I related it all to her on our return. As usual mother was very brave.

VI) <u>North American College, Rome (1949-1953)</u>

August 12, 1949, I left Iona. When I departed on the train, Mother smiled amid her tears. I went on to Milwaukee to see Eldred Lesnieski. We had a party with former Basselin students: John Tuomey, Fred Wroench, Ray Gelting, Bob Mauston, Tom Zabors, Tom Burton, and Eldred. From there I went to Chicago and then to Pittsburgh. I went to Mass at the Capachin House, then went on to see Al Giaquinto at

New Haven, CT. At his home, I met his mother, Mrs. Giaquinto, and several family members: Mary, Phyllis, Ted, Sulli, Tommy, Shirley, Patty, and Dennis.

During the afternoon, we went to a park and played with Al's nephews and nieces on the merry-go-round and slides. That evening, his mother gave us dinner. The spaghetti had so much garlic in it that I got sick. But, rather than blame the food for my sickness, I was able to explain that it must have been the many rides we had with the children.

On August 16, I took the train from Connecticut to New York City. I got a room at the Sloane House, and then took my baggage to the S.S. Washington. The next day, as I was leaving Sloane House, another guest saw the labels on my luggage. Dr. Klein was also a passenger on the S.S. Washington. We used the same taxi to the ship. We became friends and had many good discussions together.

Fr Tuomey was the chaplain on the ship. He told many stories. He disembarked at Cobb Ireland, when we landed there August 23. A day later, we landed at Le Havre, France. I was introduced to Irene Kraemer, a friend of Dr Klein, who met him at the dock.

I took the train to Paris. I had dinner with Miss Mary Dunnigan. Rented a house at Germaine. On August 26, I toured Paris, including the Louvre. August 27, I went to Sacre Couer. I saw Irene Dunn in the movie, *Mon Pere et Nous*.

I met up again with Dr Klein at Sacre Couer. I was invited to dinner at Irene Kraemer's house. Irene's father served a change of wine with each change of course during the meal. Not being used to drinking wine, I was feeling pretty good by the end of the meal.

I continued to tour Paris, including the Eiffel Tower. For a couple days, I toured more of Paris with Mary Dunnigan. On September 1 I took the train to Lourdes and stayed for four days, and then took the train to Rome.

On October 20, Bishop Edward Fitzgerald was named the Bishop of Winona.

Francis Galles as a student at the North American College in Rome

On January 10, 1950, I received *The Story of the Von Trapp Family Singers* from Bernie Dominick. When I was at Theological College, the mother of the Von Trapp family was a good friend of the rector and spoke a couple times to the college. A few years later, I visited their family home in Austria.

On January 14,1951 I met Guy Bertin from the French College and began exchanging French and Italian with him. He spoke French and Italian. One summer, for a month, George Bell had taught me French. Then, later on, I taught French to my friend, Eldred Lesniewski. When we took our test, he passed and I didn't. Guy Bertin helped me learn Italian.

John Quinn, who later became a bishop in California, was the choir director at the North American Collage and he had to tell me that I couldn't be in the choir because there wasn't enough room in the choir loft.

On May 9, 1951, I received a letter from Irene Dunn. Her name was now Mrs Francis D Griffin. I still have this letter. **On** May 11, I had a visit with Irene Dunn and her daughter, Mary Frances, and her husband, Dr Griffin. I had to get permission to go to the hotel to visit her.

Chapel at the North American College in Rome

Msgr Fulton J. Sheen spoke at the college May 28. He had been my teacher at the Catholic University for a year. I thought he was a better preacher than teacher. He is now up for canonization. In his talk he urged that we make a holy hour daily before the Blessed Sacrament and that we be kind.

On July 6, I visited the home of Maria Goretti, a young girl (13) stabbed by a man who tried to rape her. She forgave him before she died. When she was canonized, her murderer was there.

If you wanted to travel during the summer you had to go with at least two other students. So a couple other seminarians and I began our summer vacation. I visited Milan, Genoa, Berne, and Heidelburg.

I saw my first opera, *Carmen,* at an outdoor theater at Milan. Then I went to Nuremburg and saw the destruction caused by the Second World War.

On July 20, I went to Konnersreuth and saw Theresa Neumann that afternoon, while she was out on the street visiting with friends and neighbors. The next day, I went to confession, in Latin, with Fr. Nabor. Then I saw Theresa Neumann in her Friday ecstasy. Her father admitted us to her home and took us upstairs where she lay in bed. A white cloth was around her forehead and was stained with blood. There was also a blotch of blood on her breast. She had the marks of nails on her hands. She was continually responding to some aspect of the passion that Jesus went through. Fr Nabor, the pastor, was in the room with us. He explained the various stages of the passion she was then experiencing.

Therese Neumann's home in Konnersreuth

On July 22, I went on to Munich and met Ludwig Beham on the train. He was extremely kind to us and offered to take us to dinner at the train station, when we had a layover. We became friends and later, at Christmas, he sent a box of German cookies to me in Rome and also sent cookies to my parents in the States. I visited him again some years later.

On July 23, I went to the Passion Play at Oberammergau. This is presented there only every ten years. Local people were the actors.

When we left Munich, Ludwig told us to let him know when we were returning and he would come back to Munich and show us around. So, on October 25, when we returned to Munich, Ludwig met us there. He had taken the afternoon off of work, in Freising, to show us around. He was an excellent guide, and gave us a wonderful tour of Munich.

He arranged for us to stay at his mother's place in Munich. So, in the morning, a widow and three seminarians went to Mass together. She was so proud to be seen with us. After Mass, we would sightsee and, when we came back, she would have a lovely meal for us.

Ludwig even sent German cookies to us in Rome at Christmas time and also sent cookies to my parents in the United States at Christmas.

July 27, we went on to Innsbruck and a couple days later, to Salzburg.

On July 31st, we saw the von Trapp family villa at Aigen, Austria.

In August, we went on to Villach, then Trieste and Venice. We stayed several days at Venice and then went on to Padua.

On August 9, we went on to Verona and saw *La Boheme* by Puccini. The next day, we went to Trent and on the 11th, to Balogna, where we saw very fine art at the Pinocoteca. We also saw the church and cell where St Dominick had been a monk.

Then we left for Ravenna. Went to Mass at the duomo (cathedral). Saw the church of St Vitale (Byzantine) and the Mausoleum of Galla Palacidia. Went to the Academia di Belle Arti. Went to the church of

San Francesco and saw the tomb of Dante Alighieri. Saw the churches of St Apollinaire Nuovo, Santa Maria Porto and St Apollinaire in Classe.

Catholic Church at Luxembourg City

On the 14th we left Ravenna for Rimimi. Took the bus to San Marino. Saw the Palazzo del Gevorno. Took train from Rimini to Rome.

Sept 12, we went to Naples and saw the Cathedral of St Januarius. Went to the docks to meet the ship, Atlantic, that brought Roy Liturski, Fr Magee, Bob Behan, Paul Hritz, and George Duritsa, who were students, coming to Rome. Sept 14, we left Naples. Saw a cameo factory, Pompeii ruins, Palermo, Amalfi, St. Andrew grave and Sorrento.

Francis Galles in Luxembourg City - 1951

In October, Fr. John Courtney Murray gave our annual retreat, which was also my preparation for tonsure. The conferences that Fr. Murray gave were so good that years later I published the notes I had taken during his retreat. On the 10th, we accompanied Bishop Binz, who had come to Rome, to his audience with the Holy Father. Dan Tierney was Bishop Binz companion that day. Dan later became my first pastor.

On October 31, in anticipation of the declaration of the dogma of the Assumption of Mary into heaven, there was a procession from the church of Aracoeli to St Peter's Basilica. Cardinal Spellman and Clement Cardinal Micara (who ordained me as priest) and other bishops were in the procession.

The next day, the declaration (proclamation) was a tremendous experience. . It had been 90 years since the last official declaration of a dogma. There were about 500,000 people gathered in the Piazza. In front of me, a little woman was dripping tears as the Pope spoke of the hope the Assumption gives us that Mary will help us to get to heaven, too.

On November 19, at the Church of St Marcellus, I received First Tonsure, administered by Bishop Traglia, the Vice-vicar General of Rome.

In December I played the part of Mr. Gibbs in *Arsenic and Old Lace* at the college.

On December 29, I took the bus to San Giovanni in Rotundo. Attended Mass by Padre Pio. It was a rainy morning, the church was filled with people. A large number of men were in the sacristy vying for the privilege to serve Mass with Padre Pio, but two of our seminarians were chosen, Tom Mearsman and Paul Palatier. Padre Pio was very popular and he spent hours hearing Confessions. People would steal his socks as relics since they had been stained with his blood from his stigmata.

The Mass was quite ordinary except at the time of the consecration. During that time, Padre Pio spent a great deal of time giving the impression that he was actually seeing Jesus going through his passion. He did not distribute Communion during Mass, but afterward he went to the tabernacle and distributed Communion from there.

Feb 17, 1951, I was in Third Theology and received the last two Minor Orders.

In March, I took the train to Assisi and stayed at the American Atonement Sisters. Saw the Church Rufino and later San Francesco. Found the most beautiful spot in Italy. A castle overlooking the town and Umbrian Plain. Walked through Mt. Subasio. Saw the home of St Francis and his father's place of business. Saw the caskets of St Francis, Leo, Sylvester, and the refectory of St Bernadine of Sienna.

On June 3 the beautification of Pope Pius X took place.

On December 26 the students at the college presented the Greek tragedy of Sophocles: "King Oedipus." Warren Halloran directed the play. And I was the shepherd who revealed to the king his true identity.

December 27-29, I went to Perugia with Ralph Lawrence, Roy Liturski, Bob Sampon, and Jack McCabe.

January 18, 1952, I received a letter from Aunt Katie, in which she said that the family agreed to have Mother and Dad in Rome for my ordination.

On February 11, I received the orders of Exorcist and Acolyte from Bishop O'Connor.

On February 14, we had a bum run to Subiaco. The city and monastery reminded me very much of Assisi. The monastery on the slope of the mountain and sheltered by a huge rock cliff, bespoke of great peace and quiet. On the way home, we made a stop at Palestrina.

We had a bum run to Viterbo. At the Church of St Rosa we saw the incorrupt body of this saint preserved in a most beautiful reliquary. The skin is leathery and drawn, but the hands still convey a delicacy with long narrow nails and slender fingers.

St Rosa was born in 1235. From her earliest years, she gave evidence of great sanctity and performed great miracles. She went through the streets of Viterbo with a crucifix in her hands and tried to convert the infidels. For this she was exiled by Frederick II. After his death, she returned to Viterbo and was greatly revered by the populace. She tried to enter the Order of St Franciscan nuns of Domiano, but wasn't accepted. She became a Tertiary, someone who is associated with the order, but not part of it. She lived in great poverty and penance. March 6, 1252, she died at the age of 17 at Santa Maria Impogia. Her body was found to be incorrupt six years later. In 1258, amidst great solemnity, her body was removed to the Church Domiano, later renamed St Rosa.

Of the many churches we saw, I admired the Church of San Francesco, with Tudor arches, and two beautiful Renaissance tombs, one of Hadrian V and mosaic work. The columns and capitals in the cathedral (largely damaged by the war) are also very stately. Above all, I enjoyed the portico of the Pope's palace with its heavy arch and delicate colonnade above.

On March 5 I received a letter from my sister, Leona, informing me that my mother underwent an operation for rupture, February 27. Recently, she had several severe attacks. Of this, I knew nothing.

On March 28 my mother wrote that she would be glad to have me use her diamond for my chalice. She wrote, "I want to tell you how thrilled I would be to have the diamond, from my engagement ring set into the cross in your own chalice. I never wear it anyway, and that way it would perhaps save a lot of trouble later on as to who should get it." Her ring was not used in my chalice, and I do not know who eventually received the ring.

On April 15 Stan Fleming, Don Hellmann, Bob Sampon, and I, left on a bum run to the Island of Elba. On April 16 our hotel, packed us some sandwiches and wine and we started walking to Napoleon's villa, about five kilometers outside of town. The villa is located in a valley of the mountains and commands a beautiful view of the town and Portoferraio. At the approach to the villa is the quaint Bonaparte hotel. Palm trees line the drive up to the gate, which obtains an air of authority because of the fasces of rods, which form the vertical posts, and the imperial eagles overhead. Large N's of gold against red tell whose villa it was. Huge bushes of daisies fill the garden. The museum in French style, with four columns, is in front and below the original house of Napoleon. The house is very simple. Napoleon shared the house with one of his generals. Each had his own entrance, lobby, bedroom and study. Between the two apartments is the counciliers, in which each chair was distinguished by its color, and a large dining room with a large fountain and Egyptian decorations. The adjoining museum was once a Napoleonic collection, but this was sold and the articles that the museum now has have little connection with Napoleon except the graceful statue of Pauline, Napoleon's sister, by Canova. We ate our lunch in the woods back of the villa. After lunch, we returned to the road leading to Maxima Marina, and walked to the point where we could see the beach on the other side. Then we climbed one of the neighboring hills to get a good view of the surrounding country. The hills, which are wholly terraced with stone walls and intensively utilized, are dotted with purple, lavender and yellow flowers amidst the rocks and brush. The valley on this side of the island is especially luxuriant and verdant. Cutting across hills and fields, we made our way back to the main road leading to Portoferraio.

April 17 We went to see Napoleon's house in town. Napoleon built this house by joining two villas with a third central structure. It overlooks the sea and is flanked on either side by the old city fortifications built by Casimo de Medici. Here Napoleon had a library, a study, bedroom, reception hall, and so forth. The library books are of such a nature as the history of France in many volumes, Rousseau's works, the letters of Madame de Sevigne, Voltaire, and so forth. All are bound in leather. I especially liked the library. The ceilings were mostly of heavy timber. The floor was of red brick. In front of the house, toward the sea, is a garden of many flowers. The young women, who showed us through the house, had a very strong Tuscan pronunciation. All of the islanders, more or less, have this pronunciation.

Next, we went up into the nearby lighthouse. The light is supplied by a 350 watt bulb magnified by an enormous glass cylinder that surrounds it. The bulb may be replaced by using an acetylene jet. The lighthouse keeper told us the history of Elba during the recent war. He was reluctant to accept a tip. This attitude we noticed a number of times. The lack of beggars was also noticeable. At 11:30, we left by bus for Poggia.

After dinner, we began our climb to Capanne. The man at our hotel wanted to accompany us as our guide (I think not for a tip, but just for the pleasure of making the hike with us). A good path in the rocks leads to the top, which is 3,340 feet high. We walked about an hour and a half. The view from the top exceeds that from Mt Subasio overlooking the Umbrian plane. We could see the entire island from the summit, and nearly all the little fishing villages, especially along the coast with their red-tile roofed houses. This eastern portion of the island appeared more dry, but also more intensively farmed. We could also see Corsica in the haze, the mainland, Monte Crista, and several other islands, including one for prisoners. We missed the path we were to take on the return; had to go through brush and rocks and found the path just shortly before dark. It was after eight when we arrived at the hotel. We had goat's meat for supper and liked it very much

On April 24 Bishop Sheen spoke to us at the college. He stressed the importance of studying, and told us of his work on television. On April 27 Bishop Sheen spoke at St Suzanna's Church. The church was packed. I was in the sacristy. The Bishop spoke of the Good Shepherd, faith and Communism.

A sad thing happened this week. Fr Alighieri Tondi, who taught a course of higher religion at the Gregorian University for laymen, left the order and joined the Communists. There are two theories that explain his action. One, that he is mentally unbalanced; a second, that he has been in bad faith over a number of years. He was a convert and was highly praised for his work. In March, he gave a talk to a group of youths, and in a moving way, told of his conversion. It is also rumored that a woman is involved. For some time, he has been coming in late at night. The Communist papers greatly played up his attitude toward the Church and Communism, which he sees as the only hope for the world.

Today, April 28, while we were on our daily walk, a fellow pointed to us and said, "Tutti sono Padri Tondi... Conoscete Padri Tondi?" ("All are Father Tondi...Do you know Father Tondi?")

Quite by accident, we met Miss Bernadean Murphy while we were on the cam walk. Tom Duffy and Frank Stangl were with me. She said she would contact me at the college and invite the three of us to dinner.

On May 3 I went to the Angelicum to sit in on one of Fr Garrigou LaGrange's lectures. His class was quite informal. He seems to have a good sense of humor. His physical appearance didn't seem to be in proportion to his world-wide fame.

On May 7 the celluloid of Bishop Sheen's television show was shown at the Gregorian. His program seems to be much like his classes were.

On May 19 Msgr. Kramer and Fr. Grulkowski were here for dinner and we got to see them for a few minutes afterward. They left $20 for Roy Liturski and me.

Fr. Linehan, SJ, spoke on seismology on May 21. This was a very interesting talk. At the time, excavations were being carried on under St Peter's Basilica to try to locate the actual burial place of St Peter. The excavations were carried on to such an extent that the dome of St Peter's was actually imperiled and so the excavations had to be stopped.

On June 5 Cardinal Spellman, and about 790 priests on a pilgrimage to the Eucharistic Congress in Barcelona, were here for dinner.

On June 9 Frs. Mageris, McShane, Dittman and Feiten, stopped to see Roy Liturski and me.

Bill Bevington and I went out to the Good Shepherd Convent for Mass. Bill celebrated the community Mass for the girls. The sisters served us breakfast afterward. Mother Angelique and Sr Rose Virginia accompanied us in their car to the college on their way to the train station, from which Sr Rose Virginia was leaving for America. Msgr Joseph Hale stopped in to see Roy Liturski and me. He left twenty dollars for us.

I received long letter from Mother on June 21 explaining the plan that had been made for their trip to Rome and asking my advice (e.g., about where to get off the boat). Mrs Vedder has offered to pay a part of the expenses.

On Jun 29 I took my Italian friend, Vitorio Buonevenia, out to dinner at Nino's. After dinner he took me to a café for coffee and a liquore.

I began the retreat prior to receiving the Subdeaconate on July 14, 1952. The morning conference stressed that the rite of ordination admonishes the candidate of the subdiaconate to consider again and again, the 'onus,' or obligation, which he seeks in this Order. The ordaining bishop goes on to remind the one to be ordained as a subdeacon that he is yet free to go back and seek his salvation through an occupation in the world. After the reception of the Order, however, the candidate will no longer be free to retract his (propositum) proposition, but will forever (perpetuo) be bound to the service of God, who to serve is to reign! Moreover, the Subdeacon, aided by the grace of God, must observe chastity; and he is bound! (mancipatus) forever (semper) in the service of the Church.

The bishop does not urge the candidate to consider, again and again, his choice as one, who is unable to make up his mind and in this last minute will make the decision that will determine his course for the rest of his days. No, rather the bishop admonishes the candidate to consider, again and again, his dedication, so that at no time in the future, come what may, will he ever hesitate in the choice he has made. The subdiaconate retreat is not a time to decide whether or not one wants to be a priest. That decision, if it has not already been made, can hardly be made in a week. This retreat is intended, rather, to crystallize the dedication and consecration already made. The Subdeacon's life must be centered in Christ forever, and not in self.

Death was the topic for meditation on July 16. The trepidation, with which many people approach death, is due to the unknown element that lies beyond death. Man has a natural fear of the unknown, the unexperienced. However, for the Christian, that which follows death is not wholly unknown. Christ came back to tell us what lies beyond death so that we no longer fear it. We think too much on death and not enough on life. Christianity is a way of life and leads to life. If we think often of heaven and familiarize ourselves with it, we shall be eager for death, which is but the transition to life.

We may consider the death of Christ to be a good model for death. In his approach to death we find three stages:

1. The exultation of the Last Supper cf. Jn. 17. Christ speaks of His glory; the expectation He has of returning to the Father and being glorified by Him. He speaks of His joy. (Jn.17,13; Jn. 15, 11) He gives peace to His apostles as His last bequest (Jn. 14, 27). The Apostles, amidst all this joy of Christ at going home, are filled with sorrow (Jn. 16: 6, 16, 22). Christ tries to cheer them up. He promises the Paraclete; He tells of His own continual abiding with them, and also of his Father's love for them (Jn. 14: 15-27).

Christ even goes so far as to tell them that, if they really loved him, they would rejoice with him, because he's going to the Father (Jn. 14: 28).

2. The second stage in Christ's approach to death is characterized by fear and sorrow. This is his agony in the Garden. Now, the purpose, for which he is to die, slips into the background and he is confronted with death alone, which to him, who is life, appears as unjust and foreign (Lk. 22: 39sq). He is filled with grief for the sins of all men, because as man he holds communion with sinful humanity although he himself knows no sin. Now, under suffering he makes the same offering of his life as he made in the exultation in the supper room. The offering is the same; it differs only in mode.

3. The third stage is characterized by resignation to the will of his Father. This is seen in his trial and crucifixion. With St John's gospel alone it is impossible to understand the psychological change that took place between the time of the Last Supper and the arrival of the mob in the Garden. Even if we didn't have the other gospels, we might guess St John left out an important event. He does not record the agony in the Garden, which serves as the intelligible medium, connecting chapter 17 and 18 of his gospel. The suffering in the Garden and the consecration made there in agony, enable us to understand the change we see in Christ, as he is presented by St John in chapter 18. Christ rises from his agony, not heartbroken, but rather unbreakable and hard, exhibiting an indomitable will. A certain coldness descends upon him. His soul yet tingles with the emotion he had been experiencing and occasionally in his trial and crucifixion, we see these emotions flood his soul once again. He still bears with him the aftermath of intense suffering and emotion. This transition in Christ is evident in his brusque, impersonal, responses. In the Garden, he consecrated himself irrevocably. Now, in resignation, he but lives out that dedication.

On July 20, 1952 at 7:30 in the morning in the Church of XII Apostles, I was ordained to the Subdiaconate. It was a wonderful feeling to walk up to the sanctuary and know that the day had finally come when no doubt or hesitation now remained.

I was eager now to receive this Order. During the actual ceremony, I felt little emotion. I was extremely uncomfortable with the prostration, and it was hard to pray the Litany of the Saints.

When the ordination was over, it seemed so strange that in such a short amount of time, one's life could be finally determined.

On July 21 Bob Sampon, Roy Liturski, Harry Butori, and I took the 5.20 a.m. tram into Rome. Our tram left for Nice at 7.10 a.m.

Upon leaving, I had a total of $276.92 in currency from various other countries. Since we didn't have reservations in Nice, and were afraid of not getting a hotel, we stayed on the train to Carcassonne. We arrived at Carcassonne at 5:15 the following morning.

July 22 Got a room at the Hotel Terminus across from the railroad station. $39 francs. Slept in the morning. Saw the city in the afternoon. We walked nearly all the way around the city on the walls going through the various turrets and so forth. Had a nice restaurant in the old city.

July 23 Left Carcassonne at 6:40 a.m. A direct train to Ft Bau. Saw large salt works along the coast, shortly before reaching Ft Bau. We changed trains there. A hotel agent talked us into going second class and bought our tickets. Arrived at Barcelona about 3 p.m. Swamped with hotel agents upon arrival. Finally followed one to the Pension Levante.

We went to the ticket counter at the Iberia Airlines and made a plane reservation to Madrid for Sunday. Food at the Pension was plentiful and quite good - 4 and 5 courses. Dinner hour 1:30-3:00 Supper, 9:00-10.30. Wine, especially red, is very good. We got along quite well with the little Italian, French, and Spanish that we knew. Streets were very noisy until after midnight. People stroll the streets or sit on the chairs which can be rented for 50 centimes. The streets have large central boulevards. The Spanish people seem to be very clean and self-respecting with a certain sense of dignity. They are a very good-looking people. Most of the men wear a mustache. The women dress very modestly and very attractively. Begging is not allowed on the street, although occasionally it is done. Most of the old people, crippled, and so forth, have a job selling lottery tickets.

July 24 We saw the town hall, provincial council hall and cathedral. Some distinguished gentleman at the town hall went out of his way to show his good will. A guide showed us a number of beautiful rooms in the town hall. The reception was painted by the Spaniard, Satyr, who did the paintings in the Waldorf Astoria hotel and Empire State building - a very unique use of light and perspective. The provincial council hall is a very beautiful example of Catalan gothic. The cathedral is nice in its general lines, but is obstructed by the enormous rood in the center of the church. St Eulalie and I think St Raymond of Penaforte are buried there. There also is the cross, raised aloft on the ship on the Battle of Lepanto. After dinner, we went to see the Church of the Holy Family. The architect is Goudi who died in 1926. Only the crypt and side facade are finished. It should be a masterpiece when finished. The groups of statues, representing various aspects of the Holy Family, reflect great inspiration. The symbolism is plentiful and very good. We climbed to the top of the highest spire.

We saw one of the arenas now being used for "Holiday On Ice." Colorful and exciting, as I expected them to look.

July 25 is the Festival of St James, a holiday in Spain. We stopped in for a part of the High Mass at the cathedral. A whole series of bells rang at the Consecration. Went to the museum of ancient art at the exhibition buildings. After siesta, we went to the beach for a swim. The water was dirty and the beach poor. Saw a model of one of Columbus' ships. At 11:00 p.m. we went to the ice show, "Holiday On Ice." The show, with 120 artists was colorful and beautiful. The Spanish people seem to like this show. It ended at 1:30 a.m.

On July 26 at 8:a.m. we took the bus for Montserrat. The monastery is about 3000 feet high and is surrounded by jagged rocks and cliffs. There are about 200 Benedictine monks there. They are working on a new translation of the Bible. The monastery was founded in the 12th century. There were hermits living on the hills since the 7th century. St Ignatius made his retreat here. St Francis of Assisi was also there.

Columbus returned to Montserrat to give thanks for his discovery of America. The situation of the monastery is somewhat spoiled by the large hotel and other establishments that have grown up in the last few years. The church is dark - a combination of Gothic, Romanesque and Baroque. High above the altar is the famous statue of the Lady of Montserrat on a rich silver throne. It is a black Madonna in wood. The statue dates from the 12th century. The original was said to have been found in one of the caves in Montserrat. Legend has it that it is the work of St Luke. A passageway leads up in front of the statue where people may kiss the hand of the Christ child, which protrudes though the protective glass covering. We heard the monks sing a Solemn High Mass in chant. The ceremonies were slow and graceful. The stone formation at Montserrat is unique. It is said to be the deposit of what once was a lake fed by a river. The heat of the earth caused the smooth pebbles to adhere to each other forming rock. We took a funicular up one of the peaks overlooking the monastery and flat plane below.

At 1:00 p.m. a boys' choir sang in front of the Madonna at the front of the church. We ate out in the woods, the lunch the hotel had packed for us. At 3.15 p.m. we took the Path of the Rosary. Groups of statues commemorate the fifteen mysteries. At the end, is a chapel marking the spot, where the statue of our Lady was found. A guide was with us the whole day. For 11 years, he was a Christian brother. He had a number of interesting legends to tell. We left Montserrat at 6:00 p.m. and got to Barcelona at 8:00 p.m.

On July 27 at 8:45 a.m. we took the plane for Madrid. A twin-engine plane - few passengers. We followed the coast for a long way. The countryside was rocky and barren with a few green valleys between the mountain ranges. It seemed that the plane tried to follow the valleys. It became a little rough when we hit a mountain range or canyon. Near Madrid, the country became richer. We landed at 10.40 a.m.

On July 29 we took the bus at 8:40 a.m. for Toledo (69 kilometers from Madrid). At the church of Santo Tome, we saw the most famous of El Greco's paintings (The Burial of St Orgaz). Next we saw the house and museum of El Greco. The house had a very charming courtyard and garden. The Greek and Oriental influence is very evident.

The Transito synagogue is ornate with Moorish and Hebrew designs and inscriptions. Another synagogue of the 13th century was transformed into the Church of Santa La Blanca decorated in Mannesque style.

San Juan de Las Reyes is a church built by Ferdinand and Isabella in gothic style. The outside of the church is hung with chains that the Moors used to bind the Christian captives. It was a forceful reminder of similar captives in our own day.

The cathedral is 13th century gothic style. The wood carving of the choir stalls depict various stages of the conquest of Granada. The main chapel has a large painted and gilded wooden reredos, depicting New Testament episodes. The tombs of the "old Kings" are on the both sides of the altar and, on the left hand side, under the chancel, the tomb of Cardinal Mendoza, who was influential in persuading Ferdinand and Isabella to send Columbus on his way.

On the right is a statue of the Turk, who was patient when the rights of his people were being ignored by the Christians. The sacristy has a number of worthwhile paintings by El Greco, Giordano, Bellini, Goya, and others.

In the museum of San Vincente, we saw more El Greco works, including the "Assumption."

The Alcazar, or Charles V's palace, seems dear to the Spanish for its part in the recent civil war, when it was besieged by the Communists and held out against them amid great suffering until Franco arrived to relieve them. We took the bus back to Madrid.

July 30 we spent the day in Madrid. I bought a watch from a fellow on the street for 300 pesetas. Later, I found out I could have bought it cheaper at a jewelry store.

On July 31 Bob and I left by bus for El Escorial. Spent nearly the whole day seeing the huge palace and monastery built there by Philip II. Most interesting were the tombs of the kings. The several rooms of tombs are quite simple, yet very attractively conceived and executed. Charles V and Philip II share a tomb, amid many others of the kings and queens of Spain. Don Juan of Austria is also buried there. Alphonso XII is the last king buried there.

The chapel with its simplicity and elevated sanctuary is quite nice. Jose Antonia, founder of the Falangist party, is buried before the main altar. While eating dinner on the street we were told to move by a policeman. We returned to Madrid by bus at 6:00 p.m. Escorial appears to be the villa section of Madrid. The farmers were busy harvesting grain. Nearly all the work is done by hand. The grain is threshed by running a roller with blades over the grain and then sifting the grain from the chaff by throwing it into the wind. Roy and Harry went to a bullfight. We got back too late to go.

On August 1 we went to the Prado museum. There we saw an abundance of works by Murillo, Goya, Velasquez, El Greco and Ribera. We ate dinner at the Edelweiss. Got a haircut for three pesetas, six cents. Returned to the Prado. Supper at Edelweiss.

Took the train at 9.30 a.m.for Grenada. We had reserved seats, but the train was very crowded. Throughout the whole night, people kept coming to our compartment to talk to us after they found out we were Americans. We had a great time trying to carry on a conversation in Spanish. Later a girl, who spoke English, served as interpreter and put to us the many questions that the onlookers suggested. They showed little love for the English. Wanted to know where all the good-looking English girls are. They never get to see them. They were eager to know how we like the Spanish people. On August 2 we arrived in Grenada at 4:p.m. Took a taxi to the hotel Suizo.

On August 3 we became aware that many of the people are poor, more beggars than in northern Spain. Lower class of people in general.

We walked out to see the Cartuga or Carthusian monastery. The sacristy of rich marbles and in baroque style is of great beauty. It has a very pleasant effect. After dinner, we walked to see the Alhambra, an Arab palace and fortress built on top of a hill, at the foot of which flows the River Darro, and shrouded in the verdure of a wood. From the tower, a good view can be had of the city. Its several patios in the palace proper are of exquisite beauty . The Arabic style seems to maintain simplicity amid a profusion of intricate geometrical designs. The total effect is simplicity. The detail is infinite intricacy. The court of the pool and the lions pleased me most. The great variety of fine design is most astonishing. The colors used are faint and well blended. The wooden ceilings give the impression of stalagmites. No glass in the windows, only a carved wooden shutter. I must read Washington Irving's "Tales of he Alhambra". It is remarkable that the material used should have stood against the elements for so many years. Of the palace of Charles V, we saw only the circular patio.

On August 4 we went to the Generalife, the summer palace of the Moorish kings. A peaceful harmony of Moorish architecture, fountains, flowers, trees, shrubbery and gardens.

The cathedral is the first Renaissance church built in Spain. In the royal chapel lie the remains of Ferdinand and Isabel. In a corresponding tomb, are Queen Juana (Mad Jane) and Philip the Fair. Looking down upon them from the elevated altar, they seem to lie there in quiet repose awaiting their judgment, even as the most simple of people must do.

On August 5 We left Grenada by bus for Seville about 7:00 a.m. We passed practically no cars on the way. Even in the small towns there were no cars. All the houses of a town are of an almost identical pattern. All are neatly whitewashed. Even those who live in caves in the rocks whitewash the entrance. The children at the bus stops frequently ask for money. A number of the young children on the streets were naked.

We stayed at the Pension Roma. Nice atmosphere good food. It was about 3:p.m. when we arrived. We met Msgr Harrington in the cathedral and had a cold beer with him. While sitting at a sidewalk cafe, about a dozen people tried to sell us something or tried to solicit money for one reason or another. There were a number of people selling cigarettes, tobacco, flowers, shoe shines, etc.

August 6 we spent the morning at the Alcazar, built by Peter the Cruel on the site of the residence of the Almohade sultans. The work of construction was directed by Moorish architects. Very similar to the Alhambra, but lacking some of the latter's simplicity. The recent kings of Spain had residence there for some time. The variety of the gardens is interesting.

The cathedral is built on the site of the old mosque. A minaret of the 12th century is incorporated in the Giralda tower. The style of the cathedral is gothic with a blending of other styles. It suffers the disadvantage of most Spanish cathedrals - an obstructing choir screen. A modern tomb in the right transept contains the remains of Christopher Columbus. St Ferdinand III is buried in a silver urn at the high altar.

Walking through the old section of the city, we saw the quaint streets and houses with their characteristic grills, patios, and gates. Nearly all houses are built around a patio open to the air, and bright and colorful with tile and porcelain. Palm trees and potted shrubbery, together with fine furniture; give both an indoor and outdoor aspect to what appears to be the most pleasant section of the house. All of the patios have a wrought iron grill opening onto the street, which makes one think that the occupants are proud of their patio and are willing to display this portion of their home to onlookers. Many of the narrow streets are covered with a tarpaulin to shade them form the sun. In the old section, we saw the house of Murillo, where he lived all his life. After supper, we went to an open air café and Spanish dance. We had a bottle of wine in order to keep a table. The dancing was good - a real art. The use of the castanets seems very difficult. All of the dances appeared to be of a very serious nature and aimed at the interpretation of a theme. The men were equally proficient as the girls. We stayed until after 2:00 a.m.

On August 7 we saw the town from the tower of the cathedral. There is a large tobacco factory in the city. We saw Jack Weaver's group at their hotel.

On August 8 we took a bus as far as Bodajoz. Had dinner there and then took the train on to Lisbon. On the bus, we met a woman from Australia who accompanied us. We arrived at Lisbon at 11:00. We took a taxi to the Miraparc Hotel. Excellent accommodations and food.

In the afternoon of August 9 we visited the cathedral and castle from which we had a good view of the city. The well-sheltered harbor is very beautiful. Many of the houses have a porcelain-like tile covering their external walls. After supper, we went to a movie. The church near our hotel, where we went to Mass on August 10, was so crowded the men had to fill the sanctuary. We saw the park near our hotel and the conservatory of tropical plants. The city seems to be very modern and progressive. After dinner, we saw the Masterio das Jeranimas, where Vasco de Gama is buried, in the rear of the chapel.

Bob and I went to the bullfight in honor of the US Commander Rear HR Thurber. We had the cheapest seats in the house for fifteen escudos. Bullfighting horsemen: Joao Nuncia, Francisco Sepulveda and a Spaniard, Pepe Anastasia, Mexican Matador: Curro Ortega, a number of bandarilheros and a group of bullfighters led by Antonio Verga. Over half the seats were filled with American sailors. The Navy band also played. The horsemanship was interesting. The eight men who fought a bull barehanded were very amusing. Nine bulls were fought. After supper we went to a movie.

August 11 we left Lisbon about 1:30 p.m. for Fatima. Changed trains at Entruncamento. Arrived Fatima station about 4:00 p.m. No bus available. Had to take a taxi to the town - about 25 kilometers. Stayed at the Seminary of the Consolata Mission Society, which was founded by Canon Joseph Allamano. The faculty is all Italian. We gave a donation of 40 escudos for each day. When we arrived at Fatima there were, as yet, practically no pilgrims there. The Basilica is yet some distance from Fatima itself. The place of the Basilica is known as the Cava da Iria and is two kilometers from Fatima.

August 12 a Jesuit priest from the Gregorian University, who is from Portuguese India, accompanied us to the home of Francis and Jacinta. They live at Aljusterel, which is one kilometer from Cava da Iria. A number of pilgrims were speaking to the father, an old man outside his house when we arrived. He asked that only one of the group ask questions, because he gets too tired when everyone is asking questions. He is 79 years old. He was a small fellow with wrinkled leathery skin and he wore a stocking cap that hung down his back. Later his wife also came out and they stood for a picture. The mother is married a second time and Francis and Jacinta are of her second marriage. There were nine children in all. Just across the street is the house where the family lived at the time of the apparitions. A niece of Francis and Jacinta was selling some articles there and answering the questions of the visitors. Further down the street, we saw the house of Lucy and her sister, who is in charge of it and sells religious articles.

We failed to see the well near the house where the angel appeared to the children. Out in the fields, among the olive trees, we saw the spot where our Lady appeared to the children on the 19th of August, because they had been in jail on the 13th when she was to appear. Still further on, somewhat concealed by rocks, we saw the place where the angel appeared twice to the children and gave them Communion on one of those visits. The first shrine is now marked by a few stones and statue of our Lady, which is about a foot high. The place of the angel's appearance is marked by a cross scratched onto the rock. I was impressed by the simplicity of it all and by the thought that God would take such extraordinary means to try to make us understand his designs.

At dinner, there were twelve of us from the college staying at the seminary. After dinner we visited the little shrine in front of the Basilica, which marks the spot where our Lady appeared to the children. The stones around this little chapel were deeply grooved by the pilgrims constantly circling on their knees. Some of the pilgrims covered the entire length of the huge square in front of the Basilica on their knees. Many of the pilgrims come in groups singing hymns as they approach the shrine. The women carry the baggage on their heads. Many are barefoot. Throughout the afternoon the weary pilgrims sought refuge from the hot sun under the trees, within the porticos of the Basilica and wherever else shade was to be found. There they ate their lunch, which they brought with them. Within the portico of the church, one lady was cooking dinner over a small oil burner. All day pilgrims kept pouring in from all directions. Toward evening the roads were crossed with a steady stream of buses filled with pilgrims. We walked to the village of Fatima and saw the procession form at the parish church and walked to the shrine while reciting the rosary and singing.

The Portuguese Jesuit heard our confession after supper. About 11:00 p.m. the recitation of the rosary began at the Basilica. A good loud-speaking system carried the voice of the priest, who was leading it, throughout the square. The rosary was followed by a candlelight procession, which was most disorderly and lacking in all the finesse that is so evident at Lourdes. This was followed by exposition of the Blessed Sacrament in front of the Basilica. After the first hour, during which the crowd was most attentive, the people slowly began to dwindle away. Some going to their place of lodging, others just moving to the outside of the square to wrap up in their coats and blankets and spend the night out in the open. Others huddled on the steps of the Basilica and half-prayed, half-slept throughout the night. The candles, too, began to burn our and disappear. A good number kept vigil throughout the night and followed in the prayers and hymn singing, which was lead over the loudspeaker. In spite of repeated reminders that the whole square was an open church, before the Blessed Sacrament, there was considerable talking. It became quite cold as the night drew on. About 3:00 p.m. I went into the Basilica to warm a bit. What a spectacle met my eyes there! Nearly the whole floor surface was covered with baggage, sleeping children and older people lying sprawled out in every direction. Many dirty bare feet could also be seen. Others tried to move about trying to find their way through this mass of tangled bodies. Near the rear of the church, small groups of men huddled about waiting to go to confession. The crowds pressed so closely to the confessors, that they had to draw the penitents near them to avoid being overheard. At the front of the church, in either transept, where a stone marks the graves of

Jacinta and Francis, a few pilgrims could always be found saying their prayers or touching rosary beads and other objects to the graves. The air was thick with the smell of unwashed bodies.

August 13 I assisted at the 6:00 o'clock Mass out of doors after having already assisted at several Masses in the Basilica. A large square was roped off in front of the altar before Mass. Around this, the people crowded many rows deep, glad to feel the warmth of the crowd. More than thirty priests took sections near the withholding ropes to distribute Communion. The crowds, already tightly packed, crowded still closer as they tried to force their way in front to receive Communion. For several hours these priests were all distributing Communion. I would estimate the crowd at thirty to forty-thousand.

As soon as I had received Communion and made a thanksgiving, I returned to the seminary to have breakfast and go to bed. I was very tired and still chilled through. I did not get up for the Mass and procession of the sick at 11, but slept until dinner. After dinner, I again went to bed and the greater number of the pilgrims had already left Fatima when I awoke.

In the evening the Consolata Fathers showed a film at the seminary on Fatima and another on their work in the missions of Africa.

We went to an early Mass at the seminary on August 14 and then took a bus to Fatima station. From there we took the train going to San Sebastian. Train was very crowded at first and we drew a lot of attention as we made our sandwiches of cheese and onion while standing in the aisle. Later we got seats in a compartment. In our compartment was a French girl from near Paris who was on her way home after getting sick while visiting her fiancé in Lisbon. She was very friendly and eager to talk with us and was most patient with our poor attempts at French. Among ourselves we had a very interesting discussion of the labor situation. We were on the train all night. I did not sleep.

On August 15, Feast of the Assumption, we arrived at San Sebastian about 6:00 a.m. After going to Mass at the Cathedral we found rooms at 104 pts. for a full Pension.

After dinner and a siesta we went for a long walk along the beach. San Sebastian has a well-sheltered beach. The tourists have the appearance of being quite well-to-do without being really wealthy. No beggars. A high hill, surmounted with a statue of Christ, overlooks the city.

While out for a walk after supper, we saw a very fine fireworks display.

August 16 I received letters from Mother and Charlie and Doris at Cooks. Doris wrote to tell of the difficulties they have been having in trying to raise money to send the folks to Rome. Some of the family is opposed to the idea. Saw a bullfight: Gonzalas Litri

Bob and I walked up to the castle and shrine overlooking the city on August 17. Good view of the beach and the entire city. In the afternoon, Bob and I went swimming. Beach was very crowded but a nice sandy beach.

Took the train at 10:00 a.m. for Lourdes on August 18. Changed trains at Hendaya and Irun. Arrived in Lourdes about 4:00 p.m. We had a room and full pension at the St Thomas residence for 950 francs. The room satisfactory. Food quite good and plentiful. It rained, so we did not go over for the candlelight procession.

On August 19 we went to Mass at the Grotto. Spent the morning writing in my diary. Was at the Basilica for the blessing of the sick in the afternoon. An Italian pilgrimage from Naples was there. Took part in the candlelight procession. The good order at Lourdes is quite a contrast to Fatima.

On August 20 we met Fr Cleary, a Maryknoller, at breakfast. Bob and I went up to the castle overlooking the city. Good view of Lourdes, but the castle is of little interest.

We also saw the prison in which St. Bernadette's family was living at the time of the apparitions. Only a single room. The parents slept in a bed in one corner and the girls in another corner and the boy in the window box. Later the townspeople provided the family a house where the sister of Bernadette now lives. We also saw the house where Bernadette was born and the adjoining mill where her father worked.

On August 21 we made the stations of the cross following the path that led up through the woods. The life-size statues are very good. We met Ray Brown. We went to Confession, and then took the train at 5:30 p.m. for Lyon. We arrived at Lyon on August 22. We went to Mass and then asked for a room at the Foyer de Sacerdotole.

In the afternoon we took the funicular up to see the church of Notre Dame de Fuvriere. Good modern mosaics - a miraculous statue of Our Lady in the side chapel. Good view of the city.

At dinner, there was a brother of Pere Charles de Foucald. Fr. Charles de Foucald had a tremendous influence on me when I read his biography. His brother had just returned from his novitiate in Chile. He wore street clothes and wore a small wooden cross on his coat lapel as the only sign distinguishing him as a member of the congregation. We also visited the cathedral.

We moved to the Foyer de Sacerdotole on August 23. In the afternoon, Bob, Don and I went to see the Prado. A priest took us through and explained their work to us. Prado was founded by Pere Chevriere. The church was an old dance hall and the two raised platforms, now incorporated into side chapels, were once the stages for the orchestra. We saw the simple room where Chevriere used to live. His aim was to take in boys from the street, who "had nothing, knew nothing and were thought to be of no value." He differed from the Cure' of Ars in that he thought the appurtenances of the church should be as simple as the things the people themselves have. The Prado in Lyon is engaged in taking in children from the street and preparing them for Communion. The priests are secular, bound together in a society, and tending to live a community life whenever possible. They have a year of novitiate. The food at the Foyer is simple but nicely prepared. A great variety of priests and seminarians are always in for meals. It is a very stimulating atmosphere and would be much more so if one knew French well. There is a small chapel in good taste and a reading room. The bedrooms and parlor are very homey.

On August 24 Bob and I went to an early parish Mass. The Lyonese rite is used. The priests offered a very devout Mass and the congregation assisted well. We took a bus at 8:30 a.m. for Ars, arriving at 9:30. A high Mass for the parishioners was going on then. We visited the Chapel of the Sacred Heart, which has a very expressive statue of the Cure'. His face and figure, his hands, and even his garments, seem to enter into the intensity of his prayer. Before the door of the Cure's rectory is a small courtyard. In a room on the ground floor is kept the coffin where the Cure' was placed (Lead and wood), his simple confessional and other relics with him. I was impressed with the thought of all the good the Cure' accomplished in that simple confessional. Not much more than a crate. Upstairs is his bedroom and study, all in one room. A wooden bed with a canopy, a very small very rough small desk, two bookcases of books (quite a number), a fireplace, a chair, and several rather nice reliquaries and pictures completed the furnishings. Another simple room was his kitchen.

Another room across the way is now a museum of relics of the Cure'. The Cure's practice of getting the best for the church is evidenced by the several fine vestments he had.

The town must not have changed much since the Cure's time. It is still a very small farm village.

The Cure's parish church has been incorporated into the new nave of the now larger church. The pulpit, chapel of St Philomena, and so forth, still remain. In a chapel in a new part of the church in the right transept lies the Cure's body in a silver reliquary.

We assisted at a Mass for the visitors at 11:00. The priest that led the community to participate in the Mass would not allow visitors to walk about during the Mass. Giving thoughts from the Cure', he placed a number of considerations before the people. Allows periods of silence so that the congregation would not forget the Mass that was going on. He read in French the proper parts of the Mass. His short, but powerful sermon also drew attention to the Mass. He stressed the Cure's vivid realization of the presence of God especially in his fellow men and in the Mass. I derived great spiritual satisfaction from that Mass feeling a close friendship with St. John Marie.

We had a hurried dinner and took the bus back to Lyon at 12:50p.m. Toward evening, we went out to see the modern church of St Charles Borromeo. The stained glass windows, of which the dye was made in America, were most colorful and in some cases too abstract in their symbolism. They were made of rough glass held in place by some kind of mortar. On the outside, they are smooth, inside they are very rough. Even though it was toward evening and cloudy, the light shone through with great brilliance. Each window consisted of four vertical panels. The whole depicting a simple subject. The walls of the church were of reinforced concrete.

On August 25 Two students from the Pio Latino College went with us to Paray-le-Monial. We left by train at 9:00 a.m. arrived 11:30 a.m. We saw the small church where the Sacred Heart appeared to St. Margaret Mary Alacoque. The church was greatly damaged during the French revolution. The grill may be seen behind which St. Margaret Mary was when the Sacred Heart appeared before the tabernacle, more than 18 times. A large number of red lamps hang in the sanctuary. In the first chapel from the sanctuary, on the epistle side, is the reliquary of St. Margaret Mary with a beautiful wax mold of the saint.

The cathedral, which was standing at the time of the apparitions, but has no connection with them, is simple and quite nice.

In a very beautiful Jesuit church, we saw the reliquary of Bl. Fr. Columbiere, the spiritual director of St Margaret Mary. The apse had a painting of the Sacred Heart showing the place the Sisters of the Visitation and the Jesuits were to have in spreading this devotion. In the museum there is a most memorable statue of the Sacred Heart. It is of marble with an ivory head, hands and feet. It is exceptional for the very manly appearance of Christ which it presents.

I returned to the chapel of the apparitions before leaving about 3:45 p.m. We got back to Lyon about 6: p.m. Mac Deason and Stan Fleming were at the Foyer, when we got back.

Because of a lack of funds, Harry Butori, left us this morning, August 26, to return to Rome. We three left about 9:00 a.m. for Geneva, arriving about 12:30. We stayed at the Hotel Delagare Novel. After dinner, we went for a long walk along the lakefront. After supper, we went to the movie "Showboat."

On August 27 we saw the United Nations building. The assembly room has paintings by the Spaniard, Sert, whose work we came to know in Barcelona. Five joined hands signified the union of the nations. Powerful activity. Optical illusion. A relief by Eric Gill shows the creation of man after the painting of Michelangelo. The UNO building is composed of marbles, wood, and so forth, from all over the world. A Persian rug is valued at $20,000.

We sat in on a meeting of the prisoners-of-war division of the UN. The absence of the Russian delegate was referred to a number of times. A photographer took a picture of the vacant space. The delegates spoke in either French or English and then the interpreter translated into the other language.

We met Stan Fleming and Mac Deason at the train station and took them to our hotel.

Ray, Bob and I walked to the beach and went swimming - a very nice beach. Water clear as crystal. A sand beach and then a stretch of grass to lie on. After supper, we listened to an outdoor mandolin concert - very pleasing. Several bass fiddles supporting.

Aug 28 We made up a lunch, and bought a bottle of wine, and the five of us went to the beach and spent the afternoon there. We ate our lunch on the lawn and got a good suntan.

We took a bus at 8:a.m. on August 29 for Assy. Arrived about 11:00 a.m. at Via Lafayet. Beautiful view of Mont Blanc. The huge white mass is very majestic. I have never seen so much snow on a mountain. The town is almost exclusively tourists. We saw the much talked about modern church there in the construction and decoration of which a number of French artists collaborated.

The ensemble effect of the exterior is quite good. The bell tower is beautiful. The stone pillars of the facade are quite nice but apparently useless. A mosaic of our Lady in bright colors covers the façade. It is surrounded with symbols of her various titles. The interior is much too dark. The fantastic tapestry of the Women and the Beasts of the Apocalypse, which covers the apse, is colorful but hardly conducive to prayer. Some of the stained glass windows are very good. Others are terrible. The St Dominic, Matisse, is childish. The carving of the supporting beams is a unique idea. The symbolism and the color in the windows in the crypt are very good. The crucifix in bronze, symbolizing the "worm and no man," achieves its desired effect only too well. Not only is the divinity lost sight of, but also the humanity, and without these qualities Christ would not be our Redeemer.

After a poor, but expensive, dinner, we took the bus to Annecy. We left about 3:00 p.m. and arrived at La Fayette about 5:00. Changed buses there, and arrived Annecy about 7:00. A beautiful drive through the mountains. We stayed at a small pension without meals.

On August 30 we went to Mass in the Basilica, which is outside of the city. On either side of the main altar are the tombs of St Francis de Sales and St Jane Frances de Chantal. The church is Roman in style.

The city has a number of quaint sections, especially on the island formed by the split of the river. A number of the walks have overhanging arcades. The lake is very nice, but quite shallow. Mountains can be seen in the background.

We left Annecy at 1:45 p.m. Changed trains at Aix-le-Bain at 2:50. Arrived at Turin at 8:20. We stayed at Albergo Gastronnomico near the station for 500 lire.

August 31 we went to Mass at Santa Maria where St John Bosco is buried in a chapel on the right. Blessed Domenico Savio's body is also in this church in a chapel on the left near the rear. The wax mold of St John Bosco presents him with a very manly good-natured expression.

After breakfast, we visited the Cattolengo. We went through with a large group of men and a sister as a guide. I was surprised to find that we were taken right among the various mental patients. They were all around us. We first visited wards for men and women where the patients were sitting on toilets in a row on the wall. They were mental cases. In all the yards we saw the most hideously deformed and crippled people. Old people sat around on benches staring blankly into space. Some of our group would give candy to the various patients and the insane would snatch at it like monkeys in a circus. They did not seem to be at all concerned with us passing through and staring at them. The sisters in charge seemed to show infinite patience in dealing with these helpless creatures, who do not know enough to say thank you. The smell in some of the wards was sickening. We also saw hospital cases where aged patients lay in waiting with seemingly no other purpose than to wait for death. Radios in some of these wards were supplying music. Each dormitory had an altar. The laundry, bakery, etc., are modern and on an enormous scale. The institution gives the impression of a town in itself, so large it is.

We visited the main church while the nuns were still assembled after the community Mass. The church was filled with sisters. There must be at least a thousand. At the time, there were about 7,000 patients. In a chapel in the rear of the church is the body of the institution's founder, St. Joseph Catalengo. There, also, is his form. After the tour, the sisters passed out holy cards and accepted donations.

The patience and kindness of the sisters was impressive.

We had somewhat of a pranzo since it was our last day of vacation. After dinner, we went for a walk to see some of the city. The streets are all very wide, but the city is not as beautiful as Milan. There is considerable war damage.

Met an Italian on the street who criticized the British for the bombing of the city. He seemed to be quite a fanatic, ready to fight for his country, whether right or wrong. He claimed to be a Fascist and said that Italy was not dead, but would rise again. He took us into a cafe and bought us a coffee.

We saw the church where the Holy Shroud is kept in a chapel in the apse. We returned to the Church of Santa Maria to see the rest of it and also to visit the huge school of Selesions in back of the church. There are the rooms of St John Bosco and a museum of his personal belongings, including the pulpit from which he used to speak to the boys before they retired. His original church is also there. Some priests were playing soccer with the boys in the courtyard.

We had a pizza and a donut for supper. Left Turin at 8:20 p.m. by train for Rome. Arrived in Rome at 7:40 a.m. The total cost of the trip described above was $202.92.

At the end of September, seven of us visited the orphanage of Nattuno. We had a lot of gum and candy for the children. Angelo was just ready to leave for his home. We met the mother superior and Angelo's aunt. The sisters asked me to return to say a Mass for the children after my ordination, which I did two days after I was ordained when my parents and I went to Nattuno.

I received a letter from Mrs. Vedder saying that she could not come for the ordination, but that she had sent money to Mother and Dad so they could make the trip. Through American Express she is sending me $400. In my last letter to her, I asked that she reduce my allowance from $500 to $300 so that she might be able to give $200 to my folks.

On September 30th, I received the list of relatives for ordination announcements from my sister, Leona.

We began our annual eight-day retreat on October 1, which was also preparation for the deaconate. Fr. Healy, S.J. was the retreat master, and these are the notes that I took during the retreat.

Father began by giving us points of meditation: Dispositions required for a retreat: 1. Silence, 2. Peace of mind, 3. Sincerity, 4. Generosity. We seek to know ourselves, acknowledge what we are, and do something about it.

Also in a conference he gave: man was created to praise, reverence and serve God and, thus, to save his soul.

God made man in his own image and likeness (Gen 1:26). One hundred years ago, I did not exist, I was nothing. Without me, the world got along just as well as with me. The world did not need me. One hundred years ago, an insect was more than I was, because it existed, and I did not.

God called me into being. He gave me a material and spiritual element. The more we study the body in biology the more we appreciate the intelligence of God. Consider also the soul - the works accomplished through the power of the human intellect. The good and evil, which result from human will.

God made me and therefore he owns me - every part of me. Every part of me is stamped: "God's property." "What have you that you have not received?"

God could withdraw from me any part of my being. Think of the insane from whom he has withdrawn the use of their mind. Although one hundred years ago I was less than a grain of sand, now I am greater than all the material creation. All else may cease to be. I am indestructible. I shall exist forever. The average age of life expectancy is 40 years. God might have made it 1000, but, no, He saw that less time was enough to fulfill his purposes. Our life is in two parts. The first is in preparation for the second.

My body and soul are borrowed property. I must return them in good condition. God made me for a purpose. Every intelligent maker has a purpose. Why did God make man? Many people would say, "I do not know." Many make riches, pleasure, and so forth, their purpose. However, these things cannot be man's purpose, because they are not within the reach of all. Furthermore, these things are not proportionate to our noble faculties. Man is made for eternity - ultimately. Immediately, he is made to praise, reverence and serve God in this world. By praise, we acknowledge our dependence. On the one hand, creatures denote weakness, and on the other, they denote grandeur and divinity. God created us to share His goodness. To serve God is to reign. It is in serving God that we are in our proper element. God made me to do some special work. He gave me qualities, which no one else has, for this work.

Saving my soul is my chief concern in this world. This is my very own concern, because no one else can save my soul. No power on earth can control my will. I can get someone else to do many things for me, but I cannot get anyone else to save my soul. "What does it profit a man if he gain the whole world and lose his own soul?"

Reflection: God does not need our service. All the good that we do, all the things with which we cooperate with His grace, He could do directly and immediately without us. Why does He require our cooperation in bringing children into the world? Still more mysterious is the order by which men are dispensers of his supernatural grace. Does God not seek our cooperation in doing His goodness because it is a very ennobling thing for us to have such a part to play? We might draw an analogy of a father that has a large fortune in the bank. Now, he could directly dispense this money to the poor, or he might give his son access to this fortune and task him to give succor to the poor. The latter method would show the great confidence the father has in the good will and judgment of the son, and would place the son in a very exalted position.

In a conference at 6:00 that evening, Fr. Healy gave us the foundation and first principle of the Spiritual Exercises: We are to use creatures in so far as they aid toward our supernatural end. We are to withdraw ourselves from creatures that hinder us.

All creatures are capable of leading me to or away from God, depending on the use I make of them. St Paul says, "Whether we eat of drink, or whatever else you do, do all in the name of Jesus Christ."

To get a proper perspective of creatures we must view them from a distance. Creatures can be used in three ways: 1. Simple use, 2. Contemplation, 3. Abstention (sacrifice). Rules for the use of creatures: 1. Rule of the intellect: All things must be used as means only. 2. Rule of the will: I will use things only in so far as they are a help to saving my soul. These rules must be applied to all things, including all my faculties and members.

Later that evening, Father spoke of sin: The abuse of creatures. First Prelude: I see myself the sinner that I am. I see my soul imprisoned in this corruptible body. That soul is spiritual and made in the image of the Trinity. This soul has imprisoned itself. <u>Second Prelude</u>: Request the grace and confusion for sin. Sin at times <u>seems</u> to be such a little thing. Seemingly, things can, however, be immensely important. God cannot describe adequately to us what sin is. Nor can we understand. Since we cannot realize the dignity of the person offended by sin, we must study its effects.

Fr. Healy went on to describe three types of sin:

1. The sin of the angels
2. Sin of Adam
3. My own sins

God is all just and cannot punish sin beyond its due measure. Colloquy (little reflection): Gaze at Christ on the cross. Why this agonizing death? Sin.

The past is gone, but what of the future?

Christ never tried to inspire <u>undue</u> fear in his followers. He tried to lead gently, yet, frequently he reminds us of the existence of hell.

The picture that history gives us of the world at the time when Christ came to have a part in the destiny of humanity is not a very beautiful one. He came during an era of peace, which tended to heighten the evils of materialistic living. The pagan religion frequently held up immorality as virtue. Venus, Bacchus and Mars divinized unchaste love, drunkenness and violence. Children were burned on the altar of Moloch. Boys in Athens beat themselves in honor of gods until the altar flowed with their blood. In Rome, there were the gladiatorial contests. Old men were given as food to wild animals. The captives of war were most cruelly treated. One artist tortured his slave so that he might have a model of suffering for his statue of Prometheus. It was to this corrupt humanity that Christ came and made its history his history and its destiny his destiny.

The hidden life: Nazareth had a very bad reputation in its day. A proverb said that when God wants to punish someone, he gives a

Nazarene for a wife. Nathaniel well might say: "What good can come out of Nazareth?" The people of Nazareth were looked down upon by the rest of Galilee because it had its own dialect, it was less civilized and rather boorish and uncouth. We see something of this when Christ first returns to Nazareth after beginning his public ministry. The people objected to Him. "Is he not a carpenter's son?" They were too petty and narrow-minded to recognize Him as their master and teacher. Upon His second return, they took Him to the edge of a high cliff and were going to throw Him over.

Nazareth overlooked a busy and important highway that joined the East and the West. Upon this highway could be found people of all classes and races. Highway robbers lived in the hills around Nazareth and would frequently swoop down upon the rich caravans passing through and plunder them. Why did Christ choose this place for His hidden life? When St Joseph and Mary returned to Nazareth from Egypt, I wonder if any of the people still remembered them. Here, as at Bethlehem, and later in His public life, we see Christ choosing to be among the little ones, the "despised" sinners.

Not a word of St Joseph is recorded.

Retreat resolutions I made: 1. Greater effort to foster an interior life of prayer. 2. Greater application of concentration upon my work. 3. To accomplish the above two resolutions through a more serious use of the particular use of the examen (spiritual practice where, in the middle of the day, you examine your conscience, stopping to think about what you've done that day.) (I believe that this focuses too much on fault.)

After the retreat, I had a letter from Mother, in which she was greatly upset over the difficulty with her passport arising from her naturalization. (Because she was born in Luxembourg, and came as an immigrant to this country, there was a question of citizenship.) In the afternoon, I received a more consoling letter saying that the difficulty had been cleared up.

Mrs Vedder gave $600 for the folks' trip, but apparently Mr Vedder is only aware of her giving $200. I went into the city, received the $400 from American Express, which Mrs Vedder sent to me.

I called Vittorio Locke and had dinner with him at the Dinesan hotel. Locke had a brother, Giorgio, who was a resident in Nattuno and I got to know Vittorio through him. He wanted to speak English, so I would teach him English and he would teach me Italian.

We moved into the city. Deacons had "blacks". When you had house cassocks on there were red, white, and blue stripes on it. You could tell which college you belonged to. When you were wearing the cassock you could only go into a religious shop. In order to go anywhere else you had to get "black permission," which permitted you to wear a black cassock.

I got my glasses, my first bifocals. They cost 13000 lire ~ $20.80. I also got special glasses for saying Mass at a cost of 5900 lire, about $9.

We had a "scald" in our camarata (You were assigned to a camarata which had a prefect and beadle (second in command). The camarata was comprised of a section of the house. It was the responsibility of the prefect to monitor where you went. You told him where you wanted to go, and he had to decide if you could go there. He was the one that would be called to account by the vice-rector.)

We used to have what we called scalds. You were supposed to have your lights out at a specified time. We would have 6-8 individuals all in one room and block the light at the windows and door so the Vice Rector would not know we were having a party. We would share things like food from home. Mom sent cans of Spam, which we heated it up on a hotplate. Some of these scalds become very elaborate. For instance, some of the boys would pick up an entire chicken from town for our gathering.

We were having the scald in my room, when we were visited by Msgr. Burns, who was in charge of discipline. He opened the door, and, of course, the rest of the guys pealed out of there leaving me there alone. The next day I had to go see him for my punishment.

Classes began October 15 at the Gregorian University. In the plaza, there would be students from all over the world, and you could tell where they were from by the cassock they wore.

When I came there, the classes were in Latin. You would have a professor, on a dais, lecturing in Latin, over a microphone to 400 students. I didn't understand the lectures, but I could read the books and eventually came to understand classes somewhat.

Fr. McCormick, S.J., who is temporary spiritual director, since Msgr Harrington returned to the U.S., after suffering a heart attack in Spain, gave a conference in which he quoted: "He has put everything under His dominion and made Him the head to which the whole church is joined, so that the church is His body. The completion of Him, who everywhere and in all things is complete." (Eph.1:22-23)

Fr. McCormick, S.J., went on, "In what sense is Christ incomplete? He is true God sharing perfectly in the divine nature. He had a perfect human nature, but it is in His Mystical Body that He is incomplete. In becoming man, He accepted the limitations of space and time. But He hoped to overcome these limitations through His Mystical Body. By joining all men to Himself in this body, he would transcend the barriers of space and time, and in His mystical members, He would live in all places and throughout all time. He wants to live in this seminary - to work, study and pray here, but He can only do this by living in me."

On the 19th of October there was the Deaconate ordination at which I became a deacon. It took place in Leonine College Chapel, Rome. In preparation for the Deaconate, Father Jim Naughton, S.J., retreat master, presented a day of recollection.

The stole is the distinctive garment given to the deacon at the time of his ordination. Fr. Naughton spoke of the stole as a symbol of the burden which the deacon accepts - It is a symbol of the Cross. We know the priesthood as entailing a certain indeterminate burden.

Perhaps, if we knew the details of it now, we would not be strong enough to accept it. In God's plan, however, the details are not undetermined, and in the course of time, we too, shall know them. Every approach to God means a closer bond with the life of Christ in His Mystical Body. But His life was the life of the Cross. God's will sanctifies, i.e., draws us to Himself.

According to the admonition of the bishop to the candidate of the Deaconate, his new office centers around three things: 1. "Comministri et cooperatores corporis et sanguinis Domini" – co-ministers and cooperators of the body and blood of the Lord. This demands an increased study of the doctrine of the Eucharist, both sacrament and sacrifice. Also a deeper realization of the Mass as the center of the Christian life.

2. "Diaconum oportet baptizare" – the deacon is able to baptize. In this office, which directly looks to the increase of the Mystical Body, through the sacrament of Baptism, the deacon ought to foster a deeper love of the Church. Without ceasing to represent the Church in its authentic prayer and mediation, he also helps to build it up sacramentally. He must burn with a fecund love. This supernatural fecundity ought to manifest itself in a more radiant life generative of supernatural energy.
3. "Accipe potestatem legendi Evangelium" – receive the power of reading the Gospel - to communicate the Christian revelation demands of the deacon a profound knowledge of Christian thought, and an esteem of its vital values.

In the deaconate ordination, the bishop says: " Accipe spiritum sanctum, ad robur, etc." asking that the deacon may have strength or courage. St. Steven, the first deacon, has shown us the courage a deacon should have. Fortitude is the conscious undertaking of difficulties to obtain a good end. St Steven was not afraid to debate with anyone who came to him. He seems to have been able to confound them all. Steven must have known the life of Christ very well. He knew the persecution that Christ underwent, the pseudo-trial he received and the accusations brought against Him. Many of Steven's objectors, were, perhaps, the very ones that put Christ to death: surely they were of the same mind. Knowing this and knowing that preaching this Christ, who had so shortly been put to death, he would inevitably come to the same end, he did not hesitate to accept the cross, which is the badge of all disciples of Christ. When brought before the High Priest, St. Steven seems to have eagerly sought martyrdom, so that in his blood, he might give testimony of Christ. In this trial, as in the trial of Christ, how degraded these judges, who were supposed to seek justice, must have appeared.

The verdict had been formed before the trial began. St. Steven did not even bother to answer their questions, but asked them to listen to him as he summarized the history of Israel, showing the fidelity, patience, and mercy of God and the infidelity of the Jewish people in rejecting the prophets who foretold Christ and then consummated their crimes by putting Christ to death. He abruptly closes his discourse by accusing his contemporaries to be as stiff-necked as their forefathers.

The whole life of Christ was also a life of courage. It took courage to leave the solitude of His home and enter upon the tempestuous life of an itinerant preacher. His courage is forcefully manifest in driving the moneychangers from the temple. The mercy He shows on so many occasions does not lessen His constant courage, though he knew the Pharisees and scribes were plotting his death, He was not afraid to call them hypocrites and point out their evils. So much of the time He had to stay in hiding because His time had not yet come. His own people at Nazareth tried to hurl Him off a cliff. Fear is not incompatible with courage. In the garden, Christ was afraid, but He did not lose courage. Though His fear was so intense, He sweat blood, He yet concluded His prayer with "Thy will be done."

The priesthood, like every walk of life, has occasions that demand extraordinary courage, but courage is best manifest in the patience and stick-to-itiveness required in everyday life. Much of Christ's work with his apostles was devoted to giving them courage: "Do not fear, it is I." "Why do you fear, oh you of little faith?" cf. His discourse at the Last Supper, where, over and over again, he tries to build up his apostles' courage. He promises to be with them and to send His spirit upon them. It is this same spirit we receive in ordination.

On October 26, 1952, at the Leonine College of the Lazarist Fathers, on the Feast of Christ the King, I was ordained to the deaconate. Orders were conferred by Archbishop Gonfalieri. Ordination began at 7:00 a.m. and lasted till 11.10. All the orders were conferred.

Three days later, I was exposing deacon at benediction. Sensed a very unusual feeling, as I left the sacristy and realized I was in charge of the ceremony. I was so nervous I could hardly place the lunette into the monstrance. On November 3 I was deacon for the Solemn Requiem Mass at Santa Maria in Via.

On November 6 I made reservations for Mother and Dad at the Dinesen Hotel from December 19-25, inclusive, and from the 29-31, inclusive.

Beginning of priesthood retreat at the Jesuit retreat house - Borgo Santo Spirito was on December 13. Fr. Vincent McCormick conducted the retreat.

I enter this retreat with two dominant impressions: I could have brought so much more to the priesthood. I am most grateful for the grace that has enabled me to bring what I have.

Father's points for meditation: In the gospel according to John, chapter 1, John the Baptist is speaking with two of his disciples. It is the hour of evening sacrifice. Jesus appears and John points him out as the Lamb of God. The two disciples, Andrew and John, follow Christ, and ask him where He lives. Christ answers: "Come and you will see."

We ask for the grace to enter this retreat with the proper dispositions. Points for meditation:

1. "Quid quaeritis?" - What are we seeking? We want to know the will of God in our regard. This may be found: A. in the commandments of God; B. in the commandments of the Church;

C. in Cannon Law; D. through our superiors; E. in the duties in our state of life; F. inspiration of the Holy Spirit.

2. "Venite" – come. Cooperation is necessary. Our Lord asks for some activity on our part. Recollection, silence and concentration are necessary. "Train thyself to grow up in holiness" – Timothy

3. "Et videvitis" – and you will see. God is like the sun, always shining, but we can shut out this light by attachment to creatures. To follow this light will mean sacrifice, but the light of God is also warmth and life. We want the disposition of great liberality.

At 10:a.m., Fr. gave a meditation "Credo in Deum" – I believe in God. "Teach me, oh Lord, to do Thy will, because Thou art my God." - Ps. 142. St Paul always insists upon God as the "loving God." Not a mere abstraction, although transcendent.

There was a time when there was only God. That state was an eternal duration. Creation was an intrusion upon eternity. Now God is not alone. There is another being. I am. But if God was alone and I am, then I must have come from God. He made me out of nothing. Man is not life. He only continues to receive life. God cannot give being as a gift, which no longer depends on Him. That would be against His nature. God contemplating Himself saw He is infinitely imitable.

Nothing outside of God could have moved Him to create me. It must have been something inside Himself that prompted Him to create. This motive must have been love. He willed that others should know and love Himself. It was out of love of Himself that he created me. It was not because He loved me that He created me, because, before I existed, I could not be a motive for his creation.

Still more, God willed that I be elevated to a supernatural state, so that I might know and love Him face to face. Man's satisfaction and perfection consists in his powers attaining their full exercise and perfection. But this perfection of my faculties is identified with the promotion of God's glory. His purpose and my destination are one and the same. We are trying to take the measure of the length and breadth of the temple of God we are. God created me to be an eternal lover of His own infinite perfection. "Thou shalt love the Lord, thy God, with thy whole mind, thy whole heart and with all thy strength." The great commandment could not be other than the pursuit of the purpose for which He created us.

Love is a projection of oneself into another - a certain identity with another - and a consequent concern for myself in that other. This identity is most intimately realized through an identification of will. That is why we want to know the will of God. Reflection: God's work of creation, as well as redemption, manifests a great concern on His part for the "dignity" of man. He takes man to Himself so closely that he makes him a quasi creator. He endows man with a free nature and a certain potency and then lets man form himself, as it were - continue the creative act in himself. So that at the hour of death man may say: "This is also my work. I had a part in the formation of what I am. In redemption also, God has established an economy where mankind redeems mankind and a man redeems himself. How highly God esteems our dignity.

For the 4:00 p.m meditation, we were given "Tu quis es?" - Who are you? This is the question posed to St John by the priests and Levites from Jerusalem. We too might ask ourselves this question. And if we see ourselves rightly we shall see that our very constitution bespeaks dependence. Freedom from our dependence upon God would mean our annihilation. The leaves falling from the trees in autumn appear to be so free and gay, but we know that severed from the branch as they are, they are dead.

Everything created on the face of the Earth was made for man to help him obtain his end. All creatures that cross our path are positively or permissively from God and are intended as a help. That puts man between God and all creation. This world will serve God by serving man. Society itself is a creature and thus should help us to God. Thus man has a two-fold relation: to God and to his fellow men to whom he is a means to God. A priest has the position of mediator in a special way – "a priest taken from among men is ordained for men in the things that pertain to God."

As long as a creature directly or indirectly helps me to God it is not an imperfection and so the proper use of creatures is good.

From this relation of man to creatures it may be seen that man is master of all. "All things are yours, and you are Christ's, and Christ is God." (Gal.)

It is God's will that these creatures do help me to Him, even sickness, sorrow and loneliness. But many creatures can only help me by denying myself the use of them. They oftentimes offer me the opportunity to try my loyalty to God and thus can promote virtue. There must always be measure in my use of creatures. The use of creatures admits of degrees of perfection. Perfection in itself is not an obligation but a call.

At 6:30 p.m. Father's meditation was from the Mass of the third Sunday of Advent: "Modestia vestra nota sit omnibus hominibus." This "medestia," here, means reserve, self-restraint. In the preceding chapter, St Paul said that our "conversatio" is in heaven, i.e., our true home. We are strangers in this world. We must use reserve with the creatures of this world as we would with the property of a stranger whose home we were visiting.

It is not enough for us who are seeking perfection to love God with all our strength, but we must want to increase our strength, our capacity for love.

St Ignatius says that we must make ourselves "indifferent" to creatures. This indifference is not in the sense of mediocrity, nor is it in the Stoic sense of losing all sensibility – apathy. Nor is this indifference the same as resignation. Resignation shows a preference but accepts the will of God when it is manifest. Indifference is the holding of the will in abeyance. It is an equilibrium, but also a force, a power ready to reach out to that which is seen to lead to God.

In this state of indifference, my enthusiasm is not enkindled by any attachment to the creature but by attachment to the will of God. This indifference means a heart on fire with zeal. Zeal is love. Love seeks the good of the beloved. That which is the pleasure of God is the salvation of souls. Our ideal is the habitual state of indifference. This indifference bespeaks a great faith and trust in God's providence.

That evening, at 9:15, Father's meditation was: The thought of sin never left St Peter. (cf. II Pet 2) "God did not spare the angels who fell into sin. He thrust them down to hell, chained them there in the abyss, to await their sentence in torment." God's infinite justice and mercy did not spare them. For eternity they will be in hell. Sin didn't stop there. Consider the sin of Adam and Eve and the consequences. Consider a soul in hell for a single mortal sin. As for the grace of shame and confusion speak with Christ on the Cross.

At the 10: a.m. meditation: We ask for the grace of deep sorrow for personal sins. Penance is a virtue and the act of this virtue is the act of contrition. Penance is a detestation of sin with the firm resolve not to sin again. Contrition is an act of will whereby we will to undo what has been done. But this is impossible. Nevertheless, we have that state of mind that prompts us to will to undo, if possible, what we have done. This interior contrition must find exterior expression. We cannot attack the sin, but we can deal with the sinner. The pain we impose is an exterior expression of what we feel interiorly. One may doubt the depth of interior penance if it does not find exterior expression. We are composed of body and soul.

Consider the soul as a prisoner in this corruptible body. Our condition is, indeed, humiliating, because we are never secure from the temptations brought on by the body, and so we must always be on the alert. Our passions are as so many wild animals surrounding us.

(Psalm 50) David had sinned grievously – adultery and murder. The prophet Nathan came to rebuke him. In David's external expression of his interior sorrow he first makes his appeal to God as a God of mercy. Then he acknowledges his sins. He recognized the gravity of the evil he had done in God's sight: "Tibi soli peccavi." Sin is not a mere social infraction or the breaking of a law. It is a personal offence against God: "Quod malum est coram te feci." i.e., what is evil, before you I have done. Then the Psalmist asks God's mercy to restore him to the grace and friendship he had lost. He ends with a promise of reparation and sacrifice – the sacrifice of praise, reverence, and justice.

At the 4:00 p.m. conference, Father said: "It is not enough for us to be in the state of grace." Christ wishes us to grow in justification from day to day. Some means for growing in grace are the following: 1. The examination of conscience, 2. Peace of soul, 3. The avoidance of venial sin, 4. Use of a spiritual director.

That evening, at 9:15pm, the meditation was based on Hebrews 12: "Why then, since we are watched from above by such a cloud of witnesses, let us rid ourselves of all that weighs us down, of the sinful habit that clings so closely, and run, with all endurance, the race for which we are entered. Let us fix our eyes on Jesus…" The call of Christ to his kingdom. Picture Christ calling His apostles. He would make them fishers of men. We ask for the grace not to be deaf to his call, but prompt and diligent to accomplish His will. Christ is a king, and He wills to conquer the whole world and all His enemies. His is a spiritual kingdom, and a voluntary kingdom. In the economy of the redemption, Christ cannot achieve his kingdom without me, nor can I be saved without him. Just as the vine is necessary to the branches, so the branches are necessary to the vine.

At 10:00 a.m. meditation, Father said: If man is to remain free and still be saved, he must come to realize how much God loves him and what an evil sin is. To affect this and to enable man to render adequate satisfaction God decreed the Incarnation. Man would save himself according to this divine plan. Christ came to do the work of another and to do this he became that other. And now all that men had to do to be saved was to unite themselves with this God, who had become one of them.

At 4:00 p.m. meditation, Father said: The mystery of Bethlehem lies in the humiliation of God taking on the helplessness of a child. The gospels, or St Paul, do not speak of the physical sufferings of Christ at Bethlehem, but St. Paul to the Philippians speaks of the humiliation of Christ in taking the form of a servant. Leviticus 12 speaks of purification after the firstborn. Our Blessed Mother availed herself of the privilege of the poor. Simeon's prophecy was the first shadow of the cross to fall across the path of the Blessed Virgin.

It must have been an humiliation for Mary and Joseph when they were unable to find Jesus after a day's journey from Jerusalem. Mary felt the humiliation so keenly that she chided him when they found him in the temple.

At 9:15 p.m., our points for meditation were: We ask for the grace to elect that which makes for the greater glory of God. Examples of willingness or unwillingness to take the necessary means to obtain an end: 1. Christ and the rich young man. This man wanted to be perfect, but he was unwilling to use the means necessary for the achievement of perfection. 2. IV Kings, Naaman the leper was willing to take means to be cured but they were means of his on choosing. There are generous souls willing to give up many things, but unwilling to give up themselves. These other gifts are only a token of self-surrender. 3. Acts of the Apostles: Conversion of St Paul. "Lord what do you want me to do?" – unconditional surrender.

December 17: 4:00 p.m. conference : Humility. Humility is the virtue that helps me to maintain that true relationship that exists between me and God – creature-creator relationship. Humility is truth affirming the essential dependence arising from this relationship. In the physical order I cannot sever this relationship of dependence, but in the moral order I can. In the moral order I affirm this essential relationship by a unity of will with God. This bond is broken in the moral order by mortal sin. It may be strained to the breaking point by a deliberate venial sin. He who is truly humble, thus affirms this creature-creator relationship. I will suffer anything rather than weaken this bond by venial sin. Truth demands this.

This direct creature-creator relationship is not the whole truth in the present economy. Our relation to God is through a mediator. Christ is the one mediator between God and men. Our only access to God is through Christ. Thus in the present economy this creature-creator relationship finds its true expression in the complete domination of Christ over our wills. St. Paul expresses this truth when he says: "The charity of Christ presses me." The word he uses in the Greek is the same one used to express the domination of the charioteer over his horse through his use of the reins. Thus in English it might be better translated in the sense of 'dominate' or 'control'. It was this same humility that made St Paul say: "It is now not I who live but Christ who lives in me." Only when I have achieved this union with Christ will I have the true relation that exists between God and me. The order God has established demands this relationship. This means dying to self, but this dying to self is only a means to an end. The Christian life is not a dying but a life. Self-denial is a means to humility.

`December 18: 10:00 a.m. meditation: "Then Jesus came from Galilee and stood before John at the Jordan to be baptized by him." (Mt. 3:13) These few words express an event that must have great importance in the life of Christ. Think of all that Nazareth of Galilee meant to him. In this we see how Christ was perfectly at home in the world, and yet was not tied down by affections for the world. He must have been thoroughly at home in Nazareth because, when he later returned as a prophet, his townsfolk refused to believe him. He had lived too much like one of them, that now he should be their teacher. Yet, though Christ was so perfectly at home at Nazareth, when the time came for him to enter upon his public work, he hesitated not a moment, even though that meant leaving Mary behind and all that had been so dear to him at Nazareth.

John the Baptist was preaching sermons of penance. What kind of people were coming to him? What a humiliation for Christ to join this crowd. "Let it be so for the present; it is well that we should thus fulfill all due observance."

Christ began his public life with sacrifice. After sacrifice, he humiliated himself, then came a consolation: "This is my beloved Son in whom I am well pleased." Then he went into the desert to be tempted.

6.30 p.m. meditation: A day, a night and a day in Christ's life. (Mt .14. John 6) The day began with sad news. Christ heard of John the Baptist's death in prison. He wanted to be alone with his sorrow, but the crowd would not allow him. When he got to the other side of the lake, there was already a crowd there. Christ took pity on the crowd. He began speaking to them and healing their sick. The apostles tried to persuade him to get rid of the crowd by reminding him of the time and place they were in. Christ said, perhaps with tongue in cheek: "Why don't you give them to eat?" Then he called Philip, the naïve apostle, and questioned him in similar fashion. Notice how Christ performed this miracle. He allowed the apostles to pass out the bread and get credit for it. Frequently he deals with us in the same way. He allows us to receive credit for that which is truly the work of his grace. At the sight of this miracle, the crowd wanted to made Christ king. Maybe the apostles were also egging them on. Christ saw the danger in this temptation for the apostles, and so he sent them down to the boat and told them to cross over the lake: He himself would dismiss the crowd. That night, Christ when up the mountain to pray. What prayer did he make to his Father that night?

During the night, He came to the apostles, walking on the water. When they reached Capernaum, the crowd was already waiting for them. It was then that Christ promised the Eucharist. With this promise, many of his apostles walked with him no more. Peter made his act of faith: "Lord, to whom should we go? Thy words are the words of eternal life; we have learned to believe and are assured that you are Christ, the son of God."

December 19: I saw mother and dad, today, for the first time in nearly three and a half years. I was a bit surprised to see them looking so good. I had expected them to age more. They seemed very happy and had enjoyed the trip immensely. Both were dressed more richly than I'd ever seen them. Dad did most of the talking. Mother tried hard to get in her few words. We had about an hour to visit. After they left, I could not bring my mind back to the retreat meditations anymore.

December 20 1952: I awoke at 3:00 a.m. and could sleep no more. Ordination at St John Lateran at 8:30. It lasted until 1:00 p.m. There was ordination to tonsure and all the Orders. Cardinal Micara, the vicar general of Rome, was the ordaining prelate. I saw mother and dad for a minute before the ordination. They were seated right in the apse.

The Church of St. John Lateran where I was ordained

I was devoid of much emotion until the very moment of ordination. Then I felt that the silence of the church was all pressed inside of me, as if the new indwelling of the Holy Spirit made itself felt in silence and peace. Throughout the rest of the ceremony, I was choked up with such emotion that it was hard to keep back tears. It was not hard to enter into the sentiment of the Mass in concelebrating with the Cardinal. It is surprising how exhilarating happiness can be. I think my soul was most stirred when mother and dad knelt before me after the ordination and I gave them my first blessing. By the mysterious power of God, I could really bless them. Vitorio Bonavavenia met us afterwards. We went to the College where I changed cassocks, had a cup of coffee, and then the four of us went to dinner at Alfredo's. I don't think any of us were hungry, though I had been fasting all morning. After dinner, we went back to the hotel for a bit and then at 4:30 p.m. we returned to the College for a reception and the giving of blessings. George Duritsa and Roy Litursky had my room all fixed up. Mother and dad sat by as I gave blessings. And then they met most of the students. Our parents were present for Benediction. The choir sang "Tu es Sacerdos" with Bob Behan as soloist. After supper some of the fellows came around to the room and we talked until bedtime.

Fr. Francis Galles after his first Mass at St.
Peter's Basilica in Rome with his parents

December 21: I did not sleep well. Still too excited. First Mass at the altar of Blessed Pius X at St Peter's. Fr. Tom Heneghan was my assistant priest. Roy Litursky and George Duritsa served. Jack Weaver took care of my parents. Vitorio Bonavenia and his parents and brother were present. Also, Miss Alma Giovannetti and Ignatio Ramirez. Fr. Guy Bertin was there, but I did not see him. I was a little nervous in beginning Mass, but soon became quite confident. It was easier to enter into the prayers of the Mass than I had expected. The moment of consecration was so like the practice Mass that it hardly seemed I had consecrated. I was deeply moved as I gave Communion to mother. (I remember that I was very disappointed that Dad didn't receive Communion from me.)

We had dinner at the Dinesen. There were eight of us. Miss Giovannetti was with us. I had to return to the college for dinner. (I can remember we griped about that.)

After dinner, I went to the hotel where my parents were. We went first to St. Susanna's where the folks went to Confession and then to the College for the reception given to the relatives by the bishop. It was nearly over when we arrived. We had to leave shortly to take the train to Nettuno. We arrived at Nettuno at about 8:00 p.m. and were met at the station by one of the boys from the orphanage. When we got to the Casa della Divina Providenza, we were met by the superior, Suor Carmella de Micheli, the chaplain, Commodore Francesco Saverio Parisi (viale Regina Margherita 249, Roma. tel 861812) and other sisters. Five small boys in blue gowns and white collars came and recited a couple psalms welcoming us. We had a liquare, a light lunch, and then went to bed. We had the best rooms in the house overlooking the sea. It was somewhat cold, as the sisters had no heat.

December 22: Mass at 7:30 a.m. in the chapel for all the children. One of the sisters had made the alb I wore, and which was used for the first time at my Mass. My beautiful red chasuble had been worn by Pope Benedict XV. The chaplain assisted me at Mass and the children sang hymns and recited prayers. I distributed Communion to all the children. After Mass, I was given a chair at the altar steps for the "baccia delle mani." All the children and sisters came before me, knelt and kissed my hands. After breakfast, all the children and sisters were assembled for a program of poems and hymns which the children presented in our honor. I spoke a few words to the children, and then they all came up to receive an ordination holy card. Mother and dad sat on either side of me.

We then rented a car for 3000 lire and visited the home of St. Maria Goretti, saw her body at the church and visited the American cemetery. We were back at the Casa della Divina Providenza at 1:00 p.m. for dinner. The sisters had a real pranzo prepared for us. After dinner, Mr. Parisi took us through the entire house. We again saw many of the children. Suor Carmela gave me a relic of St. Joseph Cottolengo. Mr Parisi accompanied us on the train back to Rome. Mother and Dad really seemed to have enjoyed this day. I hurriedly read through my ordination mail.

December 23: Mass at the tomb of St. Catherine of Siena, offered for Aunt Katie. Dick Foley and Dave Born served. Dick Zenk took care of my parents.

Mother and Dad and Fr. Francis Galles are just to the left of Pope Pius XII, at 9:15 a.m. There were only about 35 or 40 people in our audience. I was the only priest except for a monsignor. All the other new priests and their people had their audience yesterday, and there was such a crowd that some did not get to see His Holiness. We each got to meet His Holiness individually. I presented Mother and Dad to him. After he had met everyone, we had a picture taken together. We were in the back row, and His Holiness, turning around and seeing how short we were, called us up to the front. We had breakfast at the Denesin.

Audience with Pope Pius XII after ordination. Fr.
Francis with his parents is to the left of Pope

December 24: Mass at Santa Susanna. Giorgio Bonavenia served for me.

December 25: The ordination has so eclipsed Christmas that it hardly seems like Christmas. I celebrated my three Masses with the folks at the Good Shepherd convent. Roy Liturski served. We had breakfast there afterward. We slept late, and after saying some Office, I went to see the folks at the hotel at about 11:00 a.m. We had our Christmas dinner together including a coffee and strega, and went out only to visit relics at the crib at St. Mary Major. We were at the College for solemn Benediction. I was the deacon. We had a movie in the evening.

December 26: Mass at the College. Bob Sampon served. We took Citbus to Assisi. Stayed at the Windsor-Savoia Hotel.

December 27: Mass at the Blessed Sacrament altar and the tomb of St. Francis. Rain most of the day. Mother and I wrote letters and thank you notes.

December 28: Mass at the tomb of St Clare. More rain.

December 29: Mass at the tomb of St Francis. About 40 fellows from the College arrived.

December 30: Mass at the tomb of St Francis. We took the train back to Rome.

December 31: Mass in the upstairs chapel at the College. We spent the day sightseeing and shopping.

January 1, 1953: Mass at San Andrea al Quirinale at the tomb of St Stanislas Kostka. Vitorio served. We spent the day at the hotel. It was raining.

January 2: Mass in the Confession at St Paul Outside the Walls. Met Vitorio at the Vatican museum. He took us through the whole place, and gave us an excellent tour. I returned to the College for dinner. Vitorio took the folks to dinner and then to the catacombs. I stayed at the College to see a dress rehearsal of Angel Street, directed by Roy Liturski.

January 3: Classes began again. After the third class, I went to the hotel to meet the folks and take them to the train station. Took the train at 1:43 p.m. Arrived in Naples at 4:00 p.m. Had an incident with the porter. Stayed at the Albergo Turistico.

January 4: Said Mass at the chapel in the hotel. After breakfast we went down to the boat, Saturnia. About 11:00 a.m. when we got on board. Didn't have time to finish dinner before I had to leave. Gave Mother and Dad my blessing before parting. They were up on deck when the ship pulled out at 12:00. I took a train back to Rome at 2:05. Arrived at 4:30.

January 6: I was deacon at the Solemn Mass. Movie "Detective Story". We served dinner for the old folks at the Sisters of the Poor.

January 8: Letter from Mrs Vedder saying I should order a chalice. She would send money and that Archbishop McIntyre, Monsignor Dolan, and Mr Albert Charles Berghoff would call upon me. Also had a note of congratulations from Irene Dunne: "To Francis Galles - do dear father accept our best wishes and please remember us in your prayers" – Irene Dunne Griffen

January 12: Cardinal McIntyre received his biglietto here in the auditorium. The priests served as ushers for the guests. A courier, who was sent by the Holy Father at the beginning of the Secret Consistory, picked up the biglietto at the Holy Office and then delivered it here. Cardinal Spellman, coming directly after the Consistory, arrived after the ceremony. All the guests and students had a chance to meet the new cardinal. Monsignor Dolan and Mr Berghoff asked to see me, and we talked a short time. All the old cardinals, and various distinguished people, came to visit the Cardinal in the afternoon.

January 15: Public Consistory at St Peter's. I had a good ticket, but, although I was more than an hour early, I was too late to obtain entrance my ticket entitled me to. I was about half way up the nave for the procession and left early because I could see nothing of the ceremonies from my place. Of the 24 new Cardinals, 16 received the red hat at this Consistory.

January 16: The Gregorian University had a reception for the new Cardinals. Six of the newly appointed Cardinals were alumni of the Gregorian, including Cardinal Stepinac of Yugoslavia.

January 17: Cardinal McIntyre gave a pranzo at the College for members of his party and had a reception in the afternoon. His talks are always short but perfectly sincere. He seems to be most considerate and little given to formality.

January 18: Cardinal McIntyre took possession of his titular church – St Anastasia. We were in the sanctuary and the priests came up to kiss his ring. The Cardinal gave a talk. At the dinner the Cardinal thanked us and said goodbye.

January 27: Bishop O'Connor celebrated his anniversary of Episcopal Consecration with a Pontifical High Mass, a pranzo and a movie. He seemed to be very happy. Cardinal Pizzardo was here for dinner. He read the announcement that Bishop O'Connor was named assistant at the papal throne.

February 1: (Septuagesima Sunday) I celebrated my first Solemn High Mass. George McFadden was my deacon. Dick Wempe was subdeacon. I had much more personal satisfaction from it than I expected. Fr McCormick today inaugurated a monthly day of recollection.

March 2: I received my chalice from Fumante. It has a nearly balanced cup and base with Christ and the Twelve Apostles carved in the base. The node is blood jasper. Cup and base are hammered gold. This chalice was ordered and designed by William F. Meyers of Lansing, MI, but because he delayed his ordination I was able to purchase his chalice. William Meyers was ordained July 2, 1955. He became director of the Institute for Continuing Theological Studies at the North American College in Rome where he served until his sudden death February 18, 1993.

March 4: Monsignor Burns announced that Monsignor Freking had been appointed Spiritual Director of the College. Fr Schlicte was also appointed to the faculty.

March 5: I had my chalice and paten consecrated at St Peter's by Bishop Pasini.

March 6: Used my chalice for the first time and offered the Mass for Mr. and Mrs. Vedder who donated the chalice.

March 8: My 26ᵗʰ birthday. Offered Mass at the Church of the Holy Cross in Jerusalem for my priestly perfection. Giogio Bonavenia served for me and we had breakfast afterward.

March 26: Most Reverend Theodore Suhr, Vicar Apostolic of Denmark, spoke to the community. Some observations: Many Protestants in Denmark no longer believe in an afterlife. Material prosperity has not brought happiness. Don't enter into arguments. Present Catholic doctrine. Bishop Suhr doesn't believe in much organization in Catholic action. The doctrine of the Mystical Body must be more deeply realized and lived by individuals and nations.

March 28: Last day of classes at the Gregorian University

March 29: - (Palm Sunday) I offered Mass at St John Lateren. Two German students from Innsbruck served for me: Hermann Krechting (Schubert Strasse 18, Stock I, Innsbruck, Austria) and Ulreck Derstappen (Gilmstrasse 3, Stock II, Innsbruck, Austria). I took them to breakfast afterward.

March 30: Mass at the Church of the Holy Cross in Jerusalem. My two German friends served for me.

March 31: Offered Mass at the altar of St Francis Xavier in the Gesu. My German friends served again and we had breakfast together.

Housecleaning day at the College. Day of Recollection began in the evening. A Passionist priest gave the conferences.

April 2: I was deacon for the Solemn Mass at Precious Blood convent

April 3: I made the three hours privately at the College.

April 4: I was sub-deacon for the ceremonies at Clinica Bastianelli, 277 viale Margherita Regina.

Together, with about five other students, I went to the parish of S. Euginio to bless homes. Piero Longi was my altar boy. A very interesting experience. A wealthy section of apartment houses. Many of the apartments were really sumptuous. Most of the people were waiting for us to come. After reading the prayer blessing at the door I went through the whole house sprinkling each room with holy water. If there were children, I gave them my personal blessing. Frequently, the whole family knelt for a blessing. In many homes, I also blessed eggs, cakes, and other foods for Easter.

I was quite surprised to see that the Easter preparations seldom centered in the kitchen as they do at home. No odors of baking and cooking came from the kitchens, which were frequently the smallest and unkempt room of the house.

We had dinner at the parish rectory with the pastor and assistants. A good spirit seemed to prevail in the rectory. After dinner, we took an hour siesta and then went out to bless more homes. Some of the people offered us coffee and a liquare. Without completing my section, we quit about 7:00 p.m. On the way home, many shopkeepers stopped us and asked a blessing. One man even stopped his car and asked me to bless it. We were tired at night.

April 5: (Easter Sunday) I offered Mass at the convent, Suore con Passionate Servi di Maria, via Alesandro Tortolonia 14)

At 12:00, we received our Holy Father's blessing at St Peter's. I was on top of the colonnade and had a good view of His Holiness when he appeared on the balcony and also of the entire piazza, filled with people and overflowing into the Via della Conciliazione.

I took my two German friends to the Tre Sorelli restaurant for dinner. They had enormous appetites. We went for a walk in the Pincian Gardens afterward. Upon leaving, I gave them each 1000 lire.

April 8: Gene Best, Harry Butori, Bob Sampon, and I went to Orvieto. I was greatly impressed by Signorelli paintings depicting the Resurrection and Hell. The despair on the faces of the damned is most striking. Erravimus.

April 11: Bishop O'Connor spoke to the priests. Five points he asked us to write down:

1. Modestia vestra nota sit omnibus hominibus – Our Lady of Humility – self-effacement.
2. Pare domine custodiam ari meo - pruudence, common sense, good taste
3. Integrity. Uomo di fiducia.
4. Only God can make man see. Only God can make me see.
5. Accendat in nobis domine ignem sui amoris et flamam aeternae caritatis.

April 15: Bishop Sheen spoke at the College

April 17: I received a letter from Irene Dunne while she was in NY, telling me she had dinner with Cardinal Spellman, and that he had written a letter to Count Galleazzi asking him to arrange an audience for Miss Henry and her companions, and she hoped this would not interfere with any plans I had made.

Bishop Sheen spoke on the "missionary spirit of the clergy" in the auditorium of Propaganda College. Emphasized the importance of the East in future history.

April 19: I wrote to the following priests asking them to be ministers at my first Solemn Mass at home: Fr. Majerus – deacon; Fr. Smith – subdeacon; Fr. Gengler – preacher.

April 23: Received a letter from Bishop Fitzgerald with a check for $300, which I am to pay back gradually. He approved July 12 for my Solemn Mass and would arrange my appointment for July 21st.

April 27: I wrote to Mrs. Delaney and sent the following bills for souvenirs: 14 coin purses – 18250 lire; 2 cameos – 6000 lire; a total of 224250 lire, or $39.

May 6: I showed Miss Alice Henry (Irene Dunne's aunt), Mrs Lewis, and Miss Gertrude Mulchrone around Rome.

May 7: I offered Mass at the Altar of the Chair in St Peter's for the three ladies from Los Angeles.

May 10: I went with the ladies from Los Angeles for a drive to Castel Gondolfo.

May 20: Frs. Ambrose Lane, Paul Hoddap, and Henry Russell arrived in Rome.

May 22: Written exam at the Gregorian for the STL.

I wrote on the following topic: "In quo sensu fides rationabilis dici potest."

May 23: The priests at the villa invited our whole class out for a dinner and a day at the Villa Santa Catarina

May 24: (Pentecost Sunday) I offered Mass for my own priestly sanctification at the tomb of St. Philip Neri in the Chiesa Nuova.

May 25: The College went to the beach for the day.

May 26: Roy Litursky and I took a bum run with Frs. Layne, Hodapp, and Russell to Tivoli and the castelli.

After completing my studies in Rome, I returned to the States aboard an Italian-line ship. I took the train from New York to my home town of Iona, Minnesota. Preparations were then made for my first solemn Mass at St Columba Church in Iona. Two priests from the parish, Frs. Edward Scheuring and Louis Scheuring were deacon and subdeacon at this Mass. Fr John Gengler preached the homily. The whole family along with friends joined in the celebration. It was a big event. Local boy comes home and celebrates Mass. Then I received my first assignment in the diocese July 21st. That assignment was as assistant pastor at St John Nepomucene Church in Winona. I was also assistant editor of "The Courier" from 1953 until 1962, as well as a religion instructor at Cotter High School from 1953 to 1954.

I spent most of the day at "The Courier". The office, at that time, was at the rectory. Later on the office was moved downtown.

I was at "The Courier" 9 years and at the parish 6 years.

As assistant editor of "The Courier", I wrote a number of columns in regard to the Christian Family Movement, an organization that tried to foster better family life. A group of married couples gather once a month and discus how things are going, problems they had, and they would get support from the group. I also wrote a series of editorials, and a series of articles on how I Pray my Rosary.

VII)   The Years After Ordination (1953 – 1962)

The day after my ordination on December 20, 1952, I offered my first Mass at the altar of St. Pius X in St. Peter's. I was deeply moved as I gave communion to mother, but was disappointed that my dad did not receive communion at my first Mass. The next day, we went to the church of St, Susanna and my parents went to confession. After that, dad always received communion.

After my first Mass, my parents and I took the train to Nettuno, and spent the night at the Casa della Divina Provvidenzz. The next morning, I offered Mass there with the Sisters and the orphan children who resided there. It was a quite moving experience at the end of Mass when all the children came up and kissed my anointed hands.

On Tuesday, December 23, I offered Mass at the tomb of St. Catherine of Siena for Aunt Katie. After the Mass, Mother, Dad and I went directly to the Vatican for an audience with our Holy Father, Pope Pius XII. We each got to meet his Holiness individually. I presented Mother and Dad to him. After he had met everyone, we had a picture taken together. We were in the back row, and his Holiness turning around and seeing how short we were, called us up to the front.

On December 26, we took the bus to Assisi, where I was able to offer Masses at the tombs of St. Clair and St. Francis. We returned to Rome on December 30.

My good Italian friend, Vittorio Locki took my parents through the Vatican museum and then the catacombs.

I went with my parents to Naples, January 3, and the next day, they left for home on the Saturnia.

When I got back to Rome, there was a letter from Irene Dunne in which she said, "To Francis Galles – do dear father accept our bet wishes and please remember us in your prayers – Irene Dunne Griffen."

On March 2, I received my chalice from Fumante. It had a nearly balanced cup and base with Christ and the twelve Apostles carved in the base. The node was blood jasper. Cup and base were hammered gold on silver.

I returned to the United States on the S.S. Vulcania in June, 1953.

I offered my first solemn Mass at St. Columba Church in Iona, Minnesota, on July 12, 1953. Fr. Jim Fasnacht, the pastor, was Master of Ceremonies. Fathers Ed and Louis Scheuring were deacon and subdeacon.

My first assignments were in Winona. I was Assistant Pastor at St. John Nepomecene, Assistant Editor of The Courier, and Religion Instructor at Cotter High School. I was the Assistant Pastor from January 21, 1953 until 1959, The Courier's Assistant Editor until 1962, and Religion Instructor until 1954.

Msgr. Dan Tierney, the pastor at St. John Nepomecene Parish and editor of The Courier, soon introduced me to parish work and let me do most of the work that was in the parish. He also helped me to learn how to prepare and publish a newspaper. I learned a great deal through his friendliness with people. It was unfortunate that, in my later years, because of my immaturity, our relationship became rather strained.

Shortly after my arrival in the parish, a number of couples approached me and asked if I would be chaplain if they formed a Team of Our Lady. This team of six couples became very supportive and helpful to me. They remained friends even after I left the parish.

During those early years, I wrote out my homilies and they were well received by the parish.

After six years at St. John's, Bishop Fitzgerald appointed me as Spiritual Director at Immaculate Heart of Mary Seminary, Winona. I continued on as Assistant Editor of The Courier. On July 12, 1959, I moved from the chaplain's cottage at Assisi Heights to the seminary.

In the summer of 1962, I was surprised when I returned to my room at the seminary to find on my desk a private letter from Archbishop Martin J. O'Connor, Rector of the North American College in Rome, asking if I would accept the appointment as Spiritual Director of the North American College. If I accepted, he would recommend me to Cardinal Spellman, head of the Episcopal Committee at the college.

I wrote back to the Archbishop and gave him about six reasons why I thought I should not accept his invitation, but said that I would accept the appointment if, in spite of my reasons for not accepting, he still wanted me as Spiritual Director.

He very cleverly responded to my objections and then asked again if I would accept. I sent my acceptance. The Archbishop then submitted my name to Cardinal Spellman and the Episcopal Committee.

Thus, I was destined to return to Rome.

VIII) Return to Rome (1962 – 1971)

Shortly after my appointment to the North American College, Archbishop O'Connor informed me that my classmate at Rome, Msgr. Warren Holleran from California, would serve with me as a Spiritual Director, but I would be head of the department.

Msgr. Holleran was extremely intelligent and served with me for six years. During that time, he also did further work in theology and got a PhD degree. He left Rome on October 24, 1968.

My nine years as Spiritual Director were challenging and exciting years The bishops form all over the world came to Rome for the Second Vatican Council, which was held from 1962 to 1965. Many of the bishops came to the college and some of the cardinals lived with us.

July 13, 1962,I was named a Papal Chamberlain by Pope John XXIII, and a Domestic Prelate by Pope Paul VI April 27, 1968.

I was in Rome when Pope John XXIII died June 3, 1963. I was able to view his body in his apartment even before he was displayed in St. Peter's.

I was able to do a considerable amount of travel during my time as Spiritual Director at the college. From September 10 to September 27, I visited the Holy Land with stopovers at Cairo, Egypt, and Athens, Greece.

I was in Rome when President Kennedy was shot and killed on November 22.

In January, 1964, I flew to Catania, Sicily, and rented a car and toured the whole island. I flew back to Rome on January 9, 1964.

Brother Majella Nsubuga, from Uganda, came to me when I was at the villa at Castel Gondolfo and asked if I would be his spiritual director. He began coming to me once a month for spiritual direction and we became real friends. He was instrumental in my going to Uganda and Kenya, July 24 to September 4, 1969.

I made a retreat at the Better World Center, September 16-23, 1964, and eventually became involved in giving Better World retreats at Rocca di Papa, as well as in the United States.

November 27, Bishop Francis Reh became Rector at the North American College, replacing Archbishop O'Connor. We had a farewell dinner for the archbishop, October 13, 1964.

I became acquainted with Peter Mulder, a Belgian artist, October 25,1964. He later did a very large, beautiful painting for me. I wish I had kept in touch with him.

My father, Charles Galles, died March 10, 1965, at the age of 82. Fr. Harry Gavin called me at midnight to inform me of his death. The next day, I celebrated Mass with the students at the college and then left for the States, where I celebrated Dad's funeral at St. Columba Church, Iona, Minnesota, on March 13, 1965. I returned to Rome April 24, 1965.

While I was gone, Cardinal Clement Micara, who had ordained me as a priest, died March 12, 1965.

I visited Sardinia July 14 to July 23, 1965.

Pope Paul VI paid a visit to our villa at Castel Gondolfo on September 5, 1965. I have a picture taken with him.

Fr. Robert Nagosek, Rector of Holy Cross College, Rome, gave the annual retreat at the college, January 1 to 8, 1966.

On February 10, I had a very significant discussion with Sister Mary Francis at St. Peter's Basilica, followed by dinner together. I later helped her financially to make a trip to the Holy Land with other sisters of her community.

On February 26, Bishop Fitzgerald asked me to give a Better World Movement retreat to the priests of the Winona Diocese. I suggested it would be better if it included sisters and lay people. He later agreed.

From March 6 to 12, I made a retreat at the Passionist Monastery with Fr. Barnabas Ahern, a noted Scripture scholar, as my director.

From April 11 to 17, I was on the team that conducted a Better World Retreat at the International Center of the Better World Movement. Sr. Cuthbert and Fr. Bob Nagosek were on the team with me. This was a very outstanding retreat. It was all recorded, but unfortunately, I have lost the tapes. It was at this retreat that I met Sr. Breda Lyng.

Sr. Breda Lyng with the brother of Pope John XXIII

Shirle Gordon, whom I had met in the Holy Land, came to Rome, and from April 28 to May 1, and I had a number of very significant visits with her. Erna Krueder Gordon, Shirle's mother, had committed suicide on March 1, 1966.

Shirle Gordon

Fr. Al Giaquinto, who had been so significant in my life when I was in the seminary, came to Rome June 25, and together we went to Lourdes.

I began a trip back to the United States July 11, stopping at Madrid and San Sebastian, where I had dinner with Sr. Ibone and her family. Then it was on to Paris, New York, Chicago, Minneapolis and, finally, Iona.

On July 24, 1966, Bishop Fitzgerald celebrated the 50th anniversary of his ordination. That same evening I began conducting a Christian Community Retreat at Winona. I had prepared Msgr. Joe McGinnis and Fr. Joe Haggerty to assist me as a team to give this retreat. We had 56 participants; and, though I was not feeling well, the retreat was a great success.

Immediately after the retreat I went to the Mayo Clinic at Rochester. Dr. Callahan was my doctor. After a thorough check-up, he decided there was nothing really wrong with me physically, but perhaps a bit of tension.

What was bothering me at that time diminished but persisted for many years. I think it was only when I made a 30-day retreat in 1977, and telling the director my entire life story, which I had also written, that I was freed from whatever had bothered me for so many years. I cried every day of the retreat and letting out all the hidden feelings that were within me is what healed me.

After a visit at home, I flew to New York and boarded the ship Independence as chaplain to make my way back to Naples and then to Rome. On board ship, I met St. Patrice Geuting, Sr. Agnes Horman and Sr. Carol Saussy. I spent a considerable amount of time with Sr. Saussy, especially, and it was through her that I met Sr. Meg Canty, who became a close friend of mine.

Fr. Gerald Sloyan arrived in Rome on September 17, and brought me greetings from Monika Hellwig, the former Sr. Cuthbert.

On November 3, Fr. Bartolini and I went to Pisa and then on to Luca.

December 9, I received a letter from Fay Benson, who was in Cleveland, Ohio, announcing that she would be baptized in the Catholic Church on Christmas Eve. I had met her and become friends with her at Lourdes, when I was there in July. She was later confirmed February 25, 1968.

I was with the newly ordained priests and their families for an audience with Pope Paul VI on December 19.

I was with the Sisters of the Sacred Heart on the Via Nomentana when Sisters Saussy, Horman, Geuting and Canty made their perpetual vows. It was on this occasion that my friendship with Sr. Canty really began to develop.

Lloyd and Leona Buse moved off the farm, one mile north of Iona, and into our house in Iona, on March 1, 1967. Leona was my oldest sister. This gave Mother the support and help she needed after my father's death.

Lloyd and Leona Buse (Leona is my sister)

From March 26 to April 2, I, as well as Sisters Cuthbert and Esther, was on the team for a Better World Retreat at the International Center at Rocca di Papa. There were 24 retreatants.

Lucille Herrick, who had made the Better World retreat I gave in the Diocese of Winona, was so impressed that she gave $1000 for another Better World retreat and offered to raise another $1800.

I left for the United States On August 3. In Philadelphia, I gave a retreat for the Medical Mission Sisters August 4-12.

Then, August 13 to 18, I conducted another retreat of the Christian Community at the seminary in Winona. Monika Hellwig, the former Sr. Cuthbert, was on the team with me.

On April 9, 1968, Fr. Vince Bartolini, Fr. Stan Fleming and I joined the Loyola University Tour Group to Russia, Poland and Hungary. From Moscow we went on to Leningrad. We returned to Moscow April 12 and made an excursion to Zagorsk (the holy city of Russia).

While in Moscow, I offered Mass in my hotel room with the tour group. I was later told by our guide that I could have gotten into trouble with the Communists for doing this. Later this same tour guide told me that she would like to have a Bible. I went to my suitcase and gave her the Bible I had with me. I am sure I could also have gotten into trouble for doing this.

We left Moscow by bus to go to Warsaw, April 15. It was during this long bus ride that Helen Chase, one of the Loyola students, came back in the bus and we became engaged in a very long discussion. Fr. Jim Rausch, from St. Cloud, was sitting next to me during this discussion. Later he told me that, although he did not join in the discussion, this was the most important event for him during the entire time he was with the Loyola University Tour Group. Helen and I became friends as a result of this discussion.

We also made an excursion to Czestaschowa before going on to Budapest. We returned to Rome April 20.

July 3, I returned to the United States on board the S.S. Washington.

From July 28 to August 4, I conducted a retreat for the Franciscan Sisters at Assisi Hall in Winona. Eighty sisters attended.

Fr. Bartolini came from Providence, Rhode Island, to visit me in Minnesota on July 26 and stayed until August 9.

I had lunch with Archbishop Binz and Fr. John Kinney on August 8.

I had lunch with Bishop Fitzgerald on August 13, and then visited The Courier office, where I had been Assistant Editor for nine years.

The next day, I had lunch with Msgr. Tierney, Carol King and Bob Foreman, with whom I had worked when at The Courier.

On my way back to Rome, I made a stopover at Cleveland, Ohio, and visited Fay Benson and Evelyn and Joe Kidney.

From New York, I flew to London and was met by Monika Hellwig. I stayed with David and Marianna John and family: Claire, Helen, Simon, Rachel, Sara and Matthew. Marianna, who is Monika's sister, painted a beautiful picture of Monika for me while I stayed with them.

I left the John's with Monika for London, August 23, and spent several days touring all the sights of London. I returned to Rome on August 26.

I conducted a retreat for the Sisters of Our Lady of the Missions at Rocca di Papa from August 30 to September 6. Mother Mary Joan was the superior.

Msgr. Warren Holleran, who had been a Spiritual Director at the North American College with me for six years, left Rome October 29,1969

Sr. Helen Rolfson came to Rome December 19. On December 28, she and I drove to Assisi with my nephew, Duane Galles, and Sr. Brendan Marie. After visiting all the sights of Assisi, we went on to Florence and then Sienna. We returned to Rome on the autostrada, January 1, 1969.

Bishop Reh, who had been appointed Ordinary of Saginaw on December 18, 1968, left the college as Rector January 16.

I wrote a letter to Cardinal Sheehan, January 20, advising him as regards the type of person that was most needed as the new rector.

My nephew, Dan Galles, came to Rome on January 22 and stayed until January 28.

Toward the end of January, I was doing considerable thinking about going to do missionary work in Africa after completing my time at the college.

I gave a retreat at the Casa Santa Maria, February 19 through 22, for the priests who were in Rome for graduate study.

President Richard Nixon landed in St. Peter's Square in a helicopter. When he gave an address to the college, he said that many young demonstrators today only tear down and offer nothing constructive. The young men of the church must give them a goal and meaning to their efforts.

On March 13, the installation of Bishop Loras J. Watters, as the bishop of Winona, took place.

Bishop James Hickey was named Rector of the college on March 24.

I was having a meeting with Brother Saunders of the Better World Movement on March 27, when Maureen Burke and Stephanie Rea, from England, came looking for work and a place to stay. This was the beginning of the development of a very significant friendship.

On July 14, I went with the School Sisters of Notre Dame to Assisi and conducted a retreat with them until July 16. It was on this occasion that I got to know Sr. Teresa Carroll and our friendship developed over a number of years. She was killed in an auto accident shortly before Christmas, 1979.

I flew from Rome to Entebbe, Uganda, July 24. After the six hour flight, I was met at the airport by Fr. Paul Colenda, the Rector of Katigonda National Major Seminary, and a number of other priests, who drove me directly to the Seminary at Mousaka. Although we crossed the equator, I was very cold. I stayed at the seminary during most of my time in Uganda. I met Right Rev. Msgr. Adrian Doungu, the Bishop of Masaka, and made trips to a number of places in Uganda.

I accompanied the seminarians to Sampala for Pope Paul VI's visit to Uganda. I saw the arrival of the Pope's plane and was at the Rubaga cathedral for his visit. The pope ordained twelve African bishops at Kalolo Park, August 1.

I met both Brother Majella Nsubuga and Brother Leonard Byankya.

On August 14, I visited Elizabeth Park and saw elephants, buffaloes, hippos, waterbuck, antelope, warthogs and twenty lions.

I visited the Medical Mission Sisters at Fort Portal. This was the community of sisters to which Monika belonged.

I was surprised that I met at least two dozen persons in Uganda that I knew from Rome. Some of them had made retreats that I gave.

At the Pastoral Institute at Gabe, I had a visit with Sr. Margaret McKenna, who I knew from the retreat I had given in Philadelphia. I was able to attend two of her lectures and had a long walk and talk with her.

Sr. Gertrude, a Maryknoll Sister, drove me back to Kampala.

I took the train from Kampala to Nairobi, Kenya, on August 27. I was met at the train station by Monica Muthoni, whom I had met at a retreat I gave in Rome. Monica took me to her brother's place for dinner (Mr. and Mrs. Cleopes Wangi). Their children were Jane, Oscar and Sera. Their servant was Agatha. I played games with the children. Other visitors dropped in .

I went by bus with Monica to Machakos, Kenya. There I met Rev. Raphael S. Ndingi, Bishop of Machakos. I visited the Sisters of Our Lady of the Missions and had dinner and discussion and prayer with them.

I went by bus to Niari, August 31, and then on to Fort Hall, and took a taxi to Nyeri. There I met Mother Celine and Sr. Petronilla. I gave the Sisters a conference on prayer. I stayed with the Consolata Fathers.

September 1, I celebrated Mass and gave a homily for the Sisters. After breakfast, I made a tour of the hospital with Sr. Mary Nicoletta. I met two student nurses, whom I had met at Kampala. I was given a tour of the farm, seminary and school, and then gave a conference to 49 novices. Later, I gave a conference to 30 postulants and aspirants.

That afternoon, I visited Fr. Barnabas Muragi's parish, and then gave another conference to the Sisters on spiritual development. That evening I gave a conference on prayer to the Consolata Sisters.

September 2, I celebrated Mass with the Sisters and gave a homily. After the Mass, I had a long talk with Mother Celine. The Sisters had a number of gifts for me.

I returned to Nairobi by taxi and again visited the Wangi family.

Monica had a number of gifts for me, and I bought some pineapples and mangoes. I returned to Rome, September 4.

On October 29, I received a letter from Bishop Loras Watters allowing me to continue on at the college if I wanted, but also offering many possibilities if I decided to return to the diocese at that time. That letter made me feel closer to the diocese than I had ever felt before.

I had a discussion with Bishop Hickey, October 31, about my future. He preferred that I would stay on at the college for a time to create more continuity with the faculty. There had been quite a changeover.

I had supper with Fr. Ed Malatesta, S.J., on December 27. We had a long and important discussion. He was somewhat like a spiritual director to me. In our discussion, he advised that I should make use of the gifts I have. He did not advise a long-term academic preparation. He thought I could update on my own. He suggested that I begin with parish work and move toward priestly renewal.

Pope Paul VI celebrated Mass at the college, February 22, 1970.

James and Jeraldine Gabriel, friends of mine from Sheboygan, Wisconsin, came to Rome, March 24. We had an audience together with Pope Paul VI and toured Rome extensively.

Together with Sr. Brendan we went to Assisi and then on to Florence and Siena, returning to Rome on April 3. The Gabriels left for Zurich, April 6.

Sr. Camille, a Rochester Franciscan, came to Rome, May 10 and stayed until May 12. We had a dinner together. She later became president of the the Franciscan community.

Mother Therese Courderc was canonized on May 10, 1970. The following day, I was homolist for a concelebrated Mass as part of a triduum in thanksgiving for the canonization.

Carol and Dave Steichen were in Rome, May 18 to 24. Carol is my niece, my brother Lawrence's daughter. I toured Rome with them and went with them to St. Paul Outside the Walls, St. Sebastian, Frascati, Castel Gandolfo, the Amalfi drive, Sorento and Capri.

Sr. Marie LeClerc, who came to me for spiritual direction, made a day of recollection, May 27, and the following day renewed her vows. She was a Notre Dame Sister. She later returned to the United States and left the religious community. I located her again in San Antonio, Texas, and we continued to be friends.

Sr. Mary Frances Mowe, from Singapore, whom I came to know in Rome, and who I helped financially to be able to go to the Holy Land, died on June 7. She was only 37 years old. I received word that she had received the last letter I wrote to her in Singapore and that she appreciated it very much.

I returned to the United States June 14. I made a stop at Paris and then went on to Boston. I was met in Boston by Sr. Ann Higgins and Sr. Mary Bell.

I went on to see my dear friend, Sr. Margaret Canty at Kenwood in Albany. We went to the Catskills with Sisters Higgins, Anne Byrne, Berbie Bowe, Carletta Duarte and Maura Caleher. I had some wonderful walks and inspiring talks with Sr. Canty and the other Sisters.

I flew from Albany to Chicago and called my mother from there. Then, I went on to San Francisco. I stayed at Phelan Hall, Golden Gate and Parker Ave.

I began classes at the University of San Francisco, June 18. I took a course on Hebrews, the Apocalypse, and the Johanine Epistles, by Dr. John Elliott. I also took a course on Carl Berth and Teilhard de Chardin, by Dr. James Gill, as well as a course on Contemporary Problems in Moral Theology, by Fr. Richard McCormick.

A favorite quote: *"When men have conquered the winds and rain and tides and gravity, they can begin to harness for God the energies of love, and then for the second time in the history of the world mankind will have discovered fire."* -Teilhard de Chardin

While I was in San Francisco, I visited Msgr. Warren Holleran, my classmate, who served with me as Spiritual Director at the North American College. I had supper at his sister's home: Ray and Claire Lathon, 495 Holly Ave. S, San Francisco, CA 94080. Their children were Dan, Karen, Teresa and Patricia.

I also visited my nephew, Kenny Buse, in Lompac, California. We had a beef fondue dinner and listened to Bach's Mass in B minor. Then I went on to visit another nephew, Dale Buse and his first wife, Sandi, and family. Sandi later committed suicide by burning down their house with her inside.

I flew back to San Francisco and then went to Los Gatos, July 10 to 12, to visit Fr. Ed Melatesta, who had been like a spiritual director to me in Rome. I had supper with Mr. and Mrs. Melatesta, 16480 Apple Blossom Lane, Los Gatos, CA 95030. I then returned to San Francisco.

July 16 and 17 I saw the movies "Hair," "Easy Rider" and "Last Summer".

On July 18, Warren and I went to Vallombrosa, and then on to Sausalito with Fr. Ray Lassard. The next day, I had dinner with Warren and Ray, Bishop Bernadin, Tom Madden and Ed Gaffney.

I had dinner with Fr. Godfry Dieckman, July 21. He was tremendously influential in development of Liturgy after the Second Vatican Council.

July 30, I went to Los Angeles, where I met Genevieve Vedder, who had been so helpful to me financially during my years in the Seminary. I had dinner with her and her good friends, Michael and Patricia Rye, whom I had entertained in Rome.

I went on to San Diego and El Cajon, August 2, where I had a visit with Bishop John Quinn, who had been in philosophy while I was in theology at North American College. It was he who encouraged me to publish the notes I had taken at the marvelous retreat by Fr. John Courtney Murray at North American College in 1952. I concelebrated Mass with Bishop Quinn at La Mesa convent and had supper with him. I also heard a lecture given by Fr. Alonso Schoeckel on hope based on Isaiah. I shall always remember the day of recollection which he gave at the College when he spoke on Psalms 8 and 11.

Rusty (Schoo) Fable, a classmate from grade and high schools called me and I visited her and spent the night there, August 3.

I returned to Los Angeles on August 4 where I again had visits and dinners with the Ryes, Genevieve, Kathy Smith, Mrs. Alice Rinehart and others. I was also taken on a tour of Los Angeles at night.

On August 7, I left California for Minneapolis, where I stayed with my brother, Lester, and went on to Worthington and Iona. Fr. Jim Mottel, O.P., and Dale and Sandi Buse were still at home, so I was able to also visit with them.

I was asked to conduct a retreat for the Franciscan Sisters at Tracy, namely Alice Train (from Iona), Laura Corcoran, Elaine Fritz, Catherine Grimm and Linda Wieser. I was able to have a visit and supper with Sr. Mary Jane.

I attended the Pastoral Institute at Rochester, August 17. Fr. Emil Pin, S.J., was the presenter.

I had lunch with Earl and Grace Krusemark, August 19, and, later that evening, dinner with Edgar and Rita Harrison.

I went on to Winona and had a boat ride on the Mississippi River with Fr. Bob Brom, Fr. Jim Habiger, Fr. Paul Nelson and Fr. Don O'Connell.

On August 21, I had supper with Carol King and her sister, Mrs. John Swales.

I had a visit with Bishops Watters and Fitzgerald, August 22.

I had supper with Ed Bernatz's, Paul Builders, and Snyder's, former CFM members, August 23.

On August 24, I had a pizza with Carol King and Mrs. John Swales.

I drove to the Twin Cities on August 25 and had supper with the Mondry's and Raymers.

I visited my sister, Clara, at Blue Earth, August 27, and then went on and had a visit with Fr. Joe McGinnis and Fr. Bill Bertrand at Fairmont. I also preached at Masses at Fairmont.

I went on to Iona on August 30. My bother, Eugene, and his daughter, Patty, were there at the time. It was then I learned that Nell, Eugene's second wife, had MS.

I had lunch at Jim and Gayle Buse's, August 31, and then went on the Remsen, IA, to have supper with Uncle Clem Galles and Viola.

My brother, Gerald, came home on September 4, and I had lunch with Fr. Larry Gavin.

September 7, I left home. Gerald and Mother took me to the Worthington airport. I spent the evening with Mr. and Mrs. (Ruth)

Albert Reichelt and Al, Jr, 1626B Ingleside Ave., Baltimore, MD 21207.

I went on to Washington, D.C., on September 8. There I had a visit with Dr. Monika Hellwig and Fr. Bob Duggin. The next day I had a visit with Tim and Lyn Scheuring.

On September 10, I had a visit with Vince Bartolini at Providence, Rhode Island.

I had a visit with Sr. Mary of the Cross and Msgr. Oklavikas at Manchester, New Hampshire, September 11, and concelebrated Mass for the jubilarians at the monastery, September 12.

I had a visit with Msgr.Forrester at the Boston Chancery on September 13, and met his mother, Helen, and daughters, Betty, Peggy and Helen. At the Chancery, I also met Frs. Tom Finnegan, Bob Gallagher and Tim Shea.

September 14, I had lunch with Fr. John Marshall and supper with Fr. Connie McCrea, Fr. Al Hughes and Fr. Bob Banks.

Bishop Hickey met me when I arrived back at Rome on September 16. The next day I had a visit with Srs. Brendan, Celestina and Cecilia.

September 18, I had dinner at Scoglia with Archbishop Loe Binz, Fr. Dennis Lally, Fr. Ray Lassard and Fr. Dick Mahowald.

Msgr. James Habiger and Fr. Ward arrived in Rome from Athens and I concelebrated Mass with them. On September 22, I went with them on the Amalfi drive. They left Rome the next day.

On September 28, President Nixon visited the North American College.

I flew to Munich, Germany. Klaus Schneider met me at the airport and I stayed and Klaus and Karin Schneider's home. They have two children: Claudia and Irene. I went to see the Passion Play at Oberamergan with Klaus. He also gave me a tour of Munich. The city was so different from what it was when I saw it in 1950. I returned to Rome on October 2.

On October 2, I got word that Sr. Gretchen, OFM, had spoken to Bishop Watters of the possibility of my being chaplain for the Franciscan Sisters at Rochester.

I received a letter from Miss June Forest, October 23. Then, on December 1, I had a visit with her. She was from England. We became good friends while she was in Rome, and she helped me out on a number of occasions. She offered a room where Monika Kufferath could stay when she returned to Rome. June also became a good friend with Sr. Brendan.

Sr. Canty returned to Rome with a number of her students, December 14. I had a number of visits with them, especially at Christmas. Sr. Canty and the entire group with her were at the college for dinner on Christmas. In the evening, the whole group gathered in my apartment with a number of students with which they had become acquainted.

December 26, Sr. Canty and her group left for Florence with Al Reichelt. At their departure, I had very much mixed feelings. Gratitude that I was able to see Sr. Canty again, but pain because she was leaving and I would like to have been able to spend more time with her. The presence of the whole group, together with the students from the college, prevented me from having the intimate time together that I would have liked.

At the beginning of 1971, on January 7, I went to Subiaco and Tivoli with Sr. Helen Rolfson.

On January 8, Frs. Joe LaPlant, Jerome Halloran, Leon Richards and Tom Heffernan came to Rome. They were in the service in Germany. We had a retreat together in Malta and returned to Rome January 16.

On that same day, I had a letter from Bishop Watters discussing my future work in the diocese. August 15 was set as the day for my re-entry.

I received a tape from Sr. Canty, January 18, in response to my tape. On the tape she quoted a saying by Peggy Kelly: "Goodbye means I can't be around to laugh, to sing, to share, and to love you. But I laugh, sing share and love so well because you taught me."

It was on March 10 that I was the celebrant for the community Mass at the college and gave the famous homily based on Jer. 15:18-20 and Mt. 20:17-18. The homily was based on the magnanimity of Jesus (He had just announced he was going to Jerusalem, where He would die to deliver us from our sins.) and the pettiness of the Apostles, who were arguing as to who was the greatest among them. I went on to describe how that pettiness still exists in our country, the Church and even at the college. I went on to the dramatic conclusion asking whether we were going to follow the pettiness of the Apostles or the magnanimity of Jesus to the point of the Cross. As I spoke this last line, I lifted my monsignor robes from the large painting of Jesus on the Cross that had been done for me by my artist friend, Peter Mulder, and dropped them on the floor. A profound sense of awe came over the congregation.

After the Mass, as I processed to the sacristy, the students all clapped as I went by. Bishop Hickey came up to me in the sacristy while the students were still coming up to congratulate me, and said that he needed to speak to me. It was evident that my homily had not gone over with him.

We arranged a time for a meeting. I asked if we could pray together before we discussed the homily.

We did pray. Then the bishop gave about six reasons why I should not have given that homily. He was concerned that news of it would get to the Vatican. I began to deal with each of his points, but he would interrupt. Finally, I said that if he would not give me a chance to speak, we would not have a real dialogue. He then listened. We ended up having a good discussion, but not really agreeing as to whether I should have said what I did in the homily and having dramatized it so powerfully by dropping my robes on the floor and pointing to the Cross of Jesus.

Fr. Barnabas Ahern, the famous bible scholar, spoke to the student body at the college, March 16, on "Poverty in the Priest's Life."

June Forest's mother arrived in Rome April 1. I gave them an extensive tour of Rome and environs.

Frs. Tom Furry and Fitzpatrick and Al Reichelt and I left on April 12 for Padua and then on to Venice, Verona, Trent, and Carvara. We took a chairlift to a height of 6,000 feet at Cal Alt where we had a meditation together. Three cable cars took us to Marmalotta, 10,000 feet high. We went on to Cortina Di Ampezzo and then returned to Rome April 17.

A terrible event occurred at the college April 8. Michael McCaffrey, a student at the college, committed suicide by jumping off an eight story terrazzo. A funeral Mass for him was held at the college May 12 at 10:30 a.m. His body was returned to the States.

Sr. Hildegundis, from Immaculate Heart of Mary Seminary in Winona, and her aunt, Monika, arrived in Rome May 10. On May 13, I spent the entire day sightseeing with them. At the catacomb of St. Callistus we met Monika Kufferath from Germany. A friendship developed out of this meeting that lasted for many years.

Monika Kufferath came to the college for Mass the next day and we had a good visit. Later, she wrote to me from the island of Malta asking if she could come back to the college again to participate in the Mass on Pentecost. By this time, I had come to know that Monika suffered psychologically as a result of her father's rejection. He often referred to her as stupid.

I questioned Dr. Palermo, our college psychologist, whether it would be safe for Monika to come to the college for Pentecost. He thought that as long as we would be with my friends from Munich, it would be alright. June Forest offered a place for Monika to stay.

At the Mass on Pentecost, May 30, Klaus and Karin Schneider, June Forest and Monika attended. We had breakfast together after Mass and then spent the day sightseeing. Monika had a blister on her foot and asked if I had a bandaid. She accompanied me to my apartment to get one and, at one point, reached out to embrace me. I held her firmly and she settled down.

During a walk on the beach at Fragene, later in the day, Monika took me aside somewhat and asked why I did not embrace her. I had said I loved her.

She then began saying, "The peace has left me, the peace has left me," and was quite upset. I then realized that she was sick and why the psychologist thought it was well that there were other people with us.

I later wrote to her and explained that she saw me as her father and sought to receive from me the love she looked for from her father. She wrote back and agreed that I had judged correctly. She included in her letter a bottle of pills that she could have used to take her life. At one time, she did attempt suicide. While in Rome, she thought about how she could have walked into the sea and been gone forever.

She also sent me the book "Dibs" which was about a little boy who was very shy and everyone thought he was stupid. One of his teachers took him aside and found he was very brilliant. Monika also had had a teacher who took her aside and found that she was brilliant. This teacher became such a friend to Monika that when she was dying years later, she wanted Monika at her side even more than her own daughter.

Since I would be leaving the college, there was an elaborate farewell Mass and dinner, June 9. I was able to invite the many friends I had made during my nine years in Rome. A priest from the Casa wrote me a beautiful letter afterward telling me how impressed he was with the occasion and that it greatly enhanced his appreciation for the college.

June Forest and Sr. Brendan came and helped me pack June 21 and 22. My departure from the college on June 24 was quite dramatic for me, realizing I had spent nine years there as a Spiritual Director and had made many friends.

I flew to London, where I again met Maureen Burke and Stephanie Rea and other friends.

From London I flew to Dublin, Ireland, where I was met by Sr. Brendan and Mike Ryan. I stayed with Mike and Ciss Ryan (Sr. Brendan's sister) at 10 Shandon Pk. Dublin Rd., Kilkenny, Ireland. Their children were Collum and Margaret.

I met Sr. Brendan's parents, Patrick and Kathleen Lyng, at Belly Nursery, The Rower, County Kilkenny, Ireland, on June 29. I also met Stan and Eva (Sr. Brendan's sister) Nangle, 31 Abbey Pk., Ferry Bank, Waterford, Ireland.

I rented a car on June 30 and drove to Kilarney with Sr. Brendan and Marie Nangle. On July 1, we toured the Lakes of Kilarney, the Ring of Kerry, and Glen Beigh. I returned to Kilkenny and celebrated Mass at the home of the Lyng family. Patrick Lyng was so pleased to think that Mass had been celebrated in his home.

I had a very long and significant walk with Sr. Brendan, July 5. We had a glass of sherry together and prayed together. It was a very beautiful, yet sad, farewell.

From New York, I went on to E. Aurora, N.Y., for the four week program of Community Spirituality, which was an extended Better World course.

I visited Niagara Falls, July 18, and my impression was: "How glorious is your name, Oh Lord, our God, through all the earth." I saw the falls as a symbol of the life-giving spirit that inundates us.

On July 21, I reached a turning point in the Program of Community Spirituality: "What is the question we should be asking?" I saw the need to deepen our life together. In the Liturgy, we often do not meet the "mystery." Reflecting on Ephesians, Ch.4, I came to a deeper understanding of unity – many members of one body. A real price must be paid to love: "Let your mind be renewed by a spiritual revolution."

I saw my life in stages of nine: My first appointment for nine years was to an extant a dismal failure. The sceond nine years at the North American College was a time of growth in self-identity. During that time, I came to a knowledge of special powers and charisma I had. I saw the need to work for unity on a one-to-one basis, to prepare for a new beginning, a "spiritual revolution." I had to work with community for unity.

John Fernan's nephew tickled my fancy when he asked, "How did God keep the blood inside while he was making man?"

Toward the end of the course, the presenting team gave an evaluation of each participant. In my evaluation, they saw that I needed the grace to take people where they are. Many are to threatened to be able to contemplate or begin at a deep level. I give the impression that I am analyzing them.

The team evaluated me as having a 'dignity' that keeps people from me, a contemplative character that grates with others that are seeking a different prayer experience. They saw that I had a good theological foundation and that I was capable of doing Better World Movement work.

At the farewell party, I sang "When I Get Older."

On August 20, I went to the Cenacle at Lancaster to meet Sr. Angela Murphy. I celebrated a Liturgy with the Sisters at Lancaster before leaving. Sr. Ann Lonergan came to Lancaster to take me to Brighton.

I met Fr. Dennis Sheehan at Sacred Heart Church. He took me to his home and we had supper at Hawthorne by the Sea.

I flew to Washington, D.C., on August 24, where I was met by Fr. Bob Duggin. I visited the National Shrine, the Catholic University and Theological College.

From August 25 to September 1, I joined Dr. Monika Hellwig and Fr. Bob Nagosek at St. Ann's Retreat House at Bristow, Virginia.

It was during this retreat that Dr. Hellwig made some mysterious remark that she saw me in the future carrying on a rather meaningless and ineffective ministry. Neither Fr. Nagosek nor I, when discussing this some years later, could understand what she meant or why she said it.

I gave a retreat at the Cenacle, 513 Fullerton Pkwy., Chicago, IL 60614, from September 3 to 6. Sr. Virginia Boll was Directress at the Cenacle.

IX) Diocesan Director of Spiritual Renewal and Chaplain at Assisi Heights (1971 – 1978)

I flew to Rochester, Minnesota, on September 7,1971, and was met at the airport by Sr. Marjorie Habenicht and Sr. Alcantara from Assisi Heights.

I bought a car for $723, September 8 and drove to Iona. September 20, I drove to Sioux Falls, South Dakota, and stayed with my brother, Gerald and Jeanette and George.

I was appointed by Bishop Watters as chaplain to the Franciscan Sisters at Assisi Heights and Diocesan Director of Spiritual Renewal on September 23,1971.

There was a meeting in Mankato for all the priests of the diocese, September 27. I gave a talk on the Program of Community Spirituality. Fr. John Ward, Sr. Ramona Miller and Phyllis Evens of the Better World Movement in the United States were present.

I had dinner with Carol King, Mary Swails and Fr. Dave Arnold, October 7.

I had a meeting with all the priests of Region IV at Shetak at Fr. Bernel Deslaurie's cabin, October 15.

I was present for a Region II senate meeting at St. Francis Social Hall, Rochester, October 19. Fr. Tom Adamson was the host.

Sr. Judine Klein, from Adams, came for spiritual counseling on October 28. This meeting eventually led to a lifelong friendship.

Sr. Muriel Gag began work as my bookkeeper and secretary on October 29. Sr. Gretchen Berg, as president of the Franciscan community, had appointed her to this position, which I think she never really liked. Sr. Muriel eventually left the Franciscan community.

Fr. Larry Gavin began Teams of Our Lady in the diocese, November 5,1971.

I had a meeting with Bishop Watters, November 10, to discuss the formation of a central renewal community to assist me in my work as Diocesan Director of Spiritual Renewal. We were on the same wavelength.

I conducted a weekend retreat, November 12 to 14, for the Franciscan Sisters at Columbus, Ohio.

I had dinner and discussion with Msgr. Ray Jansen, November 16, in regard to combining a 40 hours and a MBW retreat at St. Francis Parish. There was an unbelievable understanding and enthusiasm.

Kathy Smith, whom I had met in Rome, came to visit me at Assisi Heights in Rochester and left on November 26. We had discussed hiring her as a public relations person to work with me in my role as Diocesan Director of Spiritual Renewal.

Throughout November I had a number of discussions about forming a team to work for renewal in the diocese. Possible members of this team would be Virgil and Mary Noland and Sr. Valerie Usher. This fell through when some Sisters persuaded Sr. Valerie that she was too young for the work.

I conducted a pastoral weekend for the Franciscan Sisters at Chicago, January 28-30, 1972.

February 2, I led a day of quiet prayer at Calvary Episcopal Church in Rochester.

I conducted a retreat in Washington, D.C., February 18-20, for 30 Sacred Heart theologians, and, on February 21-23, I led a national conference on Teams at Sacred Heart Seminary, Detroit, Michigan.

On February 25 and 26, I led a Renewal Session at St. Adrian Convent, Adrian, Minnesota. Sr. Marlys Ann Jax had invited me.

I conducted a Renewal Program at St. Ann's Parish, Slayton, February 27.

I met with Hank and Elaine Bromelkamp and Dick and Lee Smith, February 29, to prepare for a Teams of Our Lady meeting.

From March 3 to 5, I conducted a retreat at Assisi Heights for young, unmarried women.

I led a 40 Hours retreat at St. Pius X Parish in Rochester, March 11 and 12.

On March 24-26, I led a general retreat at Assisi Heights.

Bishop Fitzgerald died on March 30,1972.

I conducted a retreat for two priests, Fr. Norb Gernes and Fr. Dave Arnoldt at Assisi Heights, April 2-8.

At St. Pius Parish, Rochester, I conducted a MBW retreat April 21-27.

I had a prayer group and council retreat at Jackson, Minnesota, April 29-30.

At a WCCW deanery meeting at East Chain, Minnesota. I spoke on the topic "MBW" on May 2. Mrs. Al (Maryann) Brixius was the contact person.

"The spirit of St. Francis in the 70's" was the topic on which I spoke at a Franciscan Family Day, May 6. 105 people were in attendance.

From May 28 to June 2, I conducted a retreat for the Sacred Heart fathers at Fairhaven, Massachusetts.

Fr. John Reed took up residence with me as Assisi Heights, May 28,1972.

I had a visit with Fr. Vince Bartolini at Warwick, Rhode Island, June 2. Then, the next day, I had a visit and dinner with Remy Paat at La Tour Restaurant in Chicago overlooking the city and the lake. She gave me "9 Symphonies of Beethoven" as a gift.

I was celebrant and gave the homily at the closing Mass for the Franciscan Sisters General Chapter, June 12.

Sr. Meg Canty came for a visit on June 15.

On July 11, I left for Minneapolis and then went on to Los Angeles for Kathy Smith's baptism. She was baptized and received First Communion at St. Paul's Church. Fr. Tom Dove officiated. There was a reception at Kathy's apartment. We had an all night discussion. Kathy had recently broken her ankle.

I also had dinner with Mrs. Genevieve Vedder at Crown of the Cock Restaurant and a drive to the sea.

I had a visit with Bishop Watters on July 20 to discuss the renewal program and the hiring of Kathy Smith as a resource. He approved, but Kathy wrote a letter to him that was very critical and asking for more pay. This ended the possibility of hiring her.

Jim and Gerry Gabriel arrived on July 21 and stayed until July 23.

July 25, I went with Sr. Gretchen and Sr. June Campion to see George Moudry.

I conducted a retreat at the College of St. Catherine, St. Paul, Minnesota, July 29 to August 6.

August 18 to 20, I attended a class reunion anniversary at Blessed Sacrament Church. Fr. Hilary La Canne was the sponsor. On the 18th, I also visited Bill and Blanche (Sylvester's daughter) Jarrett and their daughter, Kathy, in Raleigh North Carolina. Blanche was a sister of Helen (Hargrove) Galles (Gerald's wife).

Kathy Smith came from Des Moines, Iowa, for a visit on August 22. The next day was the anniversary of our first meeting in Rome in 1968. Kathy returned to Des Moines August 31.

Marguerite Liston came for a visit on August 25 and left August 28.

On October 29, I took a North Central flight to a Teams of Our Lady meeting at Stanford, Connecticut, with Dick and Lee Smith.

I attended a workshop for pastoral planners at Des Moines, October 12 to 14. I prepared a two-page summary of diocesan renewal or planning programs. I stayed with Herbert and Lillian Smith, Kathy Smith's parents.

Kathy Smith came for a visit November 6 to 13.

I had my first experience with Marriage Encounter at Prior Lake, Minnesota, November 10-12.

The former Sr. Ibone (Amaya) Beleustegigoitia and Luis Weckmann Munoz were married.

Shirle Gordon, whom I met in the Holy Land, came from New York for a visit January 12-22, 1973. Fatima Haran from Malaysia was with her.

I conducted a retreat at Fullerton Cenacle, Chicago, February 9-11. Marguerite Liston, 3243 Central St., Evanston, IL 60201, was one of the participants in this retreat. We became very good friends. She died from Amyotrophic Lateral Sclerosis September 14, 1979. Her brother, Robert Liston asked me to come to Evanston to celebrate her funeral.

I left for home, February 16,1973. The drive home was like a marking. I realized I had more joy and peace in recent years because of more faithful relation to life. I began to see prayer as listening to life. As Dag Hammarskjold said: The more faithful you listen to the voice within you, the better you will hear what is sounding outside."

I had a liturgy and afternoon of prayer for the religious priests and lay people at Holy Redeemer School, Marshall, Minnesota, February 17.

I felt it was a special privilege to be able to serve dinner for Fr. Bernard Lonergan (the noted theologian) and Sr. Gretchen Berg, March 4,1973. Fr. Lonergan was spending time at Guest House in Rochester.

I conducted a retreat at St. Mary's Hospital, Minneapolis, Minnesota, March 18-24.

April 5 to 7, I attended a Regional Pastoral Planners meeting in Milwaukee.

I attended a Teams of Our Lady weekend workshop, April 27-29.

Monika Kufferath, from Germany, came to visit me May 1-25. She accompanied me to Iona, May 7.

I attended the North American College Alumni meeting in New York City, May 8-9, and then went on to Albany, New York, to see Sr. Meg Canty, and continued on to Cleveland, Ohio, to see Fr. Jerry Blake and Mrs. Faye Benson.

I was on the team for a Marriage Encounter at Assisi Heights, May 18-20.

I had a very special meeting with Sr. Cynthia Howe on June 15, 1973. We walked to the point overlooking Rochester. We met again on July 4 and July 14.

We had a family reunion in Iona, July 29 - August 1. There were 70 people present.

I conducted a retreat for the Franciscan Sisters on an island in the Mississippi, August 2 to 6.

Fr. Gabriel Calvo was the principal presenter at a Marriage Encounter workshop at Notre Dame, Indiana, that I attended.

Sr. Breda Lyng came from Ireland to visit me August 22-31. We went together to Iona and Pipestone.

I had a Teams of Our Lady meeting and a Mass at the cottage where I lived, with 25 people attending, September 19.

Marguerite Liston came for a visit on September 24, and Kathy Smith came the same day.

Julie Otero and I attended a ballet at the Mayo City High School on September 29.

On October 4, Fr. Bill Anderson, in need of rest and recuperation, came to Assisi Heights to live with me. He had last been pastor at Adrian.

I conducted a Pastoral Weekend at St. Priscilla, Chicago, February 1-3, 1974, and visited Marguerite Liston on February 4.

February 8-10, I conducted a retreat at Longwood Cenacle, Chicago.

Sr. Breda came for a visit March 4-12.

I again conducted a retreat at Longwood Cenacle, Chicago, on April 5-7, and again had a visit with Marguerite Liston.

May 5-11, I conducted a retreat at Assisi Hall for the Franciscan Sisters.

My brother, Gerald, was shot and killed by Carl Lee Morris (831 Booth Dr., Shreveport, LA) on May 18, 1974

I attended the North American College Alumni meeting in St. Louis, Missouri, July 11-13.

Monika Kufferath came from Frankfurt, Germany, for a visit on June 17 and stayed until July 10.

Sr. Judeen Kline accompanied me to Iona on August 4 and we stayed until August 6.

I attended a World Wide Marriage Encounter in Rockford, Illinois, August 9-11, and then went on to the Marymount Sisters General Assembly in Terrytown, New York, August 14-16. I had supper with Sr. Breda on the 16th.

With Vince Bartolini, Mary Martin and Sr. Breda, I went to West Point and Bear Mountain, August 18. We left Sr. Breda off at Marymount.

Then on August 19, I went on to Manchester, New Hampshire, and visited Mary Ann Garland, Al and Alice Seifert, and John, Coral and Karen.

Together, with Fr. Jim Murphy from Rockford, Illinois, I flew to Spokane, Washington, and attended Expo '74, "The earth doesn't belong to man. Man belongs to the earth." We toured Spokane and saw the Grand Coulee Dam. On August 27, we went on to Portland to see George Bell. We stayed by the Pacific Ocean overnight and returned from the beach on August 29 and had supper at Roger and Joan Galles' home. We returned to Rochester August 30.

Sr. Judine Klien, and her sister, Delphine, visited me September 2-3.

I visited Sr. Joyce Stemper on September 4. She was very helpful in advising me on a number of occasions.

I visited Tim and Mary (Ehlringer) Halverson at St. Augustine, in Austin, September 7.

I again conducted a general retreat at Longwood Cenacle, Chicago on September 20-22, and went to see Marguerite Liston the next day.

I had a wonderful visit with Marguerite Liston on October 18. I was 47 years old at the time.

Monika Kufferath came from Germany November 13, and visited me a number of times over the next several months.

Sr. Breda arrived for a visit on November 27.

I was on the team for a Marriage Encounter, January 17-19, 1975, and again April 25-27.

Kathy Smith again came for a visit March 30.

Bernice Bertrand, who was a year ahead of me in high school, came for a visit May 9-10, 1975

I left for Manchester, New Hampshire, May 11, and stayed with Fr. Robert Kemmerry, St. Patrick's Church, 138 Coolidge, Manchester, NH. The next day, I visited Mary Ann Garland and Andy Ray.

On May 13, I went on to Buffalo, New York, and attended the North American College Alumni reunion, May 14-15.

Jovan and Vita Bea came to visit me a number of times during May, June and August, and we became quite good friends.

I celebrated the funeral Mass at Assisi Heights for Sr. Mary Jane Haefner, August 23, 1975

On September 12-14, I was on the team for a Marriage Encounter.

Sr. Margaret Canty came to Winona on September 16, and left on the 18th.

Monika Kuferath arrived November 26.

I attended a Marriage Encounter Enrichment in Mendota with Hank and Mary Clare Dorn on January 9-11, 1976.

I received a letter from Bishop Watters January 11 informing me that he was transferring the Diocesan Office of Spiritual Renewal that I was director of to an office of Pastoral Planning in Winona, and that I would also be transferred as chaplain to the Franciscan Sisters at Assisi Heights. I had a meeting with Bishop Watters January 29, 1976.

I conducted a guided retreat for the Sisters at Tau Center February 1-7.

I was on the team for a Marriage Encounter Retorno February 27-29.

On March 8-12, I conducted a retreat for the Sisters in the infirmary at Assisi Heights.

I had a meeting with Sr. Kathleen von Groll and Sr. Joyce Stemper on April 16, to discuss use of the Wilson Home, where I was living as a novitiate for the Sisters. I would then move into the house next door.

Marguerite Liston came for a visit on April 24.

I went on vacation May 9-19. First, I visited Fr. Jim Murphy in Rockford, Illinois, and then on to Baltimore, Maryland, for the North American College Alumni reunion, and then on to Indianapolis and back to Rockford.

I purchased a 1971 Ford Torino from Sterling Mestad at Universal Ford for $1674 on June 18, and sold my 1966 Ford to Donald Bartell for $100.

Sr. Breda came for a visit June 22-26.

On July 12, I moved from the Wilson Home to the cottage next door. On July 17, we had an open house to see how the cottage had been renovated to accommodate me.

Mother Teresa of Calcutta was at Assisi Heights July 20. When I came into the foyer, where she was standing in a circle of Sisters, she immediately came across the circle and greeted me as though she knew I was a priest, even though I was dressed in sport clothes.

I served supper for the Better World Movement Team, consisting of Fr. Bob Nogosek, Beth Ann Hughes and Sr. Martha McGuinness, August 24.

I was on a Marriage Encounter Retorno team, October 1-3. The other members were Fran and Herb Widener, and Chuck and Margie Jacobson.

On February 18-20, 1977, I was on the team for a Family Encounter.

I conducted a retreat for the Sisters at Tau Center March 6-12, and came to know Sr. Katarina Schuth when she came to see me on March 11.

I was again on a team for a Marriage Encounter, March 18-20.

On April 24-30, I again conducted a retreat for Sisters at Tau Center.

Marguerite Liston came for a visit May 13-16.

Emmagene (Tate) Galles and her daughter, Sylvia Gail, came to visit our family in Iona.

I had a visit with Catherine de Hueck Dougherty June 22-23.

I arrived at Gonzaga Eastern Point Retreat House, Gloucester, MA 01930, June 28, to make a 30-day Ignatian retreat.

During this retreat, I wrote up my entire life story - over 800 pages, and cried almost every day as I read my life story to my retreat director. That retreat was like a marking in my life. Many physical and psychological difficulties that I experienced in my life prior to this retreat were healed during this retreat.

When my retreat director saw how much feeling was stored up in my life, he said it was a wonder I never became an alcoholic or a suicide.

On my first retreat break day, July 13, I had a visit with Mary Ann Garland.

I spent my second retreat break day with Vince Bartolini. When the 30-day retreat ended July 31, I drove to New York and stayed with Vince and Mary Bartolini. I then went on to Albany to see Sr. Margaret Canty. I also saw Sr. Breda at Marymount.

I began my appointment to assist in pastoral ministry at St Pius X Parish, Rochester, August 4, in addition to being chaplain to the Franciscan Sisters at Assisi Heights.

Monika Kufferath accompanied me to Iona August 7.

I received news of Kathy Smith's diagnosis of MS, August 10.

Sr. Breda left for Milwaukee and New York, August 14.

Marguerite Liston came to visit me October 20-23. During that time, she went to the Mayo Clinic to get a second opinion in regard to her diagnosis of amyotrophic lateral sclerosis. She had already been diagnosed with the disease at her home hospital in Wilmot, Illinois. That was, indeed, a very sad day.

Sharon Ulrick made a retreat at Assisi Heights February 12-16, 1978.

Lloyd and Leona Buse came to visit me at Assisi Heights February 27.

I had a severe stomach ache, April 14, which resulted in my being taken to the Mayo Clinic the next day, where I underwent an appendectomy. My doctors were Dr. Stephan Deane and Dr. Peter Mucha. Bishop Watters, Sr. Gretchen and many Teams and Marriage Encounter couples came to visit me. I returned home from the hospital April 20.

I had a visit at home in Iona April 24-27. This was a rather special visit because at breakfast on the 26th, I drew out of my mother many details about her life, so much so that she became somewhat irritated that I should expect her to remember, at her advanced age (90 years old), details from her early life. Nevertheless, it was a very wonderful time of sharing.

That evening, I celebrated Mass at the parish church and in the homily, I related a number of details of my mother's life.

I attended a reunion of my class from the North American College in Chicago, May 8-11. On the 11th, I went to visit Marguerite Liston, 215 3rd St. Wilmot, IL 60091.

Sr. Breda came from Chicago on June 15 to attend a summer school at St. Mary's College in Winona. Thus, I got to see her a number of times during that summer.

I left for Gloucester, Massachusetts on June 25 to make a second 30-day Ignation retreat at Gonzaga Eastern Point Retreat House. Sr. Clairvaux McFarland, who was also going to make the retreat, accompanied me. We spent the night at Fr. Jim Murphy's rectory in Rockford, Illinois. June 26, we spent the night at Mrs. Maryann Kulka, 136 Sunset Dr., Bellevue, OH 44811; telephone 419-483-2288.

A rather freak accident occurred that evening. While Sr. Clairvaux and I were out for a walk, 5 year old Jeremy Sentaro got into his father's car, parked across the street from my car, and released the brake. The car went down the driveway, crossed the street and ran into the driver's side of my car. Although he bent my car door and the side of my car, I was still able to open the door. The boy's father's insurance enabled me to have the door replaced when I got to Gloucester.

We went on to Rochester, New York, the next day and on June 29 we visited the North American Martyrs Shrine at Auriesville. We arrived at the retreat house that evening.

Sr. Isabel Green was my director for the retreat. I was ready with notebooks to again do a lot of writing as I had done in my previous 30-day retreat. However, when I told Sr. Isabel about my experience the year before, and all the writing I had done, she suggested I not write my meditations, but simply wait for Jesus to speak to me.

This retreat, as a result, was completely different from the previous retreat. Throughout much of the retreat nothing seemed to be happening. I wanted a friendship with Jesus. July 17, I spent the entire night out on my favorite spot on the rocks overlooking the ocean. At times, I could hear some people speaking. There were dogs barking and I was somewhat afraid they might attack me. The moon came out, but other than the light of the moon, I experienced very little spiritual light and longed for the presence of Jesus which seemed to be so absent.

As I prayed and waited, I wondered what some of Jesus nights spent in prayer were like. Were they anything like I was going through?

As the sun began to rise, I heard the birds singing, but felt little emotion. Rather disappointed, I returned to my room and went to bed.

I was celebrant for the community liturgy July 19. I began to feel a bit of a breakthrough in the retreat. The next day, I began to experience a painful birth. My meditation was on Is. 26: 7-9, 12, 16-19 and Mt. 11: 28-30. I felt like a delicate child and I prayed especially to Mary.

On the retreat break day, I went to Sturbridge and had lunch with Vince Bartolini at the Publick House (1771) and saw the old Sturbridge Village with its 1830 atmosphere.

I began to experience a partial commitment on July 22.

Beginning July 24, and the following days, I began reflecting on the Last Supper, the agony in the garden, Judas, Peter, Jesus before the Sanhedrin, before Pilate. I expressed my anger to my director in my conference, July 26. She suggested I not even use the Scripture, just wait and express my anger. I questioned whether I should spend another night out in prayer, but I was somewhat afraid. About the time, while I was sitting on the rocks looking out at the ocean, a tremendous wave came crashing into the rocks resulting in a mighty spray of water. For a moment I thought it was Jesus appearing to me, but I was disappointed.

On July 28, I made a holy hour, reflecting on the passion of Jesus. With the piercing of the heart of Jesus I was expecting a breaking open of my heart. I began to realize how the dark night tends to focus our desire. God is present in the apparent absence that makes us seek Him.

I began to tell our Lord that I didn't want him to send me any more messengers. I wanted Jesus himself to appear to me. But I also began to abandon the outcome to the Lord. I began to have a feeling of being okay. I realized that I do love the Lord and He loves me.

I awoke at 1:30 a.m., July 30, and made a holy hour. I was unable to sleep afterward and I was filled with exhilaration. I then went out to the rocks to see the sunrise. Even as I went down the path to the ocean everything seemed to speak to me.

Having arrived at my favorite spot on the rocks, I began to pray Psalm 138. The words of that psalm expressed everything I had been experiencing during the retreat. "I will give thanks to you my Lord with all my heart for you have heard the words of my mouth." I was now experiencing unbelievable joy. Jesus had been present to me all along even when I did not feel his presence. Even the darkness was the gift of his presence so that I would seek and desire him more ardently.

The retreat ended with liturgy July 30. The next day, I went on to Albany and had lunch with Sr. Canty, and also saw John Grega. Sr. Canty gave me a gift of a pewter cup and plate suitable for Eucharist.

I went on to Cleveland, Ohio, August 1, and visited Faye Benson and her sister, Evelyn. I spent the evening with Walter and Margaret Anderson and Mary and gave them my account of my retreat.

The next day, I celebrated Eucharist with Faye, Walter and Margaret and then went on to South Bend, Indiana, where I met Sr. Rita Brom.

On August 3, I had a visit and breakfast with Fr. Robert Nogosek and Beth Ann Hughes of the Better World Movement.

I went on to visit Fr. James Murphy at Rockford, Illinois, August 4. During the night, someone stole the battery from my car.

August 10-13, 1978, I attended the National Marriage Encounter Convention at Milwaukee, Wisconsin, with Chuck and Sandy Jacobson and Roger Johnson.

Pope Paul VI's funeral was on August 12. The coronation of Pope John Paul I was September 3. The coronation of Pope John Paul II was October 16. 1978.

X) Pastor at St. Francis Church, Windom and St. Augustine Church, Jeffers (1978-1988)

I left Rochester on December 8, 1978, to become pastor at Windom and Jeffers. Sr. Rita Brom and Ling assisted in my moving. I had requested to be pastor at these two parishes when they were open so that I could be closer to my home in Iona, since I had always been a considerable distance from home ever since I left home to go to Loras College.

I was able to be at home in Iona, Christmas, 1978, the first time I was home for Christmas since 1961.

Sr. Cornelia Rappold died at Assisi Heights, January 11, 1979. She was 103 years old. She had been a special friend of mine at Assisi Heights.

I began to rehearse for a role in the play, "Fiddler on the Roof" on January 15, 1979 but after several months, I had to back out because of the many demands for my ministry in the parishes. I very much wished I could be in this play. As soon as I arrived in Windom and people saw me they urged me to be in the play. However, it was too much for me to learn all the music and also carry on in the parishes.

I went to Wilmette, Illinois, to visit Marguerite Liston, and Bob, Ann, Sue and Kate June 10, 1979.

Sr. Rita Brom began work as Parish Worker, August 15.

Angelo and Julie Otero returned from Texas to Rochester for a visit. I went to Rochester to see them at the Kahler Hotel September 10.

My dear friend, Marguerite Liston, died September 14, 1979 at her mother's home, 215 3rd St., Wilmette, IL 60091. Her brother,

Robert, called me and asked if I would officiate at her funeral. I was on a Marriage Encounter team that weekend so I could not leave immediately. However, after the Encounter, Sr. Rita Brom drove and we went to Wilmette, Illinois, where I officiated at the funeral on Monday, September 17.

I was present at Des Moines, Iowa, October 4, when Pope John Paul II came for a visit.

I went to the National Teams of Our Lady Weekend in Detroit, Michigan, October 26-28.

Fr. Bob Nogosek and Beth Ann Hughes came for a visit November 21.

My former teacher, Archbishop Fulton J. Sheen, died December 9, 1979

My sister, Leona, called and informed me that mother had taken a turn for the worse. I went to Iona, June 4, 1980, and took Communion to Mother. We were able to visit quite well.

Fr. Ed Scheuring celebrated the 50th anniversary of his ordination with Mass at Iona June 8. I was master of ceremonies for his reception in the parish hall. Bishop Fitzgerald was there and I told him about Mother's condition. He went over to her home and gave her a blessing.

June 9, I celebrated Mass in Mother's room with the family present. Mother was able to receive Communion for the last time.

The next day, I again celebrated Mass in Mother's room at 10:40 p.m.. I had just finished the Mass and we noticed a change taking place in Mother. At 11:40 p.m., she breathed her last.

Leona and I held hands together over Mother and Leona said she hoped I would be present when she died. As you will learn later, I was not present when she died.

We had a wake and prayer service for Mother June 12, and her funeral Mass, which I celebrated, was June 13, 1980.

When we went into church for the funeral Mass, the weather was beautiful. When we came out of the church, a great wind began to rise and increased as we went to the cemetery. At the cemetery, the wind was so ferocious that I had to cut the graveside service short to get back to our cars. Then the wind suddenly stopped and there was a great calm. I remarked that Mother had stirred up one of those Nebraska windstorms that she used to tell us about to let us know that she had just arrived in Heaven!

Leona and Lloyd Buse, together with their sons, Kenny and Dale, were on their way to Pipestone, June 19, and near Woodstock, an approaching driver suddenly made a left turn in front of them. Leona was injured and was taken to the Pipestone hospital and needed a wheelchair.

June 23, I went on vacation to New York. Sr. Breda met me and the next day we went to the beach at Coney Island.

Archbishop Oscar Romero died June 24.

I went to see Vince Bartolini on June 25. Then on to Washington, D.C., for the Teams National Family Pilgrimage, which was held June 26-28. While there, I received word that Leona had died. I returned home for the funeral, which was on June 30, 1980

Still on vacation, I flew to Los Angeles July 5 and visited Kathy Smith. On July 7, I visited Mrs. Genevieve Vedder, and then went on to Chino to see Kenneth Buse.

Kathy Smith came for a visit July 18 and stayed until July 29.

The former rector of the North American College, Archbishop Hickey, was installed in Washington, D.C.

I attended the National Marriage Encounter Convention at St. John's University in Collegeville, Minnesota, August 7-10.

Marlene Vos began working as my secretary on August 20.

I left Rochester on October 2 to attend a Teams of Our Lady meeting in Jersey, October 3-5.

Pope John Paul II was shot on May 13, 1981.

Sr. Breda came for a visit July 20-27.

I was on vacation July 26 to August 14. Fr. Jim Murphy came for a visit on August 3.

Our family reunion was on August 9.

Jean Anderson, and her daughters, Keri, Mindy and Nicole, came to visit me August 25 and we had supper together.

Sr. Bernice Jirick came for a visit September 10-11.

On September 14, I went on a hike in Kylan Woods with Jean Anderson and her children.

Eddy De Smith moved into the rectory on September 28. He paid $150 for board and $50 for a room.

I made my annual retreat in Winona, November 15-19, and visited Carol King November 16.

Eddy De Smith left the rectory on November 23 and moved into an apartment in Jeffers.

Sr. Rita Brom came for a visit December 29 and stayed until January 5, 1982.

We had a severe blizzard on January 9 and again on the 17th. The temperature, with wind chill, was as low as 103 degrees below zero.

Sr. Seton Slater came for a visit February 15-16.

I was on the team for a Marriage Encounter at Slayton, February 25-28, and again April 2-4.

Mother Josephine and Sr. Breda came for a visit April 12-17.

I attended a course in South Dakota called "The Theology of the Eucharist," by Monika Hellwig, June 14-18.

Sr. Rita Brom and her mother came for supper July 5.

I went on a picnic with Sr. Rita Brom July 20.

Fr. Bob Nogosek came for supper and stayed overnight on July 22.

There was a dance in Iona August 7, and my sister, Clara Risberg and her band played.

Joyce Back arrived August 25.

I was on vacation September 13 to October 2. I flew to New York and was met by Sr. Breda. We went to Manhattan Beach the next day, and had an eight mile walk through Brooklyn September 15.

After lunch with Sr. Breda and Mother Josephine, September 16, I left for Rome. I arrived in Rome the next day and stayed at Domus Pacis, Casa di Providenza, Via Giovanni Pratil, 00152 Rome.

On September 18, I toured the Forum, Coliseum, San Clemente, Santa Maria Maggiore, San Pietro in Vincoli, the Mammertine Prison and the New North American College.

The Teams of Our Lady Pilgrimage was September 19-24.

We had Mass at St. Peter's on August 19, and visited the catacombs of San Callisto on August 20. Had Mass again at St. Peter's on the 21st and went through the Vatican Museum.

On August 22, we went on to Assisi and had Mass at Santa Maria degli Angeli.

After Mass at St. Peters, September 23, we had an audience with Pope John Paul II, toured St John Lateran, the Holy Stairs, the North American College, Trevi Fountain, the Pantheon and Piazza Navona.

I had dinner with Srs. Annamaria Lionetti, Loretta, and Maria Terese on September 24, and then went on to Munich, where I met

Klaus and Karin Schneider and their children, Claudia and Irene. We toured the center of Munich, the city square, the Hoffbrau Haus and the Oktoberfest. We had a cookout at Schneider's on September 25.

After Mass, September 26, Klaus and I went to Dachau to see the concentration camp where thousands of people were murdered. After that, I went by train to Stuttgardt, where I was met by Monika Kufferath.

On September 27, Monika and I went to Beuron for Mass and dinner.

I wrote cards on September 28, and then saw Hans Kung's home and the university.

I went by car to Zurich, September 29, and met Hans-Albert and Doris Kufferath.

Monika took me to the Zurich airport. I went on to Frankfurt and then to Minneapolis via New York. Sr. Rita Brom and Sharon Merritt met me.

We had dinner October 1, to celebrate Sr. Rita's birthday.

I had dinner at Sharon Ulrich's home November 25.

Bill and Marge Urlick and their children, Larry and Marie, stayed overnight with me December 11.

Msgr. Dan Tierney's funeral was at St. Pius X Church, Rochester, January 3, 1983.

Sr. Bernice Jirick came for a week visit February 4.

Roy Risberg, my sister Clara's husband, died February 17.

Fr. Bob Brom was ordained a bishop on May 23.

I went on vacation with my sister, Clara. At Grand Marais, Minnesota, Diane and Fran Hartle joined us. We arrived at Saskatoon, Saskatchewan, Canada, July 6, and met Jean Bonebrake, Ron Hertzky, Scot and Noel.

Ann Bonebrake and Vern (Puff) Flath were married before a justice of the peace July 8.

On Sunday, July 10, Clara and I went to St. Paul Cathedral for Mass. When three priests came to concelebrate Mass, one of them was Fr. Bob Ogle, whom I had met at Assisi Heights years before. He was now a member of Parliament in Ottawa. We stopped at the rectory after Mass and visited with him. This developed into a regular correspondence and a lifelong friendship.

We read some of Jean Bonebrake's poems and journal back at Kiwanis Park July 12.

We left Saskatchewan July 13 and arrived at Grand Marais July 14. After breakfast, we drove on and saw the waterfalls at Kodance Creek, and arrived at Chippewa Falls in the evening, and had supper with Mary Ann Burnel.

The next day, we went on to Grandpa's Bluff Campground at Barley's Harbor, Wisconsin, and had a fish broil at La Frantera with Sr. Rita Brom and Ruth and Harlan.

We did some shopping on July 16 at Egg Harbor, Sturgeon Bay, and then went on to Door County.

We had brunch at Jacksonport July 17, and then went swimming at White Fish Dunes County Park. Sr. Rita Brom was with us until July 23.

On July 18, we went on to Ephraim, Sr. Bay, Egg Harbor and then crossed the straits to the lighthouse.

We went to Washington Island on the 19th and had a Johnson's Restaurant fish boil at Viking Restaurant at Ellison Bay.

We went for a nature walk at Ridges Sanctuary. After a steak dinner, we left for Sheboygan and returned to Windom on July 21.

The wedding of Michael Curley and Susan Luken was at Nativity Parish, Fargo, North Dakota, July 29.

Lisa Mondry and Donald Bonenberger were married at St. Lambert's Church, Sioux Falls, South Dakota on August 20.

Sr. Crescentia Ochoka, who had been a special friend of mine at Assisi Heights, died October 13.

We had such a large storm at Windom February 4, 1984, that Mass was canceled. There was another bad storm February 18 and 19.

I made a silent, directed retreat in Winona April 29 to May 5. Fr. Michael Kohler was my director.

Fr. Bob Theobold died at a very early age. His funeral was June 25.

Dave and Pat Hedelman and daughter, Joby, came to Windom apply for the Pastoral Worker position. Rose Ann Hamm was also interviewed July 20. Dave and Pat Hedelman were eventually hired.

We had a potluck farewell for Joyce Bock July 22.

I began my annual vacation July 29. I arrived in New York July 30. Sr. Breda and Mother Josephine met me at the airport.

Sr. Breda and I went for a swim at Rockaway Beach the next day, and I left for Glasgow that evening.

I arrived at Glasgow August 1 and rented a car. I drove to Loch Lomond and then on to Sterling, Scotland. On August 2, I visited Sterling Castle and then went on to Edinburg, where I saw Edinburg University the next day. I went on to Chester and drove through the very beautiful Lake region. I stopped at Windermere for tea and a walk. I had a very good visit to Chester August 4. It is a very interesting town.

I went on to London August 4 and made a stop at Coventry to see the Cathedral.

I attended Mass at Westminster Cathedral August 5, and then saw a concert and street preaching at Hyde Park. I also saw Buckingham Palace.

I toured the Tower of London August 6 and St. Paul Cathedral, Westminster Abbey, St. Margaret's and Parliament.

I drove to Windsor Castle August 7, where I saw more armor and royal apartments, and paintings by Rembrandt, Van Dyke, Holbein and Titian. I then went on to Salisbury to see the cathedral and enjoyed it more than when I saw it 32 years previously.

August 8, I arrived at Bath, where I visited Stephanie Rea, whom I had met in Rome. With Stephanie was Nigel Pollard, whom she later married. She gave me a marvelous tour of the ancient Roman baths and the entire city, which is very beautiful.

I drove on to Fishgard August 9, and then took the ferry to Rosslaire, Ireland. I rented a car there and drove to Tramor County, Waterford, and stayed with Tony and Marie (Sr. Breda's sister) Nangle.

I visited the Waterford Glass making Company August 10, and was impressed with the fantastic art.

After seeing a bit of Waterford, I drove on to Slieverue, County Kilkenny, and had lunch with Sis and Mike Ryan. I then went on to The Rower and celebrated Mass to mark Kathleen Lyng's 72nd birthday and her 48th wedding anniversary to Pat Lyng (Sr. Breda's parents). I returned to Waterford for the evening.

August 11, I drove to Swords, County Dublin, to see Patricia (Sr. Breda's sister) and Oliver Greville. I stopped at Avoca and saw the meeting of waters made famous by Thomas Moore. I then went on to Glendelough and saw St. Kevin's Church and tower.

I went to Mass August 12 at Swords and then drove on to Clones County, Monaghan, where I had supper with Josephine (another of Sr. Breda's sisters) and Hugh McGuire. I remember they had a fire in the fireplace.

I saw the butcher shop after breakfast on August 13, and then went on to Galway. I stopped at the Knock Shrine and also at Slaigo., I visited the grove of W. B. Yeats. I went into Northern Ireland, August 14, and saw the Franciscan Church, the Cathedral University,

St. Mary's College, Spanish Gate, the museum and castle, and then continued on to the beach at Salt hill. I then drove on to Kildimo County, Limerick, to see Michael and Elizabeth (Sr. Breda's sister) Keane. They also had fire in the fireplace. There, I also saw the River Shannon.

I celebrated Mass at Kilkenny, August 15, and after further visiting, I saw an abandoned castle. I then left Shannon by plane to New York. I had driven 883 miles in Scotland, England and Wales, and 600 miles in Ireland.

I served a supper at Windom on October 1 to the Better World team: Sr. Martha Ann McGuiness, Beth Ann Hughes and Fr. Bob Nogosek.

Sr. Breda Lyng came for a visit May 23-28, 1985.

On June 7, the Hedelmans announced they were not renewing their contract.

I was on vacation with Clara July 1-19. We visited my brother, Lester, July 1, and then went on to Litchfield and camped at Cape Ripley. We drove to Spicer and Green Lake, July 3, and did some fishing. We walked around Lake Ripley July 4 - about five miles. We left for Bemidji July 5, and camped at the state park. The next day, we toured Bemidji. We had dinner at Baudette July 8, and stayed at KOA. We did some fishing in the morning and caught five small walleyes and one perch. In the afternoon, we made doughnuts and had supper and sang around the campfire.

We left Baudette July 10, and went on to International Falls. We then went through the iron mine at Sudan, and then proceeded on to Ely and Grand Marais. We caught two rainbow trout July 11, and had a walleye pike supper at Windigo Lodge. We continued our travel through northern Minnesota and at Hartel, we saw twenty bears at a landfill.

I had lunch at Big Steer Restaurant July 18 with Maryann Burnell and Sr. Geraldine. This was my final contact with Maryann. I returned to Windom on July 19.

We had a farewell for Hedelmans July 28. I served them supper in the evening.

Genevieve Vedder, who had assisted me financially to become a priest, died August 23, 1985.

Jim and Gayle Buse divorced September 4.

I went to Minneapolis November 4 to see Evelyn (Paden) Meyer, formerly married to my brother, Eugene. Evelyn died December 7, 1985.

Glen Ward delivered a court summons to me April 10, 1986, in regard to the lawsuit by Sharon Ulrich. On May 13, I had a visit with Bishop Loras Watters in regard to the lawsuit. Tom Lewis was my lawyer.

I served a dinner for my family August 31, namely Lawrence and Marcella Galles, Gene and Nell Galles, Charlie and Doris Galles, Lester and Betty Galles and Clara.

Shirle Gordon, whom I had met in the Holy Land in 1963, came to the United States from Kuala Lumpur, Malaysia, October 1-30.

Bishop Loras Watters resigned as bishop of the Diocese of Winona October 14.

Fr. Andrew Olsem's funeral was November 24.

Sr. Rita Brom and her mother came to visit me January 4-6, 1987.

February 23 and 24 I went to Omaha, Nebraska, to visit Jim and Kathy Moriarity.

The funeral for Bernice Bertrand, who was a year ahead of me in high school, was April 23, 1987

Sr. Breda Lyng went to Ireland June 28, and returned to the States July 1.

I began my annual vacation June 29. I had lunch with Lawrence and Marcella Galles in Adrian and went on to Whitewood, South Dakota, where I visited with Millie Humphrey, a cousin. On June 30, I proceeded to Cody, Wyoming, and stayed at the Ponderosa campground. I toured Yellowstone, Old Faithful, Morning Glory Pond and Yellowstone Canyon July 1. I stayed at a guest house in Livingston, Montana, I arrived in Spokane, Washington on July 2, and on the 3rd, I visited Ed and Rachel Galles, and Laura, Ray and Debbie Segal, and Adam and Rebecca. The next day, I visited Mike and Milanne Galles, Jason, Jeremy and Justin, and then visited the Rose and Japanese Gardens. On July 6, I drove from Spokane to Klamath Falls, where I saw Dave and Pat Hedelman and Joby and Abram Isaiah, and took them out to dinner.

I arrived at Cupertino July 7 and met Srs. Mary Teresa, Breda and Mary Negal.

Sr. Mary Teresa Carroll

On July 8, I learned from Anatole France that "To accomplish great things, we must act but also dream, not only plan, but also believe." I went on to Carmel and had lunch at Castraville. "It is only with the heart that one can see clearly - what is true is invisible to the eye." - St. Exupery

I arrived at Ken Buse's home July 9, where we had a Chinese supper at the Crystal Palace. The wedding of Ann Leone Buse and Robert Pendley, PO Box 68, 5888 Cedar St., Rightwood, CA 92597, took place July 11.

I went to Los Angeles, California, to see Kathy smith on July 13. We had dinner at Virgilios for $83. I visited the graves of Mr. and Mrs. Vedder at Holy Cross Cemetery July 14.

I went on to Texas July 15. I arrived late at San Antonio to see Fay Bourgeois and stayed at her home. I had a Mexican breakfast with Fay July 17, and visited the Mission of San Jose. I then left for Austin to see Dick and Vera Hudson and Christine.

I left for Fr. Worth July 19 to visit Angelo and Julie Otero. On July 21, I left Otero's for De Berry, Texas. I stopped at Kilgore for lunch and then visited the East Texas Oil Museum. I arrived at Eugene Galles' home and we had supper at Ken and Vicky's. After brunch the next day, we visited my brother, Gerald's grave at Mr. Zion's, Panola, Texas. Saw Gene, Jr. Galles and Vonda, Jennifer and Christopher, Tim and Missy Bradley, Ken and Vicky Hannah, Cissy and David, Justin and Lacy.

I had breakfast with Eugene July 23, and then started for home. I had supper at a Chinese restaurant in Spirit Lake July 24 and arrived back at Windom at 8:00 pm.

The installation of Bishop John George Vlazny took place at the Cathedral in Winona on July 29. It was followed by a reception at St. Mary's College.

We had our family reunion at Gerry Buse's August 1.

A family reunion - 1986

Charlie and Doris Galles came for a visit on August 28.

The funeral of Herb Ulrich took place February 22, 1988.

Bishop Vlazny called me on April 19 about a move and a sabbatical.

I began seeing Dr. Duane Ollendick Jun 24.

My pastorate at Windom and Jeffers ended June 30, 1988. Fr. John Tighe became pastor.

Roseann Hamm and Joseph J. Voborski, Jr., were marred at St. Patrick's Church, Mauston, Wisconsin July 7. I went on sabbatical from June 30 until December. I spent part of the time with my sister, Clara, in West Concord. During this time, I purchased my first computer and began getting acquainted with using it. Fr. Dale Tupper came to visit me and was very helpful in teaching me how to use the computer. I began using Word Perfect. The early part of August I decided to spend my sabbatical with my college friend, George Bell, in Portland, Oregon. I hoped he would be able to teach me to play the piano. I started my trip to Portland August 5 with a visit to my grade school friend, Jim Larson, and his wife, Irmgard, in Cold Springs, Minnesota. I arrived at the Deetz Motel in Kite Heights, Medora, North Dakota, August 6, and at the Parkway Motel, Billings, Montana, August 7. I saw the Butte Copper mine August 8, and arrived at Charlie and Doris Galles' in Spokane, Washington, the same day. On the 12th, I arrived at George Bell's home in Portland. He began teaching me piano.

Charles and Doris Galles

One day, when I was driving with George, I asked about a turn I should make. Because of his psychological condition, he became terribly upset. I soon realized I would not be able to continue living with him or taking further piano lessons from him. Fortunately, I was going to St. Thomas Moore Church, where I met Fr. Art Dornbach, whom I knew from the North American College. When I told him about my condition with George, and my need to move, he mentioned this to Fr. Ted Webber, a priest friend of his, and Fr. Webber said he would be happy to have me come and live at his rectory, and help out at his parish. I called Fr. Ted Webber and he was happy to have me move into his rectory. Thus, I moved from George's home to Our Lady of the Lake Church, 840 Avenue, Lake Oswego, OR 97034. The telephone numbers were 503-636-4024 and 503-636-7687. This was a very fortunate arrangement. I was able to offer Mass every day and the congregation was very appreciative.

The housekeeper at the rectory was Arlene Tacke, with whom I became a good friend. Her husband, Andrew, was deceased. Their children were Andrea, Teresa, Katy and John.

I met Maurice Mettler at the parish and we became very good friends. I visited him years later, when he was dying. We corresponded frequently. I also got to know his daughter, Nancy Dowers, and her husband, Frank. Nancy's phone number was 503-231-4106.

I also because friends with Kathy and Mark Platt, who had seven children. Unfortunately, Mark later separated from Kathy.

Joy Rawitzer was the receptionist at the parish and I also got to know her very well.

I registered at Maryl Hurst College in Lake Oswego and took the course, "Perspectives in Morality," taught by Mary La Baire and also took a group piano course, where I learned the fundamentals of music, but never became a great piano player.

My nephew, Roger Galles, and his wife, Joan, came to visit me October 16, and we had dinner together in Lake Oswego.

I had breakfast at the Village Inn October 24 with Josephine Kelch, Helen Becker and Patsy and Erika Halverson.

I attended a talk by Barbara Leahy Schleman, a musician, October 31. She defined healing as "Removing anything in our lives that keeps us from being able to love God and one another and to love ourselves."

From Dominic Maruca, I picked up this interesting quote: "Our imagination is our highest faculty. It takes us into the mystery beyond the visible."

I was invited to a dinner for the Catholic Physicians Guild at the Lake Oswego Country Club November 18. One of the physicians remarked that many people pick up diseases and get ill by shaking hands. I said I thought there are more people sick from not shaking hands!

My brother, Eugene Galles, had a heart attack November 19.

On December 15, at a farewell dinner for about a dozen staff people, Arlene Tacke and I prepared a cannelloni dinner and a seven-layer salad.

I left for Spokane December 16 to see Charlie and Doris Galles. On December 19, I left Spokane to go to Preston, Minnesota.

XI) Pastor at St. Columban Parish, Preston, and St. Lawrence O'Toole Parish, Fountain, Minnesota (1988-1997)

Returning from my sabbatical at Lake Oswego, Oregon, I arrived at Preston, Minnesota, on December 22, 1988. I had been appointed as administrator at St. Columban Parish, Preston, and St. Lawrence O'Toole Parish, Fountain. Don and Harriet Osmonson greeted me and took me to their home for supper.

Eleanor Gossman became my housekeeper. Her husband was James Gossman.

I was able to celebrate the Christmas Masses at Preston and Fountain.

My brother, Lester, went with me back to Windom on December 28 to get all my belongings.

Bishop Vlazny came for Confirmation on February 26, 1989. We had dinner at Pete and Geraldine Daley's.

I made a silent directed retreat at Winona, April 23-29, and I had a meeting with Bishop Vlazny on April 27, at which time he appointed me as pastor at Preston and Fountain, effective May 1,1989

Jim and Kathy Atwood came for dinner on May 19.

The funeral for Fr. Bill Schimek was at Easton on May 23.

I purchased a Yamaha keyboard June 9 for $1,478.70.

I went to Brooklyn, New York, July 12 to see Sr. Breda. She was at St. Catherine of Alexandria Convent, 4024 Ft. Hamilton Pkwy, Brooklyn, NY 11218. Her phone was 418-853-0609. Her sister, Catherine Ryan, was with her at the time.

On July 13, we saw Central Park, the Trump Tower, St. Patrick's, Rockefeller Center, Fifth Avenue and Steubenville Glass. We also went swimming at Manhattan Beach.

We saw the Empire State Building July 15. Went from the 86th to the 102nd floor.

That evening we saw "Les Miserable" at the Broadway Theater. It was significant that Sr. Breda's sister, Catherine, who was with us, had always loved the stories by Victor Hugo when she was a child and now we were able to see one of his plays with her in New York.

On July 16, we saw the United Nations Building and Holy Family Church.

I left New York July 17 and arrived home that evening.

When I came to Preston, there was one group of people in the parish who wanted a new organ. Another group wanted to put in an elevator. At the Sunday Mass, August 13, I announced that we would have a Parish Council meeting on Wednesday, and it would be an important meeting because we had to decide if we would get a new organ or put in an elevator.

Margaret Gross' son-in-law, John Rogers, and his wife, Lois, were at this Mass. Sometime after the Mass, I was told that John Rogers wanted to see me. Thinking he might want to go to confession, I met him in the sacristy. He handed me a check for $10,000 and said it was for the organ and elevator. I never told anybody about this. At the Parish Council meeting, the two factions presented their arguments. After the discussion became rather heated, I brought out the $10,000 check. With that sum, we could now have both a new organ and an elevator. You can imagine the silence that ensued.

We were extremely grateful to John and Lois Rogers, 19100 Minnetonka Blvd., Deephaven, MN 55391, telephone 612-473-4910, for their very generous gift at a critical time.

Our family reunion was held at the Iona VFW Hall and the Iona Park, August 11 and 12, 1990.

The early part of September, Joe and Roseann Hamm-Voborski spent some time with me. Roseann underwent surgery at the Mayo Clinic September 4. She called me September 7 and informed me that her cancer had now spread to her lymph nodes. She returned home September 10.

Monica Taylor began work as Religious Education Coordinator in Lanesboro September 15.

I was very pleased when Shirley Carter, Veronica Vandermoon, Olga Burns and Lavonne Bennett, former parishioners at St. Francis Xavier Parish in Windom came for a visit October 8.

Julie Buckel began work in the parish as secretary and bookkeeper November 2.

Gayle Buse and Jim O'Brian were married March 8, 1991. I had a very serious accident on my way home from the wedding.

Joe and Roseann Hamm-Voborsky came for a number of visits in March and again in June.

Maurice Mettler called me on March 21 and informed me that he had lung cancer and was undergoing radiation treatments.

I was on my annual vacation July 21 to August 13. I visited Fr. Jim Murphy in Rockford, Illinois, and then went on to Michigan. On the way back. I visited Jim and Jerrie Gabriel at Sheboygan, Wisconsin, and then went on to Baraboo, Wisconsin, and saw the Circle World Museum. There, I met Happy the Clown (James Williams). I also stopped at the House on the Rock and was very impressed.

I visited Roseann and Joe Voborsky August 9.

Kathy Attwood began work in the parish as secretary and bookkeeper August 15, and Lisa O'Connor began work as Religious Education Coordinator the same day.

I went to see Maurice Mettler at Lake Oswego, Oregon, August 26-28. He died on August 31.

On August 31, I met Sr. Mabelle Hodges at Assisi Heights, Rochester. When I was chaplain there, she completely rejected me and even went to Mass at St. Pius X Church rather than attend the Masses I celebrated. She apparently thought she was an orphan and later found out where her parents were buried. This brought about a complete change in her character. When I visited Assisi Heights, she came up and gave me a warm hug. She also wrote to me and apologized for the way she had treated me.

James Francis Buse and Judith Margaret Kosbeb were married May 30, 1992.

I met with the Rielhe Bros. on July 17, and signed a contract for the renovation of St. Patrick's Church, Lanesboro, for $35,500. The redecoration began May 17, 1993.

I left for Dublin, Ireland, July 20. Sr. Breda Lyng and Sr. Madeliene met me at the airport. We stayed at the Rower, Kilkenny, where Sr. Breda's parents had lived. We had a delightful time together.

Toward the end of July, Sr. Breda and I flew to Zurich, Switzerland, where we were met by Monika Kufferath, who drove us to Ravensburg, Germany, where Monika lived.

During our stay with Monika, it became evident that she was jealous of my friendship with Sr. Breda. Nevertheless, we had a great time together.

On August 2, Klaus and Karen Schneider came to Switzerland from Munich. Klaus gave us a wonderful tour of Switzerland and Dachau.

I left Zurich August 6 and returned to Preston.

I had a discussion with Jeanette Fourtier, August 15, about what she would do as Religious Education Coordinator at Preston and Lanesboro, and on August 20 I had lunch with her and hired her.

On January 1, 1993, Jeanette became Religious Education Coordinator for grades kindergarten through sixth grade in addition to grades 7 through 12. She was to work 35 hours a week.

The parishes celebrated the 40th anniversary of my ordination with a very big party in Fountain January 10. I as ordained in Rome December 20, 1952.

It was on April 13 that I met Martha Greenwald. She had a stand at a city celebration in Preston and was giving massages. I bought a ticket for a future massage, and she later called and said I had won the free massage. This massage became the beginning of a lifelong friendship. I still have one of her paintings.

Eugene Galles, my brother, had surgery April 29.

Sr. Breda came for a vacation June 30, and left on July 15.

Sr. Edward Kennedy, who had been one of my excellent teachers in high school, and became a close friend when I was chaplain at Assisi Heights, died July 19. Her funeral was July 22.

I attended a North American College class reunion at the Hilton Suite Hotel, Oakbrook Terrace, 10 Drury Ln., Oakbrook Terrace, IL 60181, July 30. Present were Larry Cann, Val Gattari, Bill Houran, Dick Hughes, Dick Wempe and Dave Wheeler.

Jeanette Fortier continued as Religious Education Coordinator at Preston for $16,000 a year. She was to work 40 hours a week and 44 weeks a year.

Kathy Attwood's last day as secretary/bookkeeper was October 4.

I began taking guitar lessons taught by Jeanette Fortier on October 4.

Olga Burns, Shirley Carter and Veronica Vandermoon, from Windom, came for a visit October 11.

Morris Crawford's funeral was at Our Savior's Lutheran Church in Owatonnna on November 16.

Andy Walsh and Maggi McGinnis were married in Chatfield, December 11. Andy built and donated the altar, lector and chair for St. Columban Church.

It was on Decimeter 31, that I went with Esther Pickett and her son, James, to see the house which I later bought at 500 Preston St. NW. I again went to see Esther Pickett's home January 14, 1994. Fran Sauer, an interior decorator, was with me on this visit. Esther was asking $25,000 for the house with one lot. The appliances would be included.

The house I bought in Preston (1994) one
block from the Catholic Church

I signed the purchase agreement for the house February 23. The closing was May 24. I took possession June 4. I hired Ron Schroeder to do rather extensive renovation and also to build a garage and carport or veranda.

Fr. William Anderson, who had lived with me for some time at Assisi Heights, died June 2.

I called Arthur Adland at Westbrook, Minnesota, June 2, and purchased from him the two lots west of my house.

The 125th anniversary celebration of St. Columban Church took place June 26.

The city council approved vacating the street north of my house. Thus, in addition to the two lots I bought, I now also owned half of the street that had been vacated.

Electricians arrived July 7 to renovate the electrical wiring in my house. New windows, for which I paid $14,000, arrived July 11. The painting of the house began July 25. Paul Burland sanded the dining room floor July 28.

I bought a dining room set and other furniture at Root River Hardwoods in Preston August 1. On August 3, I bought a Lifetime cookware set from Sue Thompson.

New carpet was installed in my master bedroom August 10 and the master bedroom set was delivered. I purchased a coffee table and loveseat for my veranda August 12.

Our family reunion occurred at Mineral Springs Park in Owatonna August 13-14.

I bought box spring mattresses at Slumberland in LeRoy.

Curt Heeran delivered my computer September 1 and my freezer was delivered September 8.

Jeanette Fortier gave her two week notice letter of resignation September 15, and all three parishes had a farewell for her after a 7:30 p.m. Mass November 1.

Kenneth Buse received a pancreatic liver cancer diagnosis September 21 with two months to live.

After a meeting with Dale and Carol Schneider October 8 and 15, Carol began work as secretary/bookkeeper November 7.

Bishop Francis Reh died November 13.

Margaret Buse, Kenneth's wife, died unexpectedly November 26. We had been expecting Kenneth's death since he was diagnosed with cancer in September.

I left for Ontario, California, November 27, and was met at the airport by Jim Buse. A Vigil Service was held for Margaret Buse November 30, and I conducted an Internment Service for her at San Bernadino Cemetery December 1. I returned to Preston December 2.

Martha Greenwald called me December 19 and informed me I had won the free massage raffle which she had conducted earlier.

Sr. Cynthia's retirement at the Mayo Medical Center was December 19.

Kenneth Buse died December 24.

Rose Ann Hamm came to Preston December 27 and went to the Mayo Clinic the next day.

I had dinner for Martha Greenwald December 29.

I had a dinner for Esther Pickett January 2, 1995, to show her how I had renovated her home.

I had a series of meetings and meals with Martha Greenwald, either at my home or hers, January 15 through June 22. She gave me a beautiful silk painting of flowers August 12 the day we went together to see Mystery Cave and Meighan Store. We then had supper together.

The funeral for Fr. John Tighe, who had succeeded me as pastor at Windom and Jeffers, was February 16.

I flew to Ft. Worth, Texas, March 9, to officiate at the wedding of Kenneth Adams and Cristine Otero. There was a rehearsal dinner at the Ft. Worth Club, sponsored by Betty and Bill Adams March 10. The wedding was at Holy Family Catholic Church March 11. A reception was held at Shady Oaks Country Club. I returned to Preston March 13.

I saw four fox kits in my woods April 23.

Half of my house roof was re-shingled May 5.

Martha Greenwald had an Open House and Sale May 13.

Dave Peitz and Diane Warren were married July 22.

My salary as of July 31 was $1230, retirement was $455, and I received $589 from Social Security.

The funeral for Fr. Ed Scheuring was held in Slayton September 7.

Jean Anderson was remarried September 9.

I attended a North American College class reunion in Lisle Illinois, September 24. Present were: Dave Wheeler, Dick Hughes, Val Gattari and Bill Houran.

Ellen Whalen began work in the parish October 4.

Pope John Paul II came for a visit to the United Stated October 4-8.

Phyllis (Strie) Muller died October 17. Her funeral was held at Sacred Heart Church, Faribault, Minnesota, October 20.

Sr. Edmund Sullivan celebrated her 100th birthday at 11:00 a.m. Mass October 28.

A Preston Design Team, to make improvements in the town, was formed January 18, 1996. They held a series of meetings leading up to a presentation by the Minnesota Design Team April 20.

I went to the Irish Medieval Feast in Spring Valley with Pat Capek and Martha Greenwald March 10.

I made my annual retreat April 21-27 with Fr. Tony Kilroy as my director.

Hank and Mary Clare Doran celebrated their 40th wedding anniversary May 5.

Sr. Breda Lyng came for a visit May 31 to June 12.

I went to see "Man of La Mancha" with Carla Nemanich June 21. We also saw "Married to the Mob" together June 24.

Roger and Joan Galles came for a visit June 25-28.

The Galles/Buse family reunion was held in Iona June 29 and 30.

The Iona Centennial was held July 5-7.

Jim and Irmgard Larson came to visit me on July 12. Jim was my very dear friend in grade school. They visited again July 28-29.

Don and Lori Clasemann were married July 13. Don's previous wife was Donna.

Sr. Trudy Schommer began work as Secretary/Bookkeeper and Religious Education Coordinator at Preston and Lanesboro.

A reflection I had on August 11 resulted in the following interesting quotes: "Anyone's life can be filled with adventure, if one is seeking the Divine Mystery. Furthermore, I don't think it's the place one seeks as much as the company one keeps, which holds the power to open the hidden doors."

"When you shut down the expression of one emotion, deny it or repress it, you end up shutting down all of them."

"Pay attention to everything. If you understand the way the universe works every point along the journey is the destination, all the way there is there, if you know what I mean."

Shirley Carter, Olga Burns, Veronica Vandermoon and Betty Harrignton came for a visit October 14.

I went to the Guthrie Theatre with Carla Noack November 8 to see "Doll House."

Olga Burns died November 13, so shortly after her visit in October.

I went to Austin, Texas, for the ordination of Dick Hudson as a deacon at St. Louis Catholic Church, December 7. I also visited Fay Bourgeois while in Texas.

"The Seven Spiritual Laws of Success," by Deepak Chopra, made an impression on me:

1. The law of pure potentiality

2. The law of giving

3. The law of "Karma" or cause and effect

4. The law of least effort

a. Acceptance

b. Responsibility

c. Defenselessness

5. The law of intention and desire

a. Attention

b. Intention

6. The law of detachment

7. The law of "Dharma" of purpose in life - each has a purpose

a. Discover my true self

b. Express my unique talents

c. Serve humanity

About the same time I was struck by "The Seven Principles of Effective People," by Stephen Covey:

1. Be proactive

2. Begin with the end in view

3. Put first things first

4. Think win-win

5. Seek first to understand and then to be understood

6. Synergize

7. Sharpen the saw

A quote from Pope John XXIII: "We are not on Earth as museum keepers, but to cultivate a flourishing garden of life and to prepare for a glorious future."

I concelebrated at the Mass for the closing of St. Augustine Church, Jeffers, June 8, 1997.

There was a retirement party for me June 22. My retirement began June 30. Fr. Tom Loomis was installed as the pastor at St. Columban and St. Patrick, Lanesboro.

I first met Sr. Carolyn Marie Brockland July 12, when she came to Preston to speak for the Missionary Cooperative Plan. At that time, she was stationed at Villa Maria Center, Frontenac, Minnesota 55026. This was the beginning of a lifelong friendship.

Sr. Rita Brom's mother, Martha Brom, died July 29.

Maria Buse and Steve Snitzer were married August 16.

Vince Bertolini came for a visit August 23-28.

Bishop Vlazny celebrated Mass for the 125th anniversary of St. Patrick's Church, Lanesboro.

I served a dinner for Martha Greenwald, Phil and Heidi Dybing, Fr. Tom Loomis and Vince Bartolini August 25.

Gene and Nell Galles came to visit me August 29-31.

Mother Teresa of Calcutta died September 5.

"Do not go gently into that good night. Rage, rage against the dying of the light." Dylan Thomas

Lloyd Buse died September 22, and his funeral was on September 26 in Iona.

Alice Seifert called me in regard to her sister, Mary Ann Garland, September 29.

On December 1, I bought a 1992 Mercury Sable (59,727 miles) from Don and Marilyn Duxburg for $6850. The tax was $485. A seat was needed for my 1986 Mercury Topaz.

I went to Portland, Oregon, December 18-26, for the installation of Bishop John Vlazny as the Archbishop of Portland.

I saw Joy Fox December 20.

XII)   Retirement (1998 - present)

I went on a cruise with my sister, Clara, to the Bahamas, January 8-24, 1998. An interesting sidelight: A little girl in Winona, Remy, came up and embraced me thinking I was Santa Claus!

We visited with Rodney and Margaret Galles in Millersville, Maryland, on our way to Florida, January 10, and also met Angela, Lucinda and Ryan.

We visited Roger and Vera Fredricks in Temple Hills, Maryland, January 11.

We went on to Washington, D.C., and saw Fr. Al Giaquinto at Theological College January 12, and also the Vietnam Wall.

We went on to Orlando, Florida, and rented a car for three days, for which we paid $106.

We visited with Patty Hanson and John on January 15 and viewed the Kennedy Space Center January 16.

We went on to Ft. Lauderdale on January 17, where we saw Peter and Bee Bobyock and Gerald III and Peter.

We left Ft. Lauderdale January 18, and began our cruise which went on until January 21.

We went on to New Orleans, Louisiana January 23, and arrived back in Preston January 24.

Beginning January 27, and continuing through February and March, I saw Bob and Geri Petrillo, and their daughter, Andrea, many times.

Fr. Bob Ogle, my dear friend from Canada, died April 1 after a long illness.

Our family reunion was held August 1, and my brother, Charles, died the next day.

My classmate at the Catholic University, Fr. Raymond Brown, a noted biblical scholar, died August 8.

I went to visit Rose Ann Hamm, who was very ill, at Hospice House, Tomah, Wisconsin, September 4. She was dying, but was very angry. I prayed with her and anointed her. After that, I visited her parents, Louis and Pauline Hamm, in Mauston, Wisconsin.

When I went back September 5, to see Rose Ann Hamm again, I was amazed to see that she was now very peaceful and resigned. She died September 12, and I concelebrated her funeral Mass at Our Lady of the Lake Church, in rural Mauston. At the Mass, I spoke of the transformation I had seen Rose Ann go through in the final days of her life. How she had moved from extreme anger to a profound peace.

Jaime Jorgenson and Kristi Bromley were married at St. Joseph's Church in Owatonna September19.

My sister, Clara, and I made a trip September 22-28 to Nebraska, where my mother had lived. We stopped off at Fort Dodge, Iowa, to visit Dan and Linda Ortmann.

At Creighton, Nebraska, we went to St. Ludgers Cemetery, where we saw the grave site of Henry and Mary Boltz, my mother's parents, and also the graves of their sons, Christopher and Frank.

Fr. Francis Galles at Henry and Mary Boltz' gravesite
St. Ludger's Cemetery, Crieghton, NE

We also visited Clara Banks in Grand Island, Nebraska, and her daughters, Sandy and Mishelle.

On September 23, we went on to the Niabrara State Park and saw the Stuhr Museum of the Prairie, the Pioneer Village.

We went on to Omaha September 23, where we saw Lawrence and Ruth Anderson, and Gilbert and Geri Anderson. Lawrence and Gilbert were Aunt Catherine's sons.

Fr. Tony Kilroy, OP, who had been my retreat director, came to visit me October 1-3. His address was 2833 - 32nd Ave S, Minneapolis, MN 55406-1619.

I visited Bill and Marge Urlich October 4. They were living at 518 - 5th St., SW, Pipestone, MN 56164. Their telephone was (307)825-3283.

I played the role of the Captain on the Titanic at a dinner dance at Eagle Bluff, Minnesota, October 10. I still have the picture where I am dressed as the Captain.

I visited Lawrence and Mary Galles in Adrian, October 29 to November 11, then went on to visit Jim and Mary Cook in Worthington, November 2-5.

Bishop Bernard Harrington was named Bishop of Winona November 5, and was installed as bishop January 6, 1999.

Leola (Ehleringer) Halverson died January 3.

I was appointed as administrator of the parishes at Slayton and Lake Wilson, January 8 to February 27.

My grade school classmate, James Larson, died February 9, and a memorial service was held at St. Boniface Church, Cold Springs, May 1.

I bought a new HP computer March 6 for $1872.46.

I bought a Yamaha Clavinova CVP 92 Rosewood piano, March 26, and it was delivered March 31.

Tim Biren was ordained as a priest, June 15. I have asked him to give the homily at my funeral.

I left June 16 to officiate at the wedding of Martin Maguth and Marta Otero in Ft. Worth, Texas, June 19. After the wedding, I visited Eugene and Vicky Galles and Hannah, Brittany and Wesley.

On June 22, I went on to Marshall Texas, and had supper with Dave and Sissy, and the next night, I had supper with Gene and Vonda and Jennifer, Chris and Eileen.

I was appointed Parochial Administrator of the parishes of Spring Valley, Grand Meadow and Le Roy on July 24.

My sister, Clara, and I left for Brentwood, Wisconsin, August 18, and visited a number of places in the area, returning to Preston on August 22.

Julie Otero came for a visit October 12-15, and we were joined by Angelo on October 15.

The funeral of Sr. Genevieve Speltz was at Assisi Heights on November 24. At the dinner following, I also had the occasion to meet Michelle Walsh briefly. She was with a close lady friend of hers.

Sr. Breda Lyng went for medical tests on December 9. She called me from Ireland, December 23, to inform me she had cancer.

I met Kimberly Errigo and her son, Nicolas (Nico), at a New Years Day party in Lanesboro for the first time on January 1, 2000. We became life-long friends. I served them dinner January 9.

Knowing that my dear friend, Sr. Breda Lyng, was dying, I left for Ireland January 27, to visit her.

On the plane from Minneapolis to Newark, I sat with Julia Beaudoin, and we became friends and stayed in contact for a number of years.

In Ireland, I stayed at the home of Michael and Elizabeth Keane, and their children Eoin and Heather. Elizabeth is Sr. Breda's sister.

Their address is: Sharpallas, Pallas Kenvy, Co. Limerick, Ireland. Their phone is: 011 353 6139 3684.

Michael took me to see Sr. Breda on January 29. She was at Milford Hospice, Plassey Park Rd., Castle Proy, Co. Limerick, Ireland. Her phone number was: 011 353 61 33 1505.

There was a dinner for all the Lyng family on January 30, and at 2:30 p.m., I offered Mass and anointed Sr, Breda in the family room.

It was difficult to say goodbye knowing it would be the last time I would see Sr. Breda. I returned from Ireland on January 31.

Michael Keane called me on February 1 to inform me that Sr. Breda was confused. Sr. Laetizia called on February 3 and told me that Sr. Breda was confused at the beginning of her visit, but then revived.

Sr. Breda died on February 13, 2000.

Viola Galles, Uncle Clem's wife, died the same day.

I attended a lecture at the Mayo Civic Center Arena, February 14, by Bishop Desmond Tutu. His topic was "Education as a Vehicle for Change."

My brother, Eugene, died May 10.

Sr. Amata Schleich, my first and second grade teacher, died May 28. Her obituary was as follows:

"Sister Amata Schleich, 90, a Franciscan Sister of the Congregation of Our Lady of Lourdes, Rochester, MN, who served as an educator, died Sunday, May 28, 2000 at Assisi Heights, Rochester, MN.

Born LaVerne Gertrude Schleich on August 29, 1910 in Spring Valley, MN, Sister Amata entered the Franciscan Congregation in 1930 from St. Ignatius Parish. She made profession of vows in 1932 and began her teaching ministry at Saint Mary Academy, Owatonna, MN. She taught in various schools in Minnesota in including Iona, Lake City, Currie, Winona, Wilmont, Austin, Albert Lea, St. James, and Glencoe. She taught in Rochester at St. John's Parish from 1949-53 and at St. Francis Parish from 1977-1983. She also taught in Ironton and Portsmouth, OH, Watertown, SD, and Chicago, IL. She retired to Assisi Heights in 1983 and celebrated her diamond jubilee in 1992. Sister Amata is survived by her Franciscan Community.

A Mass of Christian Burial was held Wednesday, May 31 in the Chapel of Our Lady of Lourdes, Assisi Heights, with Rev. Francis Galles officiating. Burial was in Calvary Cemetery."

Sr. Meg Canty came for a visit September 30 to October 4.

I first met Matthew Kelly when he came to a priest's meeting at Rollingstone on October 11. He is the founder of the Dynamic Catholic Institute and the author of many books.

Shirley Carter, Betty Harrington and Gerlinda Thulien from Windom came to visit me October 24-25.

Sr. Edmund Sullivan, who had been so helpful to me when I was chaplain at Assisi Heights, died December 24, and her funeral was December 28.

I loaned Julia Beaudoin $7,000 on December 28. I had first met her on the plane from Minneapolis to Newark January 27, 2000.

A meeting was held January 17, 2001 to discuss the renovation of St. Columban Church. Peggy Lovrien was present as a liturgical advisor and the Rhiele Bros. were to do the work.

I went to Colorado Springs, CO April 16-24 to visit Julia Beaudoin. We had a very open and frank discussion over dinner at the Red Lobster April 18.

I visited Jim and Kathleen Moriarty at Woodland Park, CO April 19-20. We had supper at Yakitori, a Japanese restaurant.

I returned to Colorado Springs and had a dinner with Julia Beaudoin at the Olive Garden Restaurant. Julia was working on a draft of "Bo-Bandy - The Business Plan" while I was with her.

On Sunday, April 22, I went to Mass at Holy Apostles Church. Fr. Paul Wicker was the pastor. During the Mass he invited the guests to introduce themselves. I was very happy to do this and to mention that I had been Fr. Wicker's Spiritual Director when he was a student at the North American College.

Fr. Bob Ogle's sister, Mary Lou, from Canada came to visit me May 16-22. I took her to Spillville to see the Clock Museum. She had given me much valuable material after her bother died and I contacted her.

I went to see the play "The Quilters" at Lanesboro June 10. After the play, I met one of the actors in the play, Lori Ecker, and we became lifelong friends.

On June 21, I attended the wedding of Russell Swonger and Kimberly Anne Errigo at Spooner, WI.

Blanche Jarrett and her daughter, Kathy, visited me August 31 to September 3. Blanche is Helen (Hargrove) Galles' sister.

It was on September 11, that two hijacked planes crashed into the World Trade Center in New York and the Pentagon. Following this, a number of forums were held at the Lanesboro Public School in regard to "Why did this happen?" It was at the forum on October 24 that I first met Prathiba Varkey, one of the presenters.

I received a final letter from Julia Beaudoin on October 31, although she still owed me several thousand dollars which I had loaned to her.

I had a very significant visit with Jeannie Hertzke at St. Mary's Hospital, Rochester, January 24, 2002. I say it was significant because, in the course of our long visit, I got the impression that she might be considering to return to the Catholic Church, which she had abandoned. Jeannie was my sister Clara's oldest daughter.

However, Jeannie suddenly and unexpectedly died January 25 and her funeral was January 28 at Our Savior's Lutheran Church, 1909 St. Paul Rd., Owatanna, MN.

Helen (Hargrove) Brunning died February 20. She was formerly married to my bother, Gerald. Helen's husband, Geral Brunning, wrote to me February 27 informing me of Helen's death. Geral's address was 2399 Cool Springs Rd., Thaxton, VA 24174-3282. Telephone (540)586-4898

The kitchen of my house was reshingled May 23 by Ken Schroeder at a cost of $342.

I went to the 1952 North American College class reunion in Washington, DC, June 17-23. While there, I went to the Capital, the John Paul II Cultural Center and the U.S. Holocaust Memorial.

Our family reunion was held in Iona, August 2-4.

Maureen Burke came to visit me in Preston August 25-29.

Pilar Rick and Phylis Ann Muchiri, and their daughter, Njoki (Jacquetine) Kimonoo, visited me. They visited me again September 28.

A Craftmatic adjustable bed was delivered to my home October 3 at a cost of $4074. The sales tax was $407.47.

The painting of my house, by Bob Wherley and his family, was competed October 11.

Martha Greenwald and Randy Schenkat were married at the Cady Hayes House October 12. A reception followed at St. Patrick's. During the reception, I told how meticulous Martha always was in regard to her dog. I told her one time if her dog ever died I would be happy to take his place in her life because of the great care she had of him. However, I commented, Randy got ahead of me and got to take the dog's place. This brought down the house and Hal Cropp, who spoke after me, said he cold not compete with the talk I had given.

Kimberly Errigo, Russell Swonger, and Nico visited me October 30.

Kathy Smith and Steve Bauer were married in California November 3.

I had my right hip replaced at the Methodist Hospital in Rochester November 13. Dr. Robert T. Trousdale was the surgeon. I returned home November 18. My sister, Clara, was with me until December 6.

I ordered a Rascal Scouter for which I paid $3,499 in December. Fr. Leroy Eikens loaned me $3,000.

On December 16, I had a new water heater installed in my home by Dave McCann at a cost of $323.

I celebrated, in a rather quiet way, the Golden Jubilee of my ordination as a priest, December 20. I had been ordained by Clement Cardinal Micara at St. John Lateran Basilica in Rome on December 20, 1952.

I visited Joe Folkert at the jail in Preston, February 19, 2003. It was there that I met Lawayn Trom for the first time. She was also visiting a prisoner. I had a cannelloni dinner with her on February 24. She visited me again on March 21 and 31 and on April 28. I visited Lawayn and her husband, Douglas, and their three children: Marianne, Benjamin and Marie Rose at Blooming Prairie on May 18.

I bought a 1989 Dodge Dynasty car from Mary Mulhern, St. Paul, for $500.

Kim Kastning and Charlie Gabrelcik were married on April 1. They later divorced and Kim married Brian Hahn.

Clara Risberg celebrated her 80th birthday with a party at the Senior Center in Owatonna on April 12.

I celebrated a Mass and there was a dinner program for the closing of the St. Lawrence O'Toole Church in Fountain.

Bea Bobyock, my brother Gerald's friend, died Auguest 14.

Vince Bartolini came for a visit August 23-28.

At the Radio Show in Lanesboro, Nancy Huisinga, August 24, honored my 50th anniversary of ordination. I have a recording of it.

"Man has places in his heart which do not yet exist, and into them enters suffering, in order that they may have existence." Leon Bloy

Roger and Joan Galles visited me September 20-24.

I flew to Lenzburg, Switzerland to visit Monika Kufferath, October 5-24. Monika and I made a pan of cannelloni October 8. We went sightseeing to Lake Hallwil October 9.

Klaus and Karin Schneider, from Munich, arrived October 12 and we had cannelloni for supper.

On October 13, Monika and I went with Klaus and Karin around Uierwalestatter Lake, through Lucerne, Kussnacht, Gerson where we had lunch, Brunnen, via Axenstreet.

Klaus and Ursula Wodsak came on October 13 and brought a pork dinner with them. Ursula is Monika's sister.

We drove to Rheinfalls and to Zurich on October 14 to see Marc Chagall's windows in a church. We ate at the Schlosslengen Restaurant.

Klaus and Karin left on October 15, and Franco Barrio, a neighbor and friend of Monika, came for supper and we had Mulligan stew.

We drove to Eichberg Restaurant on October 16 and then watched the 25th jubilee of Pope John Paul II on TV.

We drove to Einsiedein Benedictine Monastery on October 17. We had coffee at Gubel and spaghetti for supper.

On October 18, we drove to Schinznath, a spa. Monika drove to the airport to meet Hans Albert and Doris returning from Egypt. Hans is Monika's brother.

The beatification of Mother Teresa of Calcutta was October 19. Monika and I went with Franco Barrio to Mass at Sacred Heart Church. Hans Albert and Doris came for dinner and we had spaghetti.

Lidia and Licio, Monika's neighbors, came for dinner on October 20. They had a small girl, Laura Benetti, with them, who was very attractive.

On the 21st, we drove to Aaron and Olten and had supper at the Hans Albert and Doris Kufferath home.

October 22 was the 25th anniversary of Pope John Paul II. We had a spaghetti dinner at Licia and Lidia Benetti.

I celebrated Mass with Santina dell Aquila and Monika on October 23.

We drove to Beromunster on October 23, and said farewell to Klaus. Ursula and Lidia brought supper.

I left Zurich October 24 at 10:45 a.m. and arrived back at Rochester at 9:05 p.m.

The wedding of Rebecca Johnson and Travis Peterson was at St. Martin's Church, Woodstock, on November 6.

On November 15, I met Treava and Kendall Lundberg at the Calumet Hotel and Restaurant where Treava was entertaining friends. Treava called the next week, November 25, and said that when they met me, they felt as though we had been lifelong friends.

Alijah (Shirle) Gordon died November 18.

Phyllis Muciri visited November 29 to December 1.

Bishop George Speltz died February 1, 2004.

Treava and Kendall Lundberg provided the entertainment at the K.C. Banquet in Preston on February 21.

I first met Elizabeth Mitchell at a DFL meeting at Peggy Hanson's on February 24. she later became my personal assistant and a lifelong friend.

I had my left hip replaced at the Mayo Clinic on May 17. Dr. Trousdale was again my surgeon. I returned to my home in Preston on May 19, and was able to go to church for Mass on May 30.

"He always had a sense of hope, he always had a sense of humor, but he had no sense that there were poor people." - Rev. Bob Edgar, General Secretary of the National Council of Churches about President Ronald Reagan.

Bishop Harrington celebrated Mass and dedicated the renovated St. Columban Church in Preston on June 13.

Julie Fabian died by suicide on June 26. She was my barber and very dear to me. At one time, she gave me an electric clipper. I celebrated her funeral Mass July 2.

Phyllis Muciri came for a visit June 25-27.

Our family reunion was held in St. James, July 23-25.

I visited Martha Greenwald with Luna Nino on August 12.

The funeral for Lawrence Anderson, a favorite cousin of mine, was held at Verdel, Nebraska, on September 16. The next day, Clara and I visited the cemetery at Verdel and saw the burial lots for Chris Anderson, 1909-1981; Mother Mary K. Boltz, 1845-1920; Father Henry Boltz, 1838-1896; Son Frank, 1868-1897; Christof Boltz, 1877-1936. The burial of Lawrence was September 18 in Niobrara, Nebraska. Buried there also were Terry Wheeler, 1950-1991; Lila (Anderson)Walsh, 1924-1961; Catherine Anderson, 1882-1958; Fred, 1882-1931.

Cardinal James Hickey, former Rector of the North American College, died October 24.

Mary (Jilk) Leighton, a teacher of mine in grade school, died November 16,

Msgr. Joseph McGinnis, on faculty with me at Immaculate Heart of Mary Seminary, died December 11.

Sr. Mary Teresa Carroll died December 22. Her former address was 345 Belden Hill Rd., Wilton, CT 068967. Tel (203)762-3318.

The inauguration of President George W. Bush, January 20, 2005, reminded me of the inauguration of President Harry Truman in 1949 which I attended.

At the K.C. banquet at St. Columban, January 29, Novella Meisner provided the entertainment. Troy Meisner was also present. Novella was one of my daughters in "Beauty and the Beest."

Fr. John Courtney Murray's retreat notes, which I published, were up for sale March 20.

I made a loan of $500 to Corinna (and Wes) Kunz on March 22.

Mary Galles, Lawrence's wife, died on April 2.

Cardinal Joseph Ratzinger was chosen Pope Benedict XVI on April 19. He was the 265th pope.

Kimberly Errigo and her son, Nico, came to visit me May 27-30. Together we visited Spillville and Niagara Cave.

I attended the North American College Alumni Meeting in Chicago with Fr. Roy Literski, June 21-23. On our way home, Fr. Literski was driving 70 miles an hour and fell asleep. He awakened when he ran onto the shoulder. It could have been a very serious accident.

On June 29, I ordered 100 copies of Fr. John Courtney Murray's retreat notes which I had published.

Karla Warner called me on July 14 to inform me that Charlie wanted a divorce. I saw the two of them for a number of times after that and they achieved a reconciliation.

Preston celebrated its Sesquicentennial July 29-31. I participated in preparing an Ecumenical Service for July 31. At my suggestion, Novella Meisner sang "The Holy City," which was a tremendous success.

I was the voice-over for the shooting of a video to advertise Preston. On the video, I said that I thought they had chosen me for my good looks, but they informed me it was because of my voice. This brought down the house at a showing of the video later in Owatonna.

I went to Norfolk, Virginia, August 12-16, where I visited Julie and Robert Keesling and Elizabeth, also Earl and Grace Krusemark, Julie, Jean, Ruth and Ed.

I met Joan Ries after she fell and hurt herself at the Rochester airport. We shared a seat on the plane. Her address was 5660 - 85th St. NW, Oronoco, MN. Her email: joanries@aol.com. We again met later.

Joan Ries

Julie Keesling took me sightseeing August 13. We saw the naval base, where there were four aircraft carriers: Carl Vinson, Theodore Roosevelt, Ronald Regan and Dwight Eisenhower. We also visited the Chesapeake Bay Bridge-Tunnel, the Shore Drive-East Beach development ocean view - old neighborhood.

On August 14, we went to Blessed Sacrament Church, 6400 Newport Ave., Norfolk, Va 23505, where Fr. Joseph Metzger III was pastor. Also met Fr. Tom Caroluzza, Fr. John Dorgen, and saw The Hermitage Museum. I returned to Preston on August 16.

I harvested three gallons of elderberries and raspberries on August 19 and 20. Elizabeth Mitchell helped me make 14 gallons of raspberry/elderberry wine, August 22.

I received $100, September 6, from Julia Boudoin as payment on the $6,000 I loaned her.

President Clinton's Global Initiative, published September 16, included these four points: 1.) Climate change; 2.) Poverty; 3.) Enhancing government; and 4.) Religious conflict and reconciliation.

Monika Hellwig died September 30.

Richard Nelson, with whom I had been involved in a number of community endeavors, died October 11.

Joan Ries, whom I met at the airport, was to come for dinner on October 16, together with Mark Abitner and their children. However, only Joan came.

Ben Love hosted a meeting for Kelly Harold for Democrats, January 27, 2006. I attended the meeting with Kay Spangler. It was at this meeting that I first heard of Gary Graft and the Enchanted Highway.

I served a dinner on February 12 for Novella Meisner, Suzie Steir-Walatski and Mark Colberson.

On February 20, I served dinner for nine Red Hatters. Rita Bezdicek arranged.

Hank and Mary Clare Doran celebrated their 50th wedding anniversary with Mass, May 5.

Louise McDermott died May 28.

Phylis Muchiri, originally from Kenya, and her mother, Mary, came for a visit July 1 and 2.

I held a Democratic house party for Tim Walz July 12. Present and assisting me were Novella Meisner, Treava and Kendall Lundberg, Val and Linn Whipple, Clara Risberg, Elizabeth Mitchell and Lawrence Galles.

The Buse-Galles reunion was held in Iona July 29-20.

Betty Galles, Lester's wife, died July 31, at the age of 79. Her funeral was held at St. Mary's Catholic Church, Little Falls, Minnesota, August 3.

I had a very serious auto accident with 77 year old Myrna Rowe (26903 - 235th Ave., Fountain, MN) while on the way to offer Masses in Pipestone, Minnesota. My 1992 Mercury Sable was totaled. Charron McLeod came to my rescue and drove me to Spring Valley, where I was able to rent, and later bought, a 2005 Buick Century from Zeimitz Motors. On November 25, I received $2758.90 from the insurance company for my totaled Mercury.

I was able to continue on after the accident to offer Masses in Pipestone, Woodstock and Jasper. Elizabeth A. Dockstader (207 W. Los Angeles Ave., Ste 315, Moorpark, CA 93021) gave me a check for $100 to help pay for my car. Her mother is Margaret Bisson (55 Circleview Dr., Jasper, MN 56144-1000). After the Masses, I went to see my brother, Lawrence, August 14. I had dinner at the Loon Restaurant in Pipestone with Treava and Kendall Lundberg, Val and Linn Whipple and Lawrence Galles.

On August 15, I offered two Masses at St. Mary's Church, Worthington. I stayed at Jim and Mary Cook's home.

I attended the farewell for Nancy Wepplo at the Good Samaritan Nursing Home on August 30.

At 6:30 a.m., I had a rectal blood hemorrhage. Jerome O'Connor took me to St. Mary's Emergency, September 12. At the Mayo Clinic, x-rays were taken to see where I was bleeding.

Prathibha Varkey came to see me September 16.

I underwent surgery at St. Mary's Hospital, September 29, to remove my colon. Dr. John R. Porterfield and Dr. Stephanie Donnelly performed the surgery. Even after the colon was removed nothing appeared to be wrong with it, but the bleeding stopped. I now had to wear a bag.

Marion and Lawrence brought me home from the hospital on October 6. Clara was with me to care for me at my home. Gwen Frabau and Helen Winslow, from Home Care, came to assist me. Clara left October 17.

Matthew Kelly spoke at the Cathedral in Winona December 13. His topic was "Perfectly Yourself: 9 Lessons for Enduring Happiness." Bethany Hawkins assisted him.

I had a rather striking prayer on December 15. I came to see that meditation on all the events of Christ's birth 2,000 years ago will inspire awe, praise, gratitude, thanksgiving, hope and love. This event will shape our future and the future of the world. It will prompt me to become the best version of myself physically, emotionally, intellectually and spiritually. The greatest gift is energy and spirit that will shape my future and the future of the world and the second coming of Jesus, the kingdom of God.

I received $350 from Daniel and Donnella Griffin for counseling their son, Nathan.

Henry Dorn, who had been a great support to me, died January 24, 2007

I served dinner to Ricardo and Arlett Kvam, and their daughter, Chelsea, on February 14. Arlett had inspired me to write my autobiography.

On February 25, a party was planned at the parish in Preston for my 80th birthday. We had a snowstorm that was so bad that few attended. Most church services were canceled that Sunday.

On March 1, I left on an extended trip to Oregon, and other places west, on the Empire Builder train. My brother, Lawrence, and my sister, Clara, went with me. We arrived in Portland, Oregon, on March 3, and visited Roger and Joan Galles. On the 4th, we visited Tiffany and William Tabbert in Corvallis, Oregon. In Newport, we saw the sea lions in Yaquina Bay. We had supper at Shark's Seafood and Steamer Co.

We left Albany on the Coast Starlight train. It was on that train, March 6, that I met and enjoyed a visit with Janna Easterling, from Kamath, Oregon. She worked with Paranormal Investigators. We arrived in Los Angeles, California, March 7, and met Bob and Marie McCann at La Quinta, California.

We had a great 80th birthday party for me March 8, 2007. We saw Sonny Bono awakens, Palm Springs; the Palm Spring Follies at the historic Plaza theater and had dinner at the Elephant Bar.

We saw "Mars Rover" at the Imax Theater March 10. That day, we also went to Mass at St. Francis of Assisi Church, La Quinta, California.

We had another birthday party March 11 for Lawrence Galles, Eric McCanna, Emily and myself.

We left Los Angeles on the Coast Starlight train March 12 and arrived at Sacramento. We visited Dale and Suzie Buse in Newcastle, California, that same day. On March 14, we left Sacramento on the Coast Starlight train and arrived in Portland, Oregon, on the 15th. We had lunch at the Newport Bay Restaurant on the 16th and left Portland on the Empire Builder train, arriving back in Winona on the 18th.

A very important event occurred on March 23 and 24. Gary Greff of Enchanted Highway fame, came to Preston and visited and spoke at the schools, and stayed at my house. Gary Greff lived in Regent, North Dakota. He saw that the town was dying and decided to do something about it. He had been a teacher and now became a metal sculptor. He decided to build ten monumental metal works on the 32 mile road between Regent and Gladstone, North Dakota, just off Highway I-94. By 1990, Gary had completed seven of the sculptures, when he visited and spoke to us. Completed were: Deer Crossing,

Grasshoppers, Fisherman's Dream, Pheasants on the Prairie, Teddy Roosevelt Rides Again, World's Largest Tin Family. Since then, he has completed Spider Webs, and is presently working on The Giant and The Dragon.

Gary was part of the inspiration for the Preston Art Council to build a 30-foot tall metal trout, called the Fintastic Trout Project. We invited local people to draw a trout that could be used as the pattern for the giant fish sculpture. Gary was the speaker at the Fintastic Trout Project, held at Eagle Bluff, March 24. Katerina Sveen, a high school student, won the $500 prize for the drawing that will be used for our 30-foot metal trout. It is expected that the sculpture will be placed on a new art center building that will be constructed, and it is hoped it will be quite an attraction for the tourists. I am proud to have had a part in this endeavor.

I visited my brother, Lester, at the St. Otto Nursing Home in Little Falls on March 26. This visit was fortunate because he died May 12. His funeral was in Little Falls, May 15, and he was buried at the Veteran's State Cemetery in Little Falls.

Bridget Ann Curley, from St. Francis Xavier Parish in Windom, was married to Jared Ray Ballinger on May 19. The Curley family had been very special to me.

A graduation party was held for Chelsea Kvam at her home May 26. Her mother, Arlette Kvam, was undergoing one of her severe times of depression at the time and didn't come out of the house to meet any of the guests, who were gathered on the lawn. However, when she heard that I was there, in spite of her depression, she came out and had lunch with me. I was very impressed.

Fatima Haron, together with Arul and Tasha Khasieb, came to visit me. Fatima was a good friend to Shirle Gordon at the Malaysian Social Research Institute, Quala Lumpur, Malaysia. She had visited me earlier with Shirle.

I visited Jim and Jerrie Gabriel in Sheboygan, Wisconsin, July 9-13. We toured the House on the Rock, in Spring Grove, Wisconsin, July 10. A very interesting place to visit.

Lori Ecker and Pat Sibley came for a visit July 28-August 2.

Gene Miller, 85-years old, died on August 15. Gene married Emmagene (Tate) Galles after her husband, Sylvester Galles, was killed on the USS Franklin in 1945.

Muriel Ann Gog died February 16, 2008. She had been my secretary for a time. She was a Franciscan nun when she was my secretary, but later left the community. Her memorial service was held April 19.

Phyllis Muchiri, with her daughter, Alisha Marie Kitutu, and her mother, came for a visit July 26-28.

Sr. Placida Wrubel, who had been my housekeeper when I was at Assisi Heights, and had been so very good to me, died August 8.

Martha (Greenwald) Shenkat died October 12, 2008

I underwent major surgery at St. Mary's Hospital, Rochester, for bowel obstruction, February 12, 2009. On February 23, I went to the Grand Meadow Nursing Home for recuperation. When I got sick again, Paul Fakler took me to the St. Mary's emergency room. After that, instead of returning me to Grand Meadow, I went to the Charter House Nursing Home on March 30, returning home April 23.

I regret that, when I moved from my home in Preston to Traditions, an assisted living home, December 1, 2015, my appointment books were destroyed and consequently I have little information in regard to what occurred in my life between 2009 and 2014. During that time, I continued to offer the daily Masses at St. Columban Church Tuesday, Wednesday, and Thursday. I also continued to fill in at parishes throughout the diocese, driving as much as 225 miles. I continued to be very active in the Preston Area Art Council and the Preston Historical Society. I was also very supportive of the Commonweal Theater in Lanesboro, and attended all their plays. I also attended all of the Knights of Columbus meetings and was the chairman for a year.

From January 16 to February 8, 2015, I lived at the Rectory in Slayton and served the parishes in Slayton, Iona and Lake Wilson.

I also had a service once a month at Park Lane Assisted Living and Traditions, as well.

Alex Jorgenson, the son of Jamie and Kristi Jorgenson, committed suicide on April 13, 2015, the day before his 16th birthday. His funeral was on April 18.

Theodore Basselin, to whom I was indebted for a three year scholarship at the Catholic University, died April 22.

Vince and Mary Bartolini came to visit me May 26-30. From June 2-5, I was at the Mayo Clinic and St. Mary's Hospital Emergency for inflammation around my stoma area.

Julie Johns, 1202 - 17 Ave. NW, #6, Rochester, MN 55901, backed into my car parked at Immaculate Heart of Mary Seminary in Winona, June 18, causing over $300 damage, which I paid so that her insurance would not be raised.

I officiated at the wedding of John Homan and Michelle Carlson in Slayton June 20.

I concelebrated at the wedding Mass for Katherine Anderson and James Just at St. Felix Church, Wabasha, Minnesota, June 27. Fr. Tom Cook officiated. I first met Katherine Anderson at the play, "Fade to Black," in Spring Valley on July 7, 2012, and we became friends.

Christie Buse, Lloyd and Leona Buse's youngest daughter, died September 19. her funeral was in Iona on September 23. She had down's syndrome and was a real blessing to the family and to all who knew her.

Lori Ecker came on her annual visit October 8-14, 2015.

I moved from my home, where I had lived for 17 years, to Traditions, 515 Washington St. NW, Preston, MN 55965, December 1, 2015. There I paid $2,220 for a living room, bedroom, kitchen and bath, $250 for services, and $40 for a garage - a total of $2510 a month. The telephone number there is (507)756-3837. My personal telephone number is: (507)676-0497. the rent charge was increased to $2520 on July 1, 2016.

My dear friend, Monika Kufferath, died January 4, 2016, at the age of 74. She was born January 29, 1942.

I held an estate sale at my house on April 1, from 7:00 a.m. To 10:00 p.m.

James and Katherine Hust came for a visit on April 16. Their son, Felix Joseph Hust, was born April 22.

Gayle Marie (Buse) O'Brian died June 29. Formerly married to Jim Buse. She was born September 5, 1943.

The Galles/Buse reunion was held at Lake Wilson July 30-31, 2016

Jared Langseth (507-360-7840) and Shona Snater (507-458-0319) bought my house. The closing date was August 16, 2016

Mother Teresa of Calcutta was canonized as a saint September 4. She was born in 1910 and died 1997.

Lori Ecker came for her annual visit October 7-11. She and Heidi Dybing gave a concert at Traditions, October 10.

My sister, Clara Risberg, died February 4, 2017. I celebrated her funeral Mass at Sacred Heart Church, Owatonna, February 18.

XIII)   185 OF MY MANY FRIENDSHIPS

(1) Lori Ecker

On June 10, 2001 I attended the play "The Quilters" at the Commonweal Theatre in Lanesboro, Minnesota. It was a Sunday afternoon. There were about 12 actresses in the play. Following the performance, I was standing outside of the theatre visiting with people. Lori Ecker was one of the women who were part of the cast, and she came outside to greet those gathered there. I was able to meet her and speak with her. We soon became friends and I invited her as a dinner guest to my home.

Lori came to dinner and our friendship grew. She was residing in New York at the time and making a living by being an actress. Our friendship grew so rapidly that the next year she came out from New York to visit me and stayed with me for three days.

Lori later moved to Indianapolis, Indiana where her mother lived. Every year since our meeting in 2001, Lori has continued to come to visit me and stay with me for three or four days. This year (2017) she will come again to see me October 7-11. During her visit with me in 2014 Lori gave a concert at Traditions which is an assisted living facility in Preston. She has a beautiful voice and interacts with the audience in a very wonderful way. In 2015, she again gave a concert at Park Lane, which is another assisted living house in Preston. She has offered to give another concert during her visit with me this year.

Lori married Ronnie Katz on October 13, 2012. Ronnie requested my presence when he asked Lori to marry him because he knew I was a good friend of hers. He paid my way to fly to Indianapolis (over $500) for me to be there for the occasion.

Lori has been a very true and good friend for many years. A very large picture of her continues to adorn my refrigerator.

Lori Ecker and Ronnie Katz wedding picture

(2) Sr. Breda Lyng

Sr. Breda Lyng was born October 26, 1937. Sr. Breda's sister, Margaret Lyng, was born October 8, 1941. Sr. Breda's mother, Kathleen Lyng, was born August 10, 1910. Sr. Breda's father, Patrick Lyng, was born December 31, 1902. (He died January 8, 1991 at 89 years old.)

Breda Lyng entered the convent on September 5, 1954 and made her first vows on April 11, 1956 as Sr. Brendan. She made her Final Religious Profession on August 26, 1961.

Beginning on April 10, 1966 I made a Four-Day Retreat at Rocca di Papa outside of Rome, Italy. Sr. Brendan Lyng from Ireland was also making this dialogue retreat. It was on this occasion that I first met her, and a beautiful friendship grew out of this meeting.

As an introduction to this retreat, all the retreatants were in a circle. Each person was invited to dialogue for five minutes with the person next to you. Then you were to introduce the person with whom you had dialogued. Only later did I learn that this was quite an unnerving situation for Sr. Brendan because I was a Monsignor.

I had occasion to speak with Sr. Brendan several times during the retreat and we became friends.

Since I was the Spiritual Director of the North American College in Rome from 1962–1971, I had the occasion to invite the retreatants living in Rome to come to the College for a reunion. This was an occasion to meet Sr. Brendan and to get to know her better. She was a Religious at the Sacred Heart of Mary Convent and lived at their house on the Via Nomentana.

As time passed she came to me for Spiritual Direction. Sr. Brendan was one of my special guests when I left the North American College in Rome in 1971.

I returned to Ireland and visited Sr. Brendan's parents and seven sisters and their families. Her father was so very proud that I offered Mass at their home in the country.

After some time and a number of meetings, Sr. Brendan expressed the concern that she was falling in love with me. Knowing that she had left her home in Ireland at a very early age to study with the Immaculate Heart of Mary Sisters in France, and later to enter their Community without ever having had a significant relationship with men, I felt it was good that she was now able to know and come to love a man, even though he was a priest. Sr. Brendan was ten years younger than I was.

Sr. Breda came to Minnesota for a visit August 22–31, 1973. We were able to go to Iona and Pipestone.

In August of 1985 Sr. Breda moved to Brooklyn, New York and was employed at St. Dominic Church, 2001 Bay Ridge Pkwy., Brooklyn, NY 11204, and was living at St. Catherine of Alexandria

Convent, 4024 Fort Hamilton Pkwy., Brooklyn, NY 11218. I visited her there on one occasion.

July 4, 1987 Sr. Breda arrived in San Francisco at St. Joseph of Cupertino Convent, 101 North De Anza Blvd., San Francisco, CA 95014. Sr. Breda left San Francisco for New York on July 12, 1987. I met Sr. Breda in San Francisco on July 7, 1987 and she returned to Ireland on August 1, 1987 and also I visited Sr. Breda when she lived at Brooklyn, New York, July 12–17, 1989.

In our sightseeing we saw the Central Park Trump Tower, not realizing that Donald Trump would become President of the United States in 2017. During this 1989 visit, we went swimming at Manhattan Beach.

We also saw "Les Miserables" at the Broadway Theater. Sr. Breda's sister, Catherine Ryan, joined us for the play. This was especially interesting because when Catherine was in high school Victor Herbert was her favorite author. She was now able to see one of his stories made for stage. This is also my favorite play.

On July 21, 1992 I met Sr. Breda at Dublin Airport. We went to Kilkenny Rower and then back to Dublin. I flew to Zürich with Sr. Breda and then on to Ravensburg to see Monika Kufferath. I left Zürich August 6, 1992 to return to Preston.

Sr. Breda went to Summer School at St. Mary's College in Winona, and consequently I was able to visit with her a number of times and she was able to meet my family. In that trip to Ireland I rented a car and Sr. Brendan and I traveled throughout Ireland, Scotland, and England.

We visited many places as I recall from my appointment books.

Sr. Breda came for a visit to Preston June 30–July 15, 1993. Sr. Brendan had now gone back to her family name which was Sr. Breda Lyng, and was living at the Sacred Heart of Mary Convent at Ferry Bank, Waterford, Ireland.

Sr. Breda went on Mission to South America in 1999. On December 23, 1999, Sr. Breda was diagnosed as having Cancer.

I was fortunate to be able to go to Ireland to see her in January, 2000 and offer Mass and anoint her with her whole family present.

Sr. Breda died in Ireland February 13, 2000. Her Patron Saint, St. Brendan died in 577. He was known as "The Light."

Sr. Breda told me at one time that she loved me more than any other person in her life.

Sr. Breda in religious habit

Sr. Breda still a religious but in secular dress

(3) Monika Kufferath

I first met Monika Kufferath on May 8, 1971. It was at the Catacomb of San Callista. I was giving a tour of Rome and the Castelli towns to Sr. Hildegundus Lang and her aunt Tanta Monika. Monika Kufferath came up to us and said she did not know what she had to do to go through the Catacomb. Her English was somewhat broken. Sister Hildegundus spoke German and so she could communicate with Monika very well. We went through the Catacomb together. Monika had polio when she was a child and was left with a somewhat deformed leg and arm and so it took her longer to make the stairs in the Catacomb.

After finishing the Catacomb Tour, we spoke to Monika for a while and then said goodbye. Later I saw her sitting on a bench at the entrance, and I wondered if she knew anyone in Rome. I asked Sr. Hildegundus if she would mind if we invited Monika to accompany us for the day since I had a good day planned. This was agreeable to Sr. Hildegundus.

I approached Monika again and asked if she would like to go with us for the day. At first she lied and said she did she had something planned for the afternoon. She later recanted and agreed to go with us.

We had a wonderful day together beginning with a dinner at Al Fico's, an outdoor restaurant.

Monika Kufferath was born January 29, 1942. She was 29 years old at the time she began to tell us about herself. Her father owned a factory in Germany that employed about 400 people. Thus the family was quite wealthy.

Monika's father showed her little affection and often told her she was stupid, however she did very well in school.

The rest of the day we toured some of the Castelli towns like Albano and Castell Gandolfo, where the Pope had a summer residence.

On our way back to Rome I asked if she wanted to go to the pensione where she was staying, or whether she wanted to stay with us and enjoy the rest of the day together.

While Sr. Hildegundus and her aunt were doing the dishes, Monika and I were sitting on the couch, and I was showing her a beautiful book I had. At one point Monika seemed to get very upset, and began shaking violently. I thought for a time she might be having an orgasm because I was being very warm and kind to her.

After a time she again settled down. She wanted to stay with us and enjoy the rest of the day together. She said she thought she had outworn her welcome and time with us, but I assured her we would like to have her remain with us.

At one point in the evening, after a small supper, we were all standing together in my room at the North American College. Monika would use an English German dictionary she had if she didn't know the English word she wanted to use. At one point she said in very broken English that I should tell her the secret of the cross. Since we were standing very close together I reached over and kissed Monika very slightly on the cheek, and then told her that I think she knew more about the cross than I did because of all she had suffered. Later I realized this made quite an impression upon her.

At the end of the evening I drove Sr. Hildegundus and her aunt to the pensione where I had arranged for them to stay. I continued to take Monika to her pensione which was quite close to the railway station. On the way, I told Monika that her eyes were very beautiful. I wanted to affirm her as much as I could because her father had always belittled her. She was not extremely beautiful but her eyes were beautiful. This, like my kiss earlier, made quite an impression on her.

When we arrived at her pensione, I said goodbye to her thinking I would not see her again.

The next day one of our seminarians from the Diocese of Winona took Sr. Hildegundus and her aunt sightseeing. When I came to the chapel for night prayers before supper, there were Sr. Hildegundus and her aunt and also Monika Kufferath.

After the Mass Monika asked if she could see me. I told her that we had supper after the Mass, but that I would be able to see her briefly.

We went up to my apartment on the third floor and Monika then gave me a letter she had written the night before regarding our day together. In her letter Monika recounted all the places and things we had seen together the day before and how much our day together meant to her.

I walked Monika to the bus stop where she would take the bus back to her pensione, and again I said goodbye, thinking I would never see her again.

The next day I conducted a day of recollection for the Seminarians, and then driving over the Gianicolo to get a haircut, lo and behold I saw Monika Kufferath on the other side of the street near the college.

When I stopped, Monika came running and asked if she could have a picture of me. I told her I was going to get a haircut, but that if she stopped at the college I would see if I could find a picture of myself for her. She didn't stop.

However some days later she wrote to me from the Island of Ischia where she had gone to bathe in the mineral waters because of the condition of her health. In her letter she asked if she could come back to the North American College once more to attend Mass there on the beautiful Feast of Pentecost.

I wrote back to her and said that she could come. Later she wrote again and said she could not find a pensione where she could stay when she came for Pentecost, and asked if I might be able to find a place for her to reside.

I related this whole story to June Forrest, a friend of mine from England, and she said she had an extra room where Monika could stay. I again wrote to Monika and told her that she could board with my friend June Forrest.

I also had some friends from Munich who were going to come to Rome and could be with me for Pentecost.

When I told our psychologist at the college all about these visits he was somewhat concerned, however he thought that because of these friends from Munich who would be with me it would probably be okay to also have Monika come and stay with June Forrest.

I also had some friends coming for the Morning Mass on Pentecost. Klaus and Karen Schneider, Monika Kufferath and June Forrest were all at the College for the beautiful Mass on the occasion.

After the Mass all of my guests joined me for a wonderful breakfast in the Faculty Dining Room. Following our leisurely breakfast we were going sightseeing. Monika asked if I had a Band-Aid. She had a blister on her foot. I said I had one in my apartment and I would go get it. Monika said she would come with me.

In my apartment Monika reached out to me and said "Take me Father, take me!" I held her tightly by her shoulder and said, "Monika, stay with me. You are all right." She soon settled down and we went sightseeing for the day. Toward the end of the day we were walking along the beach at Fragene. Monika at one point again became quite frantic and reached out to me and said, "Why didn't you take me? You said you loved me." I tried to exclaim that my love was special and not like the love that any man has for a woman.

After a time Monika settled down and we eventually got her on her way back to Germany.

Monika wrote me a long letter in which she included a bottle of pills and the book "Dibs." She explained that at one time she tried to kill herself and consumed a whole bottle of pills. She said that while she was in Rome she thought of killing herself by walking into the sea. Nobody would know what happened. She was sending me the bottle of pills to assure me that she would not try again to kill herself.

She said the book "Dibs" was the story of her own life. Dibs was also thought to be stupid and strange. He would come into the classroom, but hide under a table or desk so that nobody would see him.

One day a teacher took him aside and found that he knew everything. He was a genius!

Monika said this was the story of her life. One teacher took her aside and found she was very wise. Monika became such a friend to this teacher that when she was dying she wanted Monika present even more than her own daughter. I wrote a long letter back to Monika and explained how she had come to see me as her father, and how she sought from me the love she had always wanted from her father. She wrote back and agreed my insight was true.

Monika Kufferath and her family. Monika is on the extreme left

After a time, Monika settled down and we eventually got her back to Germany. Sometime after I returned to the United States in 1971, Monika Kufferath wrote to me and asked if she could come and visit me.

I was now Chaplain to the Franciscan Sisters at Assisi Heights in Rochester and also Diocesan Director of Spiritual Renewal for the Diocese of Winona.

Monika's father and some of her family and friends thought she was crazy for wanting to come to the United States to visit me. But I had already come to realize that when Monika set her mind on doing something, she could do it.

Monika came to see me at Rochester. I met her at the airport and we had supper together at the Wilson home at Assisi Heights where I lived. Monika stayed at the Franciscan Motherhouse at Assisi Heights.

During our supper, Monika again went into the shaking spasm that I had experienced with her in Rome. I did not know how long she intended to stay in the United States, but I realized I may be facing more of a problem than I had anticipated. After a time Monika again settled down and the rest of the evening went well.

Monika stayed about a month and almost every day when we were together she would again go into her spasm. We would then talk about what she was thinking, and it usually concerned her relationship with her father.

As the days went on it became evident that Monika was experiencing some healing by talking out what she had lived through and felt.

Toward the end of our visit Monika had a beautiful vase she wanted to give to me. However I knew she had her ticket to return to Germany and I insisted she had to leave.

Sometime after that first visit Monika wrote me that she wanted to come to United States again and to go to St. Teresa's College in

Winona. Again her father and others thought she was crazy. I knew that when Monika set her mind to something, she could do it.

I wrote back to Monika and and gave her the go ahead, but I let her know that I would not be able to alot the time to her that I had given in her first visit.

Monika came and spent a year at St. Teresa's College. For Summer School she decided to go to Loyola in Chicago. Monika visited again June 17–July 10, 1974.

While at Loyola she realized she was beyond St. Teresa's College and continued at Loyola to get a Masters Degree in Counseling.

After getting her M.A. in Counseling she wrote and told me that what happened in her first visit with me in the United States would have required 10 years of Counseling to achieve what occurred in that one month.

After getting her degree, Monika became interested in the Religious Life. In July 1977 I made a 30-Day Retreat at Glouchester, Massachusetts. When I related all that happened to me during that retreat she became very interested in making a similar one.

When I went back to Gloucester to make a second 30-Day Retreat in 1978, Monika also made a simultaneous retreat at the same retreat house.

Although Monika never found a cloistered convent that satisfied her, she continued to grow spiritually.

Monika returned to Tubingen and then Ravensburg,West Germany, where she secured a good position, and later moved to Lenzburg, Switzerland, to be closer to her favorite brother.

I visited Monika at Stuttgardt, September 26–30, 1982 in Germany and then again Lenzburg in Switzerland from October 5–24, 2003.

Monika was diagnosed with Cancer and died January 4, 2016.

(4) Marguerite Liston

When I came back to the United States in 1971 after spending nine years in Rome as the Spiritual Director at the North American College, I was in great demand to give retreats and Days of Recollection. One of those requests for me to give a retreat was by The Franciscan Sisters living in Chicago who belonged to The Franciscan Sisters with their Motherhouse at Assisi Heights in Rochester, MN where I was living at the time. This was a retreat for four days open to anyone who wanted to attend, September 3–6, 1971 at Fullerton Cenacle, Chicago.

One of the participants in this retreat was Marguerite Liston. Marguerite had been taught by the Sisters of Charity of the BVM all through school. She had formerly been a Religious Sister with the sisters of Charity of the Blessed Virgin Mary. She joined the Order September 1952. She had been a Sister for 18 years. She was among the many Sisters who at that time had decided to leave the Religious Life and enter upon a new way of life as a layperson. She worked at a publishing house in 1970.

Marguerite came to me several times for Spiritual Direction during the retreat I was giving in Chicago. I was quite impressed with her from the very beginning. Marguerite lived in Wilmette, Illinois. Her mother also lived there. She had two brothers, Robert and Jack.

We became so well acquainted during the retreat that Marguerite gave me her address and we agreed to correspond. Marguerite was born September 12, 1930 so she was three years younger than I.

Later Marguerite wrote to me and asked if she could come to Assisi Heights and make a private retreat with me. She came August 25–28, 1972 and spent three days at Assisi Heights and I directed her in a private retreat.

I visited Marguerite later at her home in Wilmette and spent three days at Assisi Heights as I directed her in a private retreat.

Marguerite came to Assisi Heights again on April 7, 1974 and later for a longer visit. We had now become very good friends.

Sometime later Marguerite telephoned to me and because of the sound of her voice I thought perhaps she had been drinking. I found out later this was the beginning of her suffering from Lateral Sclerosis.

At a local clinic Marguerite had been diagnosed as having Amitrophic Lateral Sclerosis. She now came to visit me again and to go to the Mayo Clinic for a second diagnosis as to her illness. I shall never forget when she came back to Assisi Heights on October 20, 1977 after confirmation by the Mayo Clinic that she had this dreaded disease that usually led to death after a relatively short period.

I visited Marguerite again at Wilmette on May 11, 1978 and now her voice had so deteriorated that it was at times difficult for me to understand her. She had now given up her job and was preparing for death. I offered Mass with her in her room on a Sunday.

I was now Pastor at Windom, Fountain and Jeffers when I received a call from Robert Liston, Marguerite's brother, that she had died on September 14, 1979. I was involved in a Marriage Encounter on the Sunday when I was informed of Marguerite's death.

Robert Liston told me that it was Marguerite's wish that I should officiate at her funeral.

As soon as the Marriage Encounter ended I made preparations to drive to Wilmette, Illinois, for Marguerite's funeral. Sr. Rita Brom, who was our Pastoral Worker at Windom, drove my car throughout the night so that I could sleep a bit in the car, and be ready for the funeral when we arrived at Wilmette, Illinois.

The last time I had seen Marguerite she had moved in with her mother. And she was terribly weak and deformed. Her voice was then so bad that she had to use a pen and a tablet to communicate with me.

It was terribly difficult to now see her in the coffin, very thin and quite deformed. She had been very beautiful when I first met her at the retreat in Chicago.

I knew Marguerite probably better than any other Priest and so I could give a rather laudatory homily while giving most of the time to the Scripture of the Mass that had been chosen for her funeral.

Robert, Marguerite's brother, gave a very generous stipend to me, and also gave a good sum of money to the parishes where I was serving. He also arranged hotel accommodations for me and Sr. Rita so that we could get some sleep after our long overnight drive. Marguerite's early and unexpected death was very painful for me, and I continue to miss her terribly. She was one of my dearest friends.

Marguerite's brother, Robert, moved to Florida, and I continue to have an infrequent contact with him. Robert had three children: Ann, Susan and Kathleen.

Marguerite's mother died in 1988.

Marguerite Liston when she graduated from college

(5) Fr. Al (Albert Charles) Giaquinto

I met Albert Charles Giaquinto when I was a Basselin Scholarship student in Philosophy at the Theological College and attending the Catholic University in Washington, D.C. in 1946. Al was in Third Theology, and often took me under his wing. He was a tremendous inspiration to me, especially in his last year at the college when we sat at the same table.

Fr. Gerald D. McBrearity, PSS, who was Vice Rector at Theological College, wrote the following excellent summary of Fr. Al's life at the time of his death.

In Memoriam:

Albert Charles Giaquinto, PSS
December 13, 1923-October 27, 2014
By Gerald D. McBrearity, PSS

John of the Cross once wrote, "In the evening of life we will be judged by love alone." For Father Giaquinto, love showed itself daily through his genuine interest in others and a willingness to make relationships work.

He was the sixth of eight children born in New Haven, Connecticut on December 13, 1923. A Basselin Scholar, he earned the M.A. in Philosophy (1944) and an S.T.L. from Catholic University in 1948. He was ordained a Priest on May 27, 1948, for the Archdiocese of Hartford but then became incardinated into the newly formed Diocese of Norwich in 1953. After ordination he was given the opportunity to serve as the Newman Chaplain at the University of Connecticut, an initial pastoral immersion that spawned many of his priorities as a Priest and as a future Sulpician.

Although a quiet, self-effacing and reserved man who preferred to be in the background, almost from the beginning of his Sulpician ministry, Fr. Giaquinto was asked to move into the foreground. He served on the faculty of St. Edward's Seminary, Kenmore, WA

(1956-1957) and St. Charles College, Catonsville, MD (1958-1963). He was President of St. Joseph's College, Mountain View, CA (1963-1968) and Principal of St. Joseph's High School Seminary (1967-1968). He was then President of St. Patrick's College in Mountain View, CA (1968-1969). He then moved back to Theological College where he served for the next 30 years. He was Director of the Basselin program (1970-1974) and then Rector (1982-1986). At age 44, he was elected a Provincial Consultor (1967-1973) as the Province began to implement the changes in Priestly Formation mandated by the Second Vatican Council. He was then elected again as First Consultor (1977-1982) with a new generation of leaders. In 1971, he designed and implemented the first external formation program in a Sulpician seminary. Throughout all of these activities, Fr. Giaquinto lived a life of radical simplicity.

Many experienced him as a humble, kind, dignified and thoughtful man. As many know, when the time came when he chose to speak either privately or publically, everyone stopped what they were doing, sat up and listened as he gently spoke the truth. He had a way of saying certain things that only he could get away with saying. Above all else, generations of Priests and Seminarians experienced his gift for relationships. Few escaped his friendly and affirming moniker, "fathead." He brought a sensitive pastoral presence to the entire Seminary Community, including not only the administrative staff, but also the kitchen and cleaning staff as well.

In 2000, Fr. Giaquinto retired to St. Charles Villa where he spent the evening of his life gracing the Retirement Community with his signature style of a peaceful presence and an utterly simple life. He died on October 27, 2014 in Gilchrist Hospice. On November 1, 2014, he was buried in the Sulpician cemetery at Catonsville, MD following the funeral liturgy at the Chapel of Our Lady of the Angels in Charlestown. At his Mass of the Resurrection, the Superior General, the Very Rev. Ronald D. Witherup, PSS presided, Fr. Gerald McBrearity, PSS of Theological College was the homilist, and the Provincial Superior, the Very Reverend Thomas Ulshafer, PSS led the committal service at the graveside.

For Fr. Giaquinto, love was the verb of his faith. We give thanks for his long and fruitful life that transformed the lives of so many by his wisdom honed from a lifetime of prayer and service.

Gerald D. McBrearity, PSS,
is Vice-Rector, Theological College

On August 15, 1949, when I was on my way to begin Theology Studies at the North American College in Rome I visited Fr. Al and met his family at New Haven, Connecticut.

He visited me in Rome June 25, 1966 and we went on to Lourdes together on June 30, 1966. There we concelebrated Mass together at the Grotto on July 2 and Fr. Al went on to a Sulpician meeting in Paris.

Fr. Al Giaquinto's ordination picture

(6) Monika Hellwig

Monika was born on December 10, 1929 in Breslan, Germany to a German Catholic father and a Dutch Jewish mother.

Monika, at the age of 15, began her higher education at the University of Liverpool from which she received degrees in Law (1949) and Social Science (1951).

Monika, after her Novitiate with the Medical Mission Sisters, received her MA degree in Theology at the Catholic University in 1956, and returned to CU for a Doctoral Degree in Theology in 1966.

I first met Monika Hellwig at a Movement For A Better World Retreat at Rocca di Papa in 1966. I was so impressed by her knowledge and wisdom that I thought I would never be her friend. She spoke a number of languages. I had a bit of interaction with her during the retreat.

At the end of the retreat she was invited to work at the Better World Center. She was then known as Sr. Cuthbert, a Medical Mission Sister. She invited me to the Better World Center a number of times to hear confessions and give some conferences. A friendship began to grow.

I persuaded Fr. Bob Nogosek, who was Rector at Holy Cross College Extension in Rome, to make a Better World Retreat. He was very impressed with the movement, and later he and Sr. Cuthbert and I formed a team to give a Better World Retreat at the International Center. This retreat was all recorded and it was a fantastic retreat. Unfortunately, I eventually lost the retreat conferences.

After completing her two years at the Better World Center, Sr. Cuthbert returned to her Motherhouse in Rome.

In spite of her great wisdom and broad education, the Medical Mission Sisters had her simply doing typing at the Motherhouse. Realizing that her talent and ability were being wasted Sr. Cuthbert left the Medical Mission Sisters and received a dispensation from her vows. She then went to the Catholic University in Washington, D.C. and earned a Doctoral Degree in Theology.

In 1963, Monika was sent to Rome by her Community, where she served as a research assistant to a Vatican official during the Second

Vatican Council, one of the few women allowed access as an observer at the Council Sessions.

Bishop Fitzgerald asked me to conduct a Better World Retreat in the diocese. I prepared Msgr. Joseph McGinnis and Fr. Joe Hagarty to form a team with me and conduct this retreat. This took place July 24-29, 1966.

I felt very ill at the beginning of this retreat. So much so, that I felt I had to cancel. However I went through with it, but immediately went to the Mayo Clinic afterwards. This seemed to have been nothing more than a case of the nerves.

The following year, Bishop Fitzgerald again asked me to conduct a Better World Retreat in the diocese. I asked if I might ask Monika Hellwig to help me with this retreat. The Bishop asked if this was the person who formerly had been a nun. When I said it was, he said I could not utilize her help. Later on he called me back and said that I could have her assistance.

Monika came out from Washington, D.C. and helped me with this second retreat which was from August 13-18, 1967. After the retreat Monika spent several days with me and we even drove out to my home to visit my family.

Sometime later, Fr. Bob Nogosek suggested that he, Monika, and I should make a retreat together.

It was during this retreat that Monika made some strange remark to the effect that I would return to the diocese and not accomplish much of anything. Neither Fr. Nogosek nor I ever understood what prompted her to make this remark.

Monika adopted two sons and a daughter who survived her. Monika was struck by a car before Christmas, 1968, and fractured her hip.

On June 14-18, 1982 Monika Hellwig conducted a workshop at Sioux Falls, SD, which I attended. On June 20, 1982 Monika gave a lecture at St. Francis Xavier, Windom, MN.

Monika wrote many books which I have read including "Understanding Catholicism" (1981), "Jesus, the Compassion of God" (1992), and "The Eucharist and the Hunger of the World" (1976). She was also a co-author of the Modern Catholic Encyclopedia."

As President of the Catholic Theological Society of America; in 1986 Monika co-signed a controversial letter supporting Charles A. Curran, a Catholic Priest and professor at the Catholic University of America, who had been stripped of his authority to teach at Catholic universities because of his dissent from The Church's teachings in such issues as contraception and homosexuality.

In 1996 Monika became President and Executive Director of the Association of Catholic Colleges and Universities.

Monika was also a Senior Fellow at Georgetown's Woodstock Theological Center. At Georgetown she spent six years as the Hand Distinguished Professor of Theology. Monika taught for more than three decades at Georgetown University in addition to lecturing at many other universities.

I had another visit with Monika in London, August 21-23, 1968. I stayed with Monika's sister, Marianne and David John. On August 22, 1968, Marianne painted a picture of Monika for me. See below.

How amazing that I should become a lifetime friend to this person whom I thought I could never have a friendship with when I first met her at a retreat in 1966 because of her superior wisdom and intelligence.

Monika died September 30, 2005 at the age of 75 from a cerebral hemorrhage. The National Catholic Reporter at the time of her death referred to her "near encyclopedic knowledge of Catholicism."

Painting of Monika Hellwig by her sister, Marianne

(7) Sister Rita Brom

I first met Sr. Rita Brom who was born on October 2, 1937 when I was Chaplain at the Franciscan Motherhouse at Assisi Heights from 1971-1978. Sr. Rita was running a printing press at Assisi Heights. In making use of her services I got acquainted with her and we began to be friends. She was 10 years younger than I was.

When I completed my seven years as Chaplain at Assisi Heights, and was appointed Pastor at Windom and Jeffers, Sr. Rita helped me to move out to Windom. About a year later, August 15, 1979 I hired sister Rita to be the Pastoral Worker at Windom and Jeffers. She lived at a residence owned by the parish together with a Notre Dame Sister who was the Religious Education Coordinator at those parishes. She fulfilled her ministry well and our friendship continued to grow.

After some years we did begin to experience differences in our approach to ministry. To improve the situation we agreed to have another Franciscan Sister who was in Counseling to come and help us resolve our differences.

As preparation for this meeting I had written out a complete explanation as I saw our differences. Sr. Rita resented that I had come to the meeting with such a thorough preparation, and the meeting almost broke up from the beginning. However the situation was resolved and Sr. Rita continued on as the Pastoral Worker.

In spite of our differences, our friendship remained intact through the years, but perhaps at a lesser degree.

Sr. Rita was a most definite asset to the parishes. She was a very accomplished artist in addition to being a good organizer of Community.

(8) Sr. Mary of St. Louis

Sr. Mary of St. Louis (Aunt Katie), one of my mother's sisters had a great influence in my life. She belonged to the Good Shepherd Sisters and was stationed in Los Angeles during the time I knew of her. She was born March 16, 1882 and entered the convent November 21, 1901. The Good Shepherd Sisters cared for delinquent girls, often sent to them by the courts.

Sr. Mary of St. Louis was an extern at the convent, which gave her considerable contact with the outside world. The other sisters were quite cloistered.

During the depression when my family was very hard up, Sr. Mary of St. Louis was a great help to us. As the extern sister she had contact with various people outside the convent. She knew many movie stars and wealthy people. I was able to visit one of these famous stars, Irene Dunne and her daughter when I was a student at the North American College in Rome. I have three letters written to me by Irene Dunne.

Sr. Mary of St. Louis was often able to get clothing and other things from these wealthy people, and she would send huge boxes of clothing and other items to my family.

When Sr. Mary of St. Louis heard that I might study to be a priest, through her connections Mr. and Mrs. Milton and Genevieve Vedder offered to pray for my education. They assisted me financially when I went to Loras College in Dubuque, Iowa. Then since I received the Theodore Basselin Scholarship to the Catholic University for three years they did not have to give me as much aid. The Diocese of Winona paid for my four years at the North American College in Rome, but Mr. and Mrs. Vedder assisted me with money so that I could travel during the summers.

I was able to meet the Vedders when mother and I went to Los Angeles to visit aunt Katie in June 1944. They had a beautiful house in a large orange orchard. Mrs. Vedder toured part of Los Angeles with us.

Mother and I also met a number of wealthy people whom aunt Katie knew.

I was privileged to serve Mass at the convent where Sr. Mary of St. Louis lived. She was, of course, very pleased when I was ordained as a priest in Rome on December 20, 1952.

Sr. Mary of St. Louis died October 17, 1955, and her funeral was October 19, 1955.

I regret that I was never able to see her after I was ordained as a priest and to offer Mass with her present.

Francis Galles, Sr. Mary of St. Louis and Mrs. Charles Galles in California June 1944

(9) Sr. Margaret Canty

I met Sr. Margaret Canty on December 12, 1966. Sr. Saussy Carroll whom I had met on the ship from New York to Naples introduced me to her. Sr. Canty was in Rome to make a 30-Day Retreat in preparation for taking Final Vows. She was born September 8, 1934.

I was present at the Marymount Motherhouse when Sr. Canty and her companion Sisters made their Perpetual Vows on February 3, 1967.

I felt honored when Sr. Canty told me even before she told the other Sisters where she was going after taking Perpetual Vows. She was going to Belgium to take special courses to prepare for the work she would be doing in the future. I regretted that she would be leaving Rome and would be gone for a year.

After the year in Belgium, Sr. Canty returned to Rome and she was now in charge of the program to prepare the Sisters to take their Perpetual Vows. Now that she was back in Rome I got to see her quite often and a very deep friendship developed.

On one occasion when we enjoyed a long visit in my apartment at
the North American College where I was now the Spiritual Director,
I asked her how Jesus was Present to her in her life. She put her head
down in her lap for a long time and when she came up she said that
when she prayed she had no image of Jesus, but that she experienced
a desire to live and to love, to create, to go beyond herself, to do more
and be more, to rise again when she had fallen, and this, she said. is the
presence of Jesus to her. This statement had a profound effect upon me.

Playing the devil's advocate, I asked "How do you know this is
the Presence of Jesus? Is this not the very elon of life itself?" Sr. Meg
said in reply, "My God if I am wrong in this my whole life is a loss."
Then she said, "I know this is the presence of Jesus because when no
human person is present I have this experience."

A passage of Scripture that became a favorite for the two of us
was Colossians 2:27. According to the Jerusalem Bible translation
this says: "Christ is in you. Yes, Christ is in you which means you
will share in the glory of God."

There were so many other times when Sr. Meg's presence made
me want to know and love Jesus more. In 1970 when I returned to the
U.S.A. to attend Summer School at the University of San Francisco,
I made a stopover and visited Sr. Canty on June 14-16 at Kenwood
in Albany, New York.

On July 15, 1972, Sr. Meg Canty came for a visit.

After Sr. Margaret returned to the U.S.A., and I was also back to
the United States she came out to Winona to attend Summer School
at St. Mary's College, a program of Community Spirituality, and I
was able to see her a number of times and even have her come to Iona
with me to visit my family.

When Sr. Margaret made her first 30-Day Retreat at Glouchester,
Massachusetts, she inspired me to make one also and I attended at
the same place where she had made hers. She also made a second
30-Day Retreat. Sr. Meg came to visit me in Preston on September
30, 2000. I was also able to visit Sr. Margaret one time when she was

at Albany New York. Her friendship, which still continues by letter and phone calls, has truly been a great blessing to me.

Margaret Canty with college friends.
Margaret is the second from the left

(10) Kathy Smith

Kathy Smith with two other ladies came to visit me in Rome on September 11, 1969. As happened so often, Kathleen heard of me from a couple of her friends who had visited me earlier, and I showed them around Rome; that was our only connection. I gave them a good tour and we enjoyed a dinner together. Kathy wrote to me from France and we began a correspondence. Born in 1947, she was 22 years old when I met her. Before we met, she had undergone surgery to remove a breast due to Cancer.

Kathy was living in Los Angeles, California, where she had a very good job in Advertising. She came to visit me at Assisi Heights in 1971. She was very impressed with the Sisters and also the Catholic Church. Later I was with her in California when she was baptized and received into The Church on July 12, 1972 at St. Paul's Church.

Kathy Smith came from Des Moines, Iowa for a visit August 22-31,1972.

I attended a workshop for pastoral planners at Des Moines, Iowa October 12-14, 1972 and stayed with Kathy's parents Hebert and Lillian Smith

November 6-13, 1972 Kathy Smith came for a visit at Assisi Heights.

She was Jewish. Her parents, whom I later met, lived in Iowa.

Having a background in Public Relations, Kathy has used hundreds of young people in her work in this field. When I became well acquainted with her we had some serious discussion about hiring her to help me in my work as Diocesan Director of Spiritual Renewal. Although she was earning a big salary in her role in Public Relations in Los Angeles, she was willing to accept a very modest salary to help me.

I discussed with Bishop Waters the possibility of hiring her and he was in agreement. The whole thing fell through however, when she wrote to the Bishop herself and critcized him for not offering a more reasonable salary. Kathy again came for a visit on July 5, 1980.

When my sister, Clara, and I made a trip out west to California and other places in 1987, I visited Kathy at Culver City, California. Unfortunately she had not continued in her Catholic faith.

At one time time she wrote to me and asked if I would officiate at her funeral in the event of her death. I felt I could not do this unless it was a Catholic funeral which she did not want.

On August 10, 1977 I received word that Kathy had been diagnosed as having multiple sclerosis. This began to limit her greatly in her work.

Kathy married William J. Frost on May 28, 1983. He was partially blind and they were able to help each other. However this marriage ended.

On November 3, 2002 Kathy married Steve Bauer but they later separated.

Kathy died December 26, 2013.

Kathy Smith when I first came to know her

(11)   Kimberly Errigo

I first met Kimberly Errigo at a New Year's Party on January 1, 2000. She had with her Nicolas (Nico), her son, who was conceived out of wedlock while she was in Colombia, South America. Her parents live in Northern Wisconsin.

Kimberly was with the Peace Corps in Panama and later traveled in Colombia. After returning to the United States she lived in Minneapolis, St. Paul, Lanesboro, and in Wisconsin, and presently lives in Santa Cruz, California.

After we met at the New Year's party, I asked Kimberly and Nico to join me for dinner at my house. At that dinner I was impressed not only with her beauty but also her outgoing personality. Kimberly had lived in Colombia and traveled widely, and had a very interesting background.   At the time I met her she was working as a Certified Life Coach. She was born in 1970 and had lived in northern Wisconsin, Panama, Colombia, Lanesboro, Minnesota, Minneapolis and St. Paul, Minnesota, Viroqua, Wisconsin. She is presently in Santa Cruz, California.

Later on, when we traveled to the cave in Spillville, I watched her speak with a young man who had some problems and was really struck by her ability to give him her undivided attention and genuine interest and concern, even though he was only a stranger. I noticed her gift and it reminded me of Jesus in his ability to focus on people. This is why people followed Jesus, because they were impressed by his attention on them. They saw something special in him, and I saw that in Kimberly that day.

Kimberly and I have very different backgrounds, and I think we learn from each other. We come from very different religious traditions. Kimberly was trained in shamanism and that makes her a very special and unique person to me. Even though she and I weren't in agreement about religion, we shared a deep understanding about spirituality which brought us together.

I continue to enjoy her friendship and look forward to her coming to visit me again when she returns to Minnesota and Wisconsin to see her parents later this year.

(12)   Kendall and Treava Lundberg

I met Kendall and Treava Lundbergh on November 15, 2003. I was offering the Masses at St. Leo's Church in Pipestone, Minnesota that weekend. The organist invited me out for dinner at the Calumet Restaurant Saturday evening. Kendall and Treava were entertaining the guests. Treava was playing the piano.

After a time they both came around to each table to greet the guests. I was very pleased to meet them and we chatted for some time. I gave them my calling card before they moved on.

I was amazed the next week when I received a letter from Treava. She said that when they met me it felt as if they had known me for a lifetime. This was the beginning of a friendship. They lived at Lake Benton which was not too far from Iona, my hometown.

On another occasion I was back to Pipestone and I went to see the Lundbergs at their beautiful home.

Kendall and Treava came to Preston and performed at the Knights of Columbus banquet on August 29, 2004. Treava played the piano and sang at Spring Valley. We have continued to keep in touch and I still treasure their friendship.

(13)   Elizabeth Mitchell

I met Elizabeth Mitchell at a Democratic meeting in Lanesboro on February 24, 2004. We seemed to have similar political viewpoints and a friendship grew out of that.

We met on a number of occasions and later, when I was in need of a personal assistant, and she was available, I hired her and paid her $15 an hour. She usually only worked one day a week and that was on Wednesdays. She was very helpful. Among many things, she provided secretarial and computer help.

Elizabeth was very knowledgeable about the computer and typed up a lot of material useful for my autobiography. In addition to the help she gave me, I enjoyed her company.

After several years Elizabeth asked for the $3 raise. That seemed rather high and, since I no longer needed a secretary so much, I did not agree to the raise, and so Elizabeth terminated her work, but we have continued to be friends. Now, she is helping me get my autobiography published.

(14)   Fr. Bob Ogle

It was probably in November or December of 1978 that I met Fr. Bob Ogle at Assisi Heights in Rochester. I was on the team for a Marriage Encounter at Assisi Heights.

Sr. Joyce Stamper had heard that I was going to be on the team for this Marriage Encounter. Usually when I was on a Marriage Encounter the Sisters would try to get another Priest to offer the Mass for them. Sr. Joyce Stamper told me that her uncle, Bishop Stamper, from New Guinea would be able to offer the Mass, but he would not be strong enough after surgery to give a homily. A Sister who was at our same table overheard the remark and said she would be able to give the homily.

Ordinarily I would not have gone down to the Main Chapel for the Mass, but I wanted to hear that Sister's homily. She gave it on the Scriptures of the Mass with Bishop Stamper sitting on a chair before the Tabernacle. I decided to stay for the rest of the Mass. After the Mass Sr. Alcantara brought Fr. Bob Ogle and Sr. Margarita Findlay who was with him to introduce them to me.

Fr. Ogle made some remark about the Mass that prompted me to ask if he had time to go for a cup of coffee. We went to the dining room and about half dozen sisters also joined us. In the course of our discussion Fr. Ogle recalled a story about the two models of the Church that had been bantered about by the Bishops at the Second Vatican Council, namely the Town Model of The Church and the Covered Wagon Model of the Church.

The Town Model of the Church sees The Church like a town with nice straight streets, square blocks, and a fence around each house. The Town Model of the Church is very neat and clean but there isn't much life in it except at the local bar where there are dancing girls. Proper people are not inclined to go there. The Town Model also has a court and a judge. When people are out of order they are brought before the judge who judges right and wrong. Everything is black and white, never any grays. All is neat and clean.

The Covered Wagon Model of the Church is like a covered wagon moving out west. God the Father is simply the horizon. Jesus is the scout who goes ahead to find the right trail to take. The Holy Spirit is like the buffalo hunter who supplies the caravan with food. The caravan people gather around the campfire at night with food and singing and dancing with much joy and laughter.

I was greatly struck with this comparison of the two types of Church, and I told Fr. Ogle so.

On the way out of the Dining Room I took Fr. Ogle aside and told him that I had a letter from the Bishop telling me that he was moving me from Assisi Heights but I did not want yet tell the sisters about this. Fr. Ogle told me that I should tell the Bishop that I would like to go to the smallest and most insignificant parish. If I did some of the good work I had done at Assisi Heights, people would soon be looking at this insignificant parish and asking what was happening in that stinking little place. It seems that Fr. Ogle was quite prophetic because that was exactly what began to happen in the small parishes at Windom and Jeffers where I was sent.

Some years later my sister Clara and I and other members of her family went to Canada to visit Clara's daughter Julie who had lived in Saskatoon, Saskatchewan.

On a Sunday morning Clara and I went to the Mass at the Cathedral there. When three Priests came out to celebrate the Mass and they were introduced, one of them was Fr. Bob Ogle. I told Clara that I knew him, and she couldn't believe that I was friends with this Priest up in Canada.

When I first met Fr. Ogle in Rochester he mentioned that he had spent six years in the Missions in Brazil. He was on a sabbatical and would spend a year in India to study the effect of Catholic Aid to India.

After the Mass, Clara and I stopped at the Rectory and met Fr. Ogle. I recalled for him how I had met him at Assisi Heights. He was now a member of Parliament in Canada. He spoke of Fr. Drinan and the Priest from Massachusetts who had stepped down from Congress under Vatican pressure. Later Fr. Ogle also had to withdraw from the Parliament in Canada under Vatican pressure.

I left my calling card with Fr. Ogle and he wrote to me on July 11, 1983 and said how happy he was about our visit at St. Paul's Cathedral. He also sent me a copy of the book "When the Snake Bites the Sun," which he wrote after his sabbatical year in India.

But this was still not the end of my relationship with Fr. Bob Ogle. Fr. Frank Morrissey, a Canon Lawyer, conducted a workshop for us in the Diocese of Winona in June 1988. Fr. Morrissey was from Canada, so I asked him if he knew Fr. Bob Ogle. He said he was living with him and knew him very well. I gave Fr. Morrissey my calling card and told him how I had met Fr. Ogle in Rochester and again there in Saskatoon.

On June 28, 1988 Fr. Bob Ogle wrote me the following letter:

Dear Father Frank,

Father Frank Morrissey, Canonist, gave me your card today. He told me he had received it from you in Winona, Minnesota and that you had talked about meeting me in Saskatoon years ago.

Now as Frank may have told you, I have had a brain tumor which is now in remission after radiation, but I have lost a great deal of my memory and I have difficulty remembering you. Your name comes to me like a hazy dream.

Maybe if you have time you could fill me in. I like keeping in contact with people and a book which I wrote last year I dedicated to my sister, Mary Lou, and my 10,000 closest friends.

I imagine Minnesota is burning up like Saskatchewan. It seems we are inches away from disaster.

God bless.
Bob Ogle

In reply I wrote a long letter to Fr. Bob Ogle in which I told him about my first meeting with him in Rochester when he spoke of the Two Models of The Church and how this affected me. Then I wrote about our second meeting in Saskatoon.

Fr. Ogle replied to my letter on July 21, 1988. This is what he wrote:

Dear Frank,

It was a great pleasure to receive your letter and to make contact again. As you know I have a brain tumor which is growing and, as the medics say, allowing me only a few more days. However I am continuing to live "day by day" as if there were 10,000 years to go. My memory is all but gone due to the tumor and radiation, so I could not remember you at all until you outlined our short encounter. It was like an old dream coming back. I would have been in Rochester then to visit a close friend, Msgr. John Robinson, dying from cancer. The nun was a Notre Dame, Indiana College colleague and Sister of St. Joseph. She has since left and married a Grade One classmate and former Priest, Jack John O'Connor. They are living in Saudi Arabia and teaching English under contract commute. I was actually between India and Brazil. It was my sabbatical year and I had gone on Fellowship to study the effects of Canadian Aid.

I can't recall our meeting in Saskatchewan at Saskatoon at all. It must have been at St. Paul's Cathedral, where I lived when I was a Member of Parliament.

Your experience though is not unique. I could tell several stories too about how the Spirit moves through the lives of others. Nobody ever knows when they will be influenced or when they will influence. Your story of peace coming to your life through the almost insignificant event of your coffee break has been acted out in my life as well. It almost always has taken place at the time of change of appointments--- right down to the Vatican squeezing me out of Parliament.

I'm still a great supporter of the "Wagon Train" Model of Church---God the Father is still the horizon, Jesus the scout well out in front, the Spirit the hunter and provider, the Priest the cook, the liturgy is the campfire and singing. But everybody has given up the security of a picket fence and a weekly salary. They are in this insecurity of traveling into the future, of living in faith that the Kingdom is ahead.

In the next month or two, I plan to move back to Saskatoon. My sister is arranging a place at St. Ann's home. I am being told that I am due for a massive stroke or death as the tumor now surrounds my spinal cord and jugular vein.

I am sending you my recent book written since the cancer has been diagnosed and also a few petitions to give your "rich" friends. B.I.U. Will carry on. We have a good Board Meeting and have accepted the fact that "The seed has been sown. They will have to nurture it."

I am so happy you have a sabbatical. Use it well. A great time for reflecting on the marvel of being alive and the speed of life.

I write this on an Air Canada flight between Ottawa and Saskatoon. An Ogle Reunion is being planned next week near Seattle, Washington. The medical people here have told me to take in all these human events as long as I can. I will be happy to see you again--- if not there, then in the Kingdom.

Peace and love,
Bob

The book he sent me was "North/South Calling" describing how the Northern Hemisphere has caused many of the problems in the Southern Hemisphere.

On August 30, 1988 Fr. Ogle wrote the following letter to me, still in his own handwriting:

Dear Frank,

I'm still writing letters. Tomorrow I go to the hospital again for a devastating set of brain tests and scans. They will inject dye into my brain and from previous experience, I have had tremendously negative side effects from the procedures. But that is the marching order as of today. My sister from Saskatoon is with me. On Sunday the rector of the seminary and staff celebrated The Sacrament of the Sick with me and two friends also suffering from Cancer. About 50 of my friends and relatives were present and it was most supportive. As a matter of fact I feel fairly well today---much better than I will feel tomorrow, I know.

I truly appreciate your letter and supportive message and prayers. I'm glad that you enjoyed my book and I'm enclosing one for the Bishop too, in case he might read some of it. Your $100 will be put to work and in due course you will receive an official receipt for it.

My hope for you is that your wish to study music and computer will come true. But maybe in my Wagon Train Model---that may not be the horizon which may involve (you) in some other way--- remember, however, the Wagon Train Model celebrates with spontaneous music and song and from what you write, it seems you are already doing that.

I was very happy to know the cook was living the "most Spirit-filled time of his life." My prayer for you will accompany you through the darkest canyons---who knows we still may have that long friendly visit again.

In the Lord,
Bob.

In November, Fr. Bob Ogle again wrote to me in his own handwriting:

Dear Father Frank,

This notice to thank you for your continued support and to assure you that your donation is bearing fruit. Broadcasting for International Understanding is progressing and several new programs will be aired before Christmas.

My personal health has been a problem so a new director, Raymond Vander Bewkes, has been hired. He comes with the long experience in development work. I will act as Founding Director and continue to promote B.I.U. as well as fundraise, as my health permits.

We hope to be able to send you a more detailed newsletter before Christmas. Thanks for your prayers and moral support.

Sincerely,
Fr. Bob Ogle

With this letter Fr. Ogle also sent an article that appeared in Home Missions entitled "Just a Little Bit of Time...A Terminally Ill Priest Reflects On Life's Wonder." The article read as follows:

We are all alive, but we are also all dying. Nobody knows the day or the hour when human life will end, and death will win the contest.

I have had the privilege of having time to get ready for that day. An inoperable brain tumor changes one's perspectives quickly. I have lived with the knowledge that a tumor exists in my brain since July 1986.

The experience has focused my life in a way that nothing else could have. On two different days, I felt that my spirit was about to leave my flesh. Those days were positive and mystically joyous in a way that I would previously never have imagined.

What is best about these extra days is that it is much easier to see life as it is--- to separate the grain from the chaff --- to identify what is worthwhile and to call trivia "trivia."

For me it has been a time to marvel --- to marvel at creation in all its glory: to see sky, smell grass, hear speech, touch reality, taste life in a way that had never before been so focused.

Now I know that in this moment of time which is my life, I have nothing better to do than just stand with my mouth open and marvel at the wonder of it all. Geraniums, salmon, Canada geese, amoebas can't do that. Only me and my fellow humans know we are creatures of the Father.

The notion of time has always fascinated me --- springtime, being on time, history time --- particularly Creation time...

Love and Peace,
Bob Ogle

The last letter I received from Fr. Ogle, he wrote from St. Ann's place in Saskatoon, Saskatchewan on January 11, 1997. He wrote:

Dear Francis:

Thanks for your message. The Spirit seems to have given you a good year in 1996. I have been wondering what you did for Christmas. For me, today is the "Third Day Out of the Hospital" after the "Twelve Days of Christmas in the Hospital." On Christmas day I fell in my apartment, couldn't get up to tell anybody, and waited for my sister to arrive to go out for dinner. (A four hour session on the floor) Then ambulance and emergency entrance.

I passed 12 days in the University Hospital battling pneumonia and other problems including prostate gland. Finally I was let out with a prescription against depression. My theory on that is that after this kind of holiday experience, if you were not depressed, you must really be sick.

All in all, I have lost a bit of strength in my legs, so I am using a walker to get around the apartment, but I was able to shower and make breakfast today, so I am semi-back to normal. My brother Chuck and his wife set out for Arizona this morning. My friend Fr. Al Dietch is soon to follow. I am now traveling, the last journey being to an Ogle's 50th Anniversary in Calgary on Labor Day. It was actually Anniversary for me too. I left for the Seminary 50 years ago on the weekend that Rusty and Betty were married. I am just slightly younger than you, 68 in December.

My serious wish for you is that 1997 will be an upper.

Love and Peace,
Bob Ogle

I don't know how or when I heard of Fr. Bob Ogle's death. He died April 1, 1998. He was 70 years old, having been born on December 24, 1928.

As soon as I learned of Fr. Ogle's death, I wrote a letter to his sister (at the time I did not even know her name.) I addressed the letter to Fr. Bob Ogle's Sister at the last address I had for him. Fortunately she received the letter and wrote back to me.

His sister, Mary Lou Ogle, wrote to me on January 1, 1999 and told me a bit about how difficult his final years and days were. She also sent me a tremendous number of personal mementos of Fr. Bob and newspaper articles about him and also articles he had written.

Mary Lou also sent me books based on the letters Fr. Ogle wrote to his father during the years he was in Brazil.

Sister Torero Therese Sullivan of Gary, Indiana, collected all these letters by theme:

Page 1 ... The Land: Brazil
Page 8 ... The Effort: What Fits ... What Doesn't
Page 14 ... The Work: Development of Peoples
Page 23 ... The People: Fermentistas
Page 31 ... The Culture: Poverty
Page 43 ... The Flood: Afterwards
Page 54 ... The Priest

Mary Lou Ogle also sent me the beautiful book "A Man of Letters" containing all the letters Fr. Bob wrote to his father and others during his year in India.

In addition, Mary Lou gave me the book Fr. Ogle wrote as his Doctoral Dissertation entitled "The Faculties of Canadian Military Chaplains"

Mary Lou Ogle also came from Canada to visit me at Preston for four days. Together we toured a number of sites in the area.

Eventually I just I lost contact with Mary Lou and I expect she died. She was born August 22.

Fr. Bob Ogle

(15)   Sr. Judine Klein

Sr. Judine Klein was living at Assisi Heights in Rochester when I became Chaplain there in 1971.

She came to me for Spiritual Direction during many of my years at Assisi Heights. We became very close friends, and she even accompanied me to Iona and met my family.

She became a much more outgoing person during the years that I knew her. Even after I left Assisi Heights our friendship continued.

(16)   Sr. Gretchen Berg

Sister Gretchen Berg was President of the Franciscan Community at Assisi Heights. When she heard that I would be returning from

Rome to the Diocese of Winona she went to Bishop Fitzgerald and asked if I might be appointed as Chaplain to the Franciscan Community. Bishop Fitzgerald apparently responded to her request and from 1950-1971 I was appointed Chaplain to the Franciscan Community at Assisi Heights and also Diocesan Director of Spiritual Renewal.

I enjoyed a very good relationship with Sister Gretchen all during the years she continued as President of the Franciscans, and my good relationship continued even after she was replaced by Sister Kathleen Van Groll.

Sister Gretchen and I seemed to be very similar in our thinking. She arranged to have dinner at my residence at Assisi Heights together with Fr. Bernard Lonergan.

(17)   Delphine Voss

Delphine Voss lived on a farm near Wilmont, Minnesota. During my high school years I was introduced to her by my brother Lester's wife, Nettie.

Delphine and I became steady friends for a couple of years.

Eventually I suggested that we terminate the relationship because I thought it might hinder my vague intent at that time to become a priest. I think this was rather difficult for Delphine.

I met Delphine several times much later when I was a priest. She seemed to have a very good life with a husband and family.

(18)   Sylvia Platt

Sylvia Platt was a steady girlfriend of mine in my later years in high school. Her family lived on a farm a couple of miles from Iona, Minnesota. My family had good relations with all the Platt family. Sylvia's brother, Charlie, who died in 2016 was a classmate of mine and a good friend in grade school. He did not go on to high school.

I was going with Sylvia at the time I decided to leave high school and to attend Loras College in Dubuque, Iowa to begin my studies for the Priesthood. It was rather dramatic when she and all my high school classmates came over to my house to say goodbye.

Sylvia later married Max Gunderson and apparently had a rather difficult life because he became an alcoholic. They had a number of children, one of whom was partially blind.

(19)   James Larson

James Larson was very a close and dear friend of mine all during grade school. His family moved away for a time but James came back during part of my high school years. He was probably the closest friend I had during my younger life.

James was later in the military service and married a German girl named Irmgard. I met the two of them in later years, but I do not think their marriage was a very happy one. I think he wished he had not married.

James Lloyd Larson died February 9, 1999.

(20)   Martha Greenwald

Martha Greenwald lived in Lanesboro, Minnesota. I met her at a fair in Preston April 13, 1993 where she was giving massages. She was offering one FREE half-hour massage to the winner of the drawing. She called sometime later and told me I had won the one half-hour FREE massage. Since I had never had a massage I told her I would come for the half-hour FREE massage but I would also pay for an additional half-hour.

The massage at her home in Lanesboro on May 7, 1993 at 9:30 a.m. was a very pleasant experience, but even more enjoyable was the conversation we had during the massage.

A friendship developed as a result of this FREE gift and I invited Martha for dinner. She reciprocated and our friendship increased.

Martha later began coming to the Catholic Church and joined the Church.

Martha had a dog that she cared for with meticulous care. The dog would just need to move and she would jump up to care for her. I told her once that if that dog ever died I would volunteer to take the dog's place so that I could get all the care and attention that the dog received.

Martha married Randy Schienkat on October 12, 2002. At the reception I told how I had met Martha and that later she became a Catholic. I also spoke of the care she had for her dog and that I had volunteered to take the dog's place if ever the dog died. I then went on to say that Randy Schienkat got ahead of me and managed to take the dog's place before I did!

Martha and I had many visits in the course of our friendship. Martha became ill with cancer and went through a long period of therapy to try to overcome it, but eventually she died on October 12, 2008. She was born September 8, 1954.

In addition to her many other gifts, Martha was a painter. I have a very beautiful painting of flowers which she gave to me.

(21)   Alice (Scully) Knutson

Alice Scully was two years ahead of me in high school. I was very attracted to her and still remember the lilac perfume she used and the red dress she wore. She never seemed to pay much attention to me, but favored other older classmates like Bob Spartz.

Alice's brother, Joseph, was a good friend of mine. I somewhat knew and admired all of her family. They lived on a farm several miles from Iona. Joseph married a very small lady and later ran a filling station in Iona.

On one occasion I attended a dance at Slayton together with my brother, Lester. Alice Scully was at the dance also, and Lester, knowing that I liked her, suggested I might ask to take her home. I

did so, but she let me know that she would go home with her brother
James.

Alice married a Knutson from Slayton and I think she had a
rather good life and raised a number of children. Even after her
husband died, she remained very active at St. Ann's Parish in Slayton.
I continued to see her quite frequently when I was offering Masses
at St. Ann's. She was always very attractive and in good health even
in these later years.

Alice continues to live at Slayton and is very active in St. Ann's
Parish.

(22)   Eunice (McCormick) Meadow

Eunice McCormick was a classmate of mine in grade school. I
had quite a crush on her. One time I danced the Virginia Reel with
her as a part of a school play. She and two of her sisters were well
known in the area for their tap dancing.

Eunice was younger than my class in high school. She married
John Meadon, and I think had a rather good and happy family.

I saw her many years later when I was a priest. We had a fairly
good conversation at a dinner at St. Anne's Parish in Slayton. I regret
that I did not know or remember more about her.

(23)   Bernard Dominick

Bernard Dominick was a rather good friend of mine when I was
at Theological College and studying there at the Catholic University
in Washington, D.C. He was in Theology while I was in Philosophy.

Our relationship continued on a bit after we left Theological
College. I remember that he sent me a book when I was at the North
American College in Rome.

(24) Eldred Lesniewski

Eldred Lesniewski from Milwaukee was a classmate and a rather good friend of mine when I was at the Catholic University in Washington, D.C. Eldred was a Theodore Basselin Scholarship student, as was I.

What I remember about him especially was our relationship over French. We both required a reading knowledge of either French or German for the Masters Degree at the Catholic University in Washington, D.C. George Bell, a good friend of mine from Kentucky whom I knew from Loras College in Dubuque, Iowa came one summer and spent a month with me in my home in Iona to teach me French.

When I went back to the Catholic University in Washington, D.C., Eldred also wanted to know French for the Masters Degree. Thus I taught him French for about a month.

Eldred and I went over to the Catholic University to take the hour-long test to see if we had a reading knowledge of French. He passed and I flunked! I think the reason I flunked was because I tried to translate the passage that was given to us, instead of just getting the meaning, and consequently I was only able to answer about half of the questions.

At a later date I went back and took the exam again and passed.

On my way to Rome I stopped off at Milwaukee and again got to see Eldred Lesniewski.

(25) Henry Schneider

Henry Schneider from North Dakota was a fellow classmate when I was a Basselin student at the Catholic University in Washington, D.C. I only remember that he was a very down-to-earth person and a rather good friend of mine during our three years together. He was also ordained a priest for his diocese which I think was Bismarck.

(26)   Joyce Back

Joyce Back became the Secretary-Bookkeeper or Pastoral Worker at Francis Xavier, Windom, and St. Augustine, Jeffers on August 25, 1982.

She played the guitar which was helpful at liturgies.

We had a potluck farewell dinner for Joyce Back on July 22, 1984.

(27)   Sherilyn Bahnemann

I had major surgery at St. Mary's Hospital in Rochester for bowel obstruction on February 12, 2009. Sherilyn Bahnemann came to visit me on March 27, 2009. Her visit was so special that I have never forgotten it.

Sherilyn is an extremely beautiful person and I could not help but admire her good spirit in carrying out the ministry of visiting those who were in the hospital.

I remember how honored she felt in bringing communion to a monsignor.

Though infrequently, we have kept in contact. I also met her husband Steve. They have a son, Brandon.

(28)   Vince Bartolini

Fr. Vincent Bartolini from Providence, Rhode Island joined the faculty at the North American college as a Repetitor in 1964. We soon became very good friends and often we would spend one day a week off at Fragene where a number of faculty had rented a house near the beach.

We would often take food from the kitchen at the North American College. I would cook the food and Vince would prepare the drinks. We would also go swimming or take walks on the beach. Father

Vincent and I usually saw eye to eye when there was a difference of opinion among the faculty at the college.

After returning to the USA, Vince married and they had a son, Daniel Martin.

Vince visited me several times in Minnesota and with Mary, his wife, also. I visited Vince at Warwick, Rhode Island on June 2, 1972.

Vince visited me August 23-28, 1997.

(29)   Julia Beaudoin

I met Julia Beaudoin born May 4, 1956 on a plane flight from Minneapolis to Newark.

Julia lived in the East at the time, January 27, 2000. She was on her way to the Twin Cities to see her father. She later moved to Colorado Springs, Colorado. I later visited her in Colorado and spent several days with her.

At a time when Julia was in need of money I helped her out with $7,000.

Julia was formerly married to John P. Kuklinski on July 14, 1984 and divorced.

She had a sister, Diane S. Morris who lived in New York at the time and owned Bag Linens, a very successful enterprise. She later moved to Woodside, New York.

Something I wrote to Julia at one time, she misinterpreted and thus broke off the relationship. She never repaid the loan I had made to her. Her last letter to me was written October 31, 2001.

Julia Beaudoin

(30)   Fay Bourgeois

Fay Bourgeois was formerly a Notre Dame Sister with the religious name of Sister Marie LeClerc. It was as a Sister that I came to know her when I was the Spiritual Director at the North American College in Rome.

Sr. Marie LeClerc first knew me through a retreat I had given. Subsequently she came to me for Spiritual Direction quite frequently.

Sr. Marie later left the convent and returned to the United States. I was fortunately able to locate her some years later when she had now gone back to her name as Fay Bourgeois. She had one serious relationship with a man, but never married.

Her last address was San Antonio, Texas. Together with my sister, Clara, we visited her after 1981. She has continued to be active in the Church and involved in the RCIA with about 40 people attending.

Fay Bourgeois

(31)   Sr. Carolyn Marie Brockland

Sister Carolyn Marie Brockland, an Ursuline Sister, came to St. Columban Church to preach a Mission Collection for the Ursuline Sisters on July 12, 1997. At first she was rather cautious of me, but we kept in contact and became friends. She was with the Ursuline Sisters at Frontenac, Minnesota, when I first met her. Later she moved to St. Louis, Missouri, and then to New Orleans, Louisiana.

(32)   Chris & Jeralyn Buchan

I was on my way back to Rochester, Minnesota and had a rather extended layover in Chicago. At the airport in Chicago I met Chris and Jeralyn Buchan. Jeralyn had a tumor on the brain that horribly disfigured her face, she was so hideous that it was difficult to look at her. They were on their way back to get help at the Mayo Clinic. When we boarded the plane they were across the aisle and about five seats ahead of me. All the way to Rochester I prayed that Jeralyn would get help at the Mayo Clinic and be cured. We parted at Rochester but exchanged addresses and emails. They lived at Lumpkin, Georgia.

We kept contact by mail and email. They had two small children, Amelia and Hannah, about three and six years old.

In my Christmas letter of 2015 I wrote that I was moving into Traditions, assisted living. In response they sent me a large, beautiful box with a blanket to keep me warm and a huge quantity of various candies and cookies. I was very impressed.

Knowing that they must have terrible medical bills and other expenses (Chris also had surgery), I sent them $1,000 on one occasion and $2,000 on another occasion.

This last October, 2016, they sent me another large box with an unusual bucket for tricks and treats, and again a huge bag of candy.

Hannah who is now 11 years old and Amelia who is eight years old each wrote me a letter and sent pictures. Jeralyn sent a picture of herself taken with her grandmother on her 90th birthday celebration. Jeralyn's face is greatly improved, but her mouth and jaw are still somewhat distorted. In an earlier letter she mentioned how she used to love to sing in the choir, but she is no longer able to do that.

In an earlier letter Jeralyn sent me a copy of a talk she gave at a church meeting describing all she had gone through, but how the Lord had also been with her through it all.

(33)   Julie Buchel

Julie Buchel began secretarial work with me on November 2, 1990. Julie was married to Chuck Buchel. They had three children: Heather, Christopher, and Melissa.

We got along very well, and at times her children would join her at work.

I remember one time I corrected her on the way she wrote out checks. She mentioned that she had learned from her teacher how to write checks. She was somewhat surprised when I pointed out that she did not need to write "dollars" after the amount because that was already on the check.

Chuck and Julie were married June 18, 1971.

(34)   Dr. Maureen Burke

On September 27, 1969 I was having a meeting with Brother Saunders at Rocca Di Papa. Maureen Burke and Stephanie Rea from England stopped by. They had left England with the expectation of work teaching in Germany. When they arrived in Germany they found the job was not available. Rather than returning directly to England they decided to do some traveling.

This is what brought them to Rome. Accidentally they stopped in at our meeting. They were looking for work and a place to stay. I thought I might be able to help them out. They waited until the end of our meeting. We had dinner together and they then followed me into Rome.

Sr. Breda got a job for Maureen, and Stephanie got a job taking care of the child of a prostitute.

Maureen and Stephanie became good friends of mine. I often showed them around Rome. They stayed in Rome about a year. We kept in contact even after they left. Maureen later moved to Australia and married but her husband died.

Stephanie returned to England and married. I later visited her. Both Maureen and Stephanie visited me in Preston.

(35)   Patricia Capek

Patricia Capek was the Religious Education Coordinator at St. Columban Parish in Preston when I became Pastor there. She was born March 8, 1939.

At Christmas time I went into her Religious Education classes and mentioned that we never got Christmas presents because we couldn't afford them. Patricia mentioned this to her son, Edward, who is an artist, and he said that he was going to give me a Christmas present. He gave me one of his paintings which depicted a group of young people playing "Ring around the Rosey." Later I bought another of his paintings, "A Farmer Plowing With Two Horses."

Patricia and I became friends and the friendship even continued when she moved from the rural house she had at Chatfield, to a residence in Winona, Minnesota.

(36)   Shirley Carter

Shirley Carter and her husband, Al, were parishioners at St. Francis Xavier Parish at Windom when I was pastor there.

Shirley became quite special to me. Often I would find at my back door a package of garden vegetables that she had raised. Her husband ran the local filling station where I got gas and had my car serviced. He was always very good to me.

After I moved to Preston, Shirley on a couple of occasions brought a number of women from the parish to visit me.

Our friendship continued through visits, letters, and telephone calls.

(37)   Don Clasemann

Don Clasemann became the Pastoral Worker at St. Francis Xavier Parish, Windom, and St. Augustine Parish, Jeffers, when I was Pastor of these parishes. He was an excellent Pastoral Worker and we became friends.

His wife at the time was Donna and she was also a good friend to me. They had three sons: Joel, Jon, and Cory.

Donna later divorced Don and remarried. Don then married Lori with a dispensation from the Catholic Church. He later became the Pastoral Worker at Hector, Minnesota, and went on to get a Masters Degree at St. Mary's College in Winona.

We continued friendship through mail.

(38) Jim and Mary Cook

Jim and Mary Cook from Worthington, Minnesota made a Marriage Encounter at Rochester when I was on the team conducting the Encounter. The Marriage Encounter had a profound influence in their lives and we became friends.

Mary made a whole set of Mass vestments for St. Columban Parish, and also made a very elaborate bedspread for me.

Jim and Mary came to visit me a number of times and we continued to be very good friends.

(39) Dharmini Cropper

I became friends with Dharmini Cropper from Lanesboro. She used to bicycle to Preston and would quite often come to Mass and then visit me at Preston.

Dharmini married Brennan Voboril on July 7, 2007 but divorced shortly after. She moved to Los Angeles, California and we continued to correspond.

(40) Mike and Sue Curley

Mike and Sue Curley were parishioners at St. Francis Xavier Church, Windom, when I was pastor. They were also social friends and gave me great support.

Their children were Bridget, Thomas, and John Patrick. Sue and the children came to visit me at Preston. Bridget stayed in contact with me even after she married.

(41)　Glen and Mary Ann Davis

Glenn and Mary Ann Davis belonged to the parish at Grand Meadow, where I celebrated Mass quite frequently. Numerous times as I greeted the parishioners after Mass, Glenn would squeeze a $100 bill into my hand as he shook hands.

(42)　Jean (Andersen) DeWall

Jean Anderson was a member of St. Francis Xavier Parish in Windom, Minnesota. Her husband, Randy, died at an early age.

Their children were: Carrie, Mindy, Nikki, Jay, Whitney, and Briana.

The family were special friends, especially because of the early death of the father, and Jean being left with the responsibility of such a large family.

Jean later married Tom DeWall. Their last address was Zimmerman, Minnesota.

(43)　Hank (Henry William) and Mary Clare Doran

I became friends with Hank and Mary Clare Doran when I was Chaplain at Assisi Heights in Rochester. They introduced me to Marriage Encounter and were strong supporters of the movement.

Their children are Terrie, Colleen, Debra, and Bill.

Hank died at the age of 71 on January 24, 2007 in his favorite rocking chair, in the family cabin at Lac du Flambeau, Wisconsin.

(44)   Phil and Heidi Dybing

I first met Phil and Heidi through Heidi. She played piano for a concert at Lanesboro which I attended. After the concert I went to the White Café and was in a booth with a number of friends. When Heidi came into the restaurant she surprised me by coming over and joining our table.

I was invited to their rural home on a number of occasions.

In more recent times Heidi was the pianist for concerts given by my friend, Lori Ecker.

Both Phil and Heidi are entertaining people with a wide variety of interests.

(45)   Sylvia Gail (Galles) Ellsworth

Sylvia Gail Galles was the daughter of Sylvester Galles and Emmagene Tate. Her father, Sylvester Galles, was killed on the USS Franklin in 1945. Emmagene Tate was pregnant with Sylvia Gail at the time and Sylvia Gail was born after her father's death.

Sylvia Gail visited our family with her mother when she was about two years old. Both Sylvia Gail and her mother accompanied us on a trip made with Lloyd and Leona Buse. Among other places, we visited Yellowstone Park.

Emmagene married Gene Miller who died August 15, 2007 at the age of 85.

Sylvia Gail married Roger Ellsworth and they had two children, Tim and Martyn.

Emmagene had five children: Sylvia Gail, Larry, Dennis, Rodney, and Paul.

Sylvia Gail Ellsworth and sons Tim and Martyn

(46)   Sr. Agnes Fleming

Sr. Agnes Fleming was a Sister of the Sacred Heart of Jesus and Mary whom I came to know in Rome. It was through Sr. Breda Lyng that I came to know Sr. Agnes Fleming.

My friendship with Sr. Agnes Fleming continued when she returned to the United States and was stationed at the Marymount Convent in Tarrytown, New York.

(47)   Jeanette Fortier

Jeanette Fortier became the Religious Education Coordinator at St. Columban Parish, Preston, St. Lawrence Parish, Fountain, and St. Patrick Parrish, Lanesboro, on August 20, 1992.

On January 1, 1993, Jeanette became Religious Education Coordinator for Grades K-6 in addition to grades 7-12, working 35 hours a week.

In addition to being a good Pastoral Worker, Jeanette played the guitar and even gave me a few lessons on the guitar. She writes the most beautiful Chancery Script I have ever seen.

Jeanette was born May 20, 1952.

(48) Joy Fox

Joy Fox was Secretary at a parish in Lake Oswego, Oregon. We became friends during the time I stayed at the parish while on sabbatical.

She was married and had a number of children.

(49) Carolyn Freese

Carolyn Freese was a beautiful singer whom I came to know at Lanesboro. I have some of her CDs.

Her husband is Jeff Freese and they have five children: Yvonne, Sarah, Christopher, Isaac, and Allison.

(50) James and Jerrie Gabriel

Geraldine Gabriel worked at The Courier Office for a short time when I was appointed Assistant Editor in 1953. She had taken instructions from Msgr. Tierney, the Editor, and became Catholic. Jerrie married James Gabriel on October 15, 1955 and they had five children: Paul, Ann, Eric, Jennifer and Daniel. I visited them a number of times at Sheboygan, Wisconsin, where they lived. James was an architect.

Unfortunately, Jerrie became involved with an Evangelical group and left the Catholic Church.

James died after a lingering illness.

Jerrie and James visited me in Italy March 24-April 6, 1970, and I was able to show them around Rome and also travel with them to Assisi, Florence and Siena.

I have continued to see Jerrie and enjoy friendship with her. While still having her home at Sheboygan, Jerrie also took up residence at Green Valley, Arizona.

(51)   Leola and Viola Ehleringer

Leola and Viola Ehleringer were twins who lived just a few houses south of our home in Iona. We became friends while I was in high school. Their brother, John, was also a good friend of mine. Their sister, Marion, a couple years ahead of me in school, was the first girl with whom I ever danced.

Leola and Viola, although about four years older than I, were a great help to me when we moved into town and no longer had a car. They would often take me to dances or plays when I had no way to get around. I had quite a crush on Leola especially.

They were twins and married twins. Leola married Harold Halverson and Viola married Henry Halverson.

Harold and Leola had four children: Mary, Barbara, Joseph, and Teresa.

Henry and Viola had five children: Michael, Tom, Paul, JoAnn, and Jean.

Leola died January 3, 1999.

(52)   Leo and Joanne Hanson & Kathy

I became friends with Leo and Joanne Hanson through a Marriage Encounter which they made.

Leo and Joanne had eight children: Kathy, Mark, Dave, Mary Jo, Michael, Thomas, Patrick, and Susan Veronica.

Leo and Joanne visited me a number of times when I was a Spiritual Director at Immaculate Heart of Mary Seminary.

Kathy once visited me in Rome. I regretted that she seemed more interested in shopping then in seeing the treasures that are in Rome.

Later Kathy had the very unfortunate experience of being picked up when she was hitchhiking, and she was held captive and abused for a period of time. Her parents spent practically all their savings to rescue her.

(53)   Fatimah Herron

Fatimah Herron from Malaysia, accompanied Shirle Gordon when she came to visit me in Rochester.

On May 27, 2007 Fatimah came to visit me with two of her sons, Arul and Tasha Khasieb, and their wives. The sons were living in Northern Minnesota.

Fatimah was a dear friend of Shirle Gordon and deeply involved in Shirle's work at the Malaysian Sociological Research Institute, at Kuala Lumpur, Malaysia.

(54)   Blanch (Hargrove) Garrett

Blanche Hargrove was a younger sister of Helen Hargrove who was married to my brother, Gerald. I met Blanche when she was a young teenager and I had quite a crush on her.

Blanche married William Garrett who was a minister.

Blanche and her daughter, Kathy, came to visit me at Preston. The visit was quite unsatisfactory. They seemed little interested in anything we went to see. After this visit Blanche wrote to me and requested that I would respect her wishes and no longer correspond.

Several years later she wrote and apologized for her earlier reaction.

The daughter Kathy had married a Davis who was a Catholic and she began attending RCIA as preparation for becoming a Catholic. Blanche, as I last heard, did not know about this.

Blanche was in poor health.

(55)   Don and Elsa Hofmeister

I first met Elsa Hofmeister when she was a patient at the Windom Hospital. I was struck by her beauty. I became friends with both Don and Elsa and the friendship has remained, even once they moved to Burnsville, Minnesota.

They have four children: Elizabeth, Andrew, Francis and Joseph.

Elsa wrote a book which I have read.

(56)   Msgr. Warren Holleran

Msgr. Warren Holleran from California was a classmate of mine at the North American College, and was ordained at the same time I was. After I was invited to be the Spiritual Director at the North American College, Msgr. Holleran was also invited to be the Spiritual Director. He was much more of a scholar than I was and while he was there as Spiritual Director, he continued his studies in Theology and obtained a Ph.D. at the Gregorian University.

Having been invited first as a Spiritual Director, I was Head of the Department. At one time I felt Msgr. Holleran was usurping my position as Head of the Department. I mentioned this to Archbishop O'Connor the Rector, and he met with both of us and straightened out the situation. Msgr. Holleran was very gracious and accepting of this insight.

When my father died on March 10, 1965 I returned to the States for his funeral and I took vacation at the time so I could spend more time with my mother.

Although I had already taken my vacation at the time of my father's death, Bishop Reh, the Rector, insisted that I still take my vacation in the summer.

From July 14-23, 1965 I went to Sardinia. Msgr. Holleran was gracious enough to insist that I take his car to Sardinia, which I did.

After six years as Spiritual Director at the College, Msgr. Holleran left there on October 29, 1968 to return to the United States. He continued to serve at St. Patrick's Seminary at Menlo Park, California.

We met again when I attended a North American College Reunion.

(57)   Sr. Cynthia Howe

Sr. Cynthia Howe was a nurse at St. Mary's Hospital for many years. She was born October 29, 1930 so she was three years younger than I was.

I met Sr. Cynthia while I was Chaplain at Assisi Heights. We soon became friends and enjoyed numerous visits.

Sr. Cynthia was an avid reader and gave me a list of the hundreds of books she had read over the years.

One night, June 15, 1973 we walked out to the point at Assisi Heights. The moon was shining and it was just a beautiful evening. We realized then that we both loved each other very much.

We had dinner together at the Wilson home, on October 20, 1978. Cynthia had very long black hair, which she did up into a very beautiful bun on the top of her head.

Later when Cynthia was transferred to Assisi Heights and no longer was doing the nursing work at the Mayo, she found it very difficult to adjust. She had arranged for me, at one time, to observe an open-heart surgery which was very impressive and interesting.

Sr. Cynthia Howe

(58)   James and Katherine (Anderson) Hust

I met Katherine Anderson at a play given at the Community Center in Spring Valley on July 7, 2012. The play was "Fade to Black" about Jodi Huisendroit. We had a long talk together and exchanged email addresses. Catherine was not a Catholic at the time.

At college she met James Hust who is from a strong Catholic family. They became friends and often discussed religion.

James and Catherine were married at St. Felix Catholic Church, Wabasha. I had become friends with both of them.

Their son, Felix Joseph, was born on April 22, 2016.

Catherine's grandmother is Kay Wold.

(59)   Rose Ann Hamm

Rose Ann Hamm came from Wisconsin and applied for the job as Pastoral Worker at St. Columban Church shortly after my arrival as Pastor in 1988. She spent a weekend with me.

I found her to be very a talented and interesting person, but the Parish Council decided to choose a married couple that had applied for the job rather than Rose Ann.

Although Rose Ann moved to Texas shortly thereafter, we kept in touch.

She married Joe Voborsky shortly after that, and they lived in Wisconsin. Joe and Rose Ann visited me on January 22, 1989.

Rose Ann came to the Mayo Clinic in August 1990, where they discovered she had cancer in her lymph glands. She underwent surgery September 4, 1990.

Joe and Rose Ann or Rose Ann alone came for numerous visits to the Mayo Clinic and stayed with me throughout 1990-1993. They also went to New York and other places seeking help.

I became aware that the marriage relationship was not going well. On April 29, 1993 Joe called me to let me know that Rose Ann had initiated divorce proceedings.

On August 1, 1993 I visited Rose Ann at Mauston, Wisconsin. On October 10, 1993 Rose Ann came to visit me and went to the Mayo Clinic the next day. April 7-10, 1994 she stayed with me again.

Rose Ann Hamm and Alan Johnson visited me on October 6, 1994. On December 27-29, 1994 Rosanne again visited me and went to the Mayo Clinic.

I visited Rose Ann on September 27, 1995.

Rose Ann and Clifford Albright visited me on February 7, 1996. Rose Ann and Clare Tracy came to see me on May 7, 1996.

I visited Rose Ann at Hospice House, Tomah, Wisconsin on September 4, 1998. She was very angry as she was facing death.

I again visited Rose Ann on September 5, 1998 and she was now very resigned and peaceful.

Rose Ann died on September 12, 1998 at 10:30pm. I attended the funeral on September 16, 1998 at Our Lady of the Lake, rural Mauston, Wisconsin.

(60)   Michael and Elizabeth Keane

Elizabeth Keane was a sister to my dear friend, Sr. Breda Lyng.

When Sr. Breda was dying, I went to Ireland and stayed at the home of Michael and Elizabeth Keane. They were very gracious to be.

I offered Mass for the entire Lyng family with Sr. Breda shortly before her death at Milford Hospice, and celebrated the Sacrament of Extreme Unction January 30, 2000.

Michael and Elizabeth had two children, Eoin and Heather. Michael was very gracious in taking me to a number of sites in the area. He called me February 1, 2000, and reported that Sr. Breda was now quite confused. She died on February 13, 2000.

(61)   Francis Kelly

Francis Kelly was a student and a counselee of mine at the North American College. After his ordination he kept in contact with me. His address at the time was 1419 Skunk St., Philadelphia, PA 19145. His phone number was (215) 426-2600.

Francis indicated that he greatly appreciated the help I had given him as his Spiritual Director. At Christmas each year he was very generous in sending me a gift of money.

In recent years I have no longer heard from him. I wonder if he has died.

(62)   Sister Mary Elizabeth Keyser

Sister Mary Elizabeth Keyser came and presented a talk on behalf of the Maryknoll Sisters at St. John's Parish in Winona when I was Assistant Pastor there. We kept in contact. She went on Mission to South America.

Upon her return to the United States we continued correspondence. My last address for her is: Sr. Mary Elizabeth Keyser, Maryknoll sisters, PO Box 311, Maryknoll, NY 10545-0311. Her telephone number is: (914) 941-1575.

I sent a considerable amount of money to the Maryknoll Sisters through her. At present her eyesight is very bad and she can hardly write.

(63)   Fr. Tony Kilroy

Father Tony Kilroy was my Retreat Director for a number of years.

I came to feel he was a real friend. He is a Dominican Priest.

My last address for him is: Fr. Tony Kilroy, O.P., 2833 32nd Ave. South, Minneapolis, MN, 55406-1619. His telephone number is (612) 724-3644.

He has suffered from a leg injury.

(64)   Carol King

Carol King, born December 25, 1935 was The Courier Secretary when I was appointed as Assistant Editor in 1953. She had just graduated from high school and I saw her as very attractive. We were both learning Journalism together under Msgr. Dan Tierney, the Editor.

In my immaturity at the time, I was jealous that she showed so much more attention to Msgr. Tierney than to me. This built up to develop a very serious situation in the office. It would perhaps had been better if Msgr. Tierney had brought the situation out into the open and discussed it. The immaturity and jealousy just continued to grow and develop to the point where I was often doing very little work, and silence reigned. Toward the end these were some of the worst years of my life.

After nine years as Assistant Editor, the Peter Principle came to play when I was asked to be the Spiritual Director at the North American College in Rome.

Prior to this appointment my distance with Carol King increased when Carol Cada was also employed by The Courier, and she became somewhat like my Secretary. I showed favoritism to Carol Cada oftentimes to spite Carol King. I even helped Carol Cada to learn how to drive my car, and she drove with Carol King as a passenger.

On my return trips to the United States from Rome, I usually got to see Carol King who continued on at The Courier, but eventually became Secretary at the Cathedral in Winona. On one of these trips home Msgr. Tierney invited me and Carol King out to dinner.

After I returned to the United States in 1971, I tried to keep in contact with Carol King and even sent her money.

The relationship ended when I wrote a letter to Carol for Christmas and included a check for $100. She effectively let me know that she was not interested in any friendship with me. Without a written word she enclosed my letter to her and the check in an envelope. She did not even write my address on the envelope, but simply cut out my return address from my letter and pasted it on the envelope which she sent to me with my letter and check enclosed. Thus without words she spoke a very powerful message, and any further relationship was ended.

I have seen her at a distance on several occasions, but we have never had words together. I continue to pray for her and wish her well.

She has never married.

(65)   The Obritsch Family

I am extremely grateful that the Obritsch family came into my life. Wesley and Julie Obritsch have two lovely daughters, Sarah and Olivia.

I first met Sarah when I was offering Mass at Chatfield and Sarah was the sacristan who helped me by setting up the altar, etc. I was very impressed with her friendliness and I engaged her in conversation.

I again had a significant contact with the family when Sarah and Olivia were both in the play "Leaving Iowa" in February 2013. I attended the play and met both Sarah and Olivia afterwards.

Then I attended the play "Fiddler on the Roof" in 2014 and Julie and both her daughters were also in that play. The performance was really outstanding.

In the summer of 2013 Julie and Sarah came to my home and helped me make cannelloni.

Wes and Julie and Olivia came on another occasion and spent the whole day helping me make 10 pans of cannelloni.

I continue to cherish the friendship of the whole family. Sarah and Olivia are both in college at the present time.

(66)   Arlette Kvam

I was celebrating Mass at Spring Valley with Arlette Kvam as Lector. At the end of Mass I complemented her on how well she read. Then facetiously I asked if she would be willing to be the Lector at my funeral. She said she would need a lot more practice.

We sat together at a dinner that was served after the Mass and had a discussion that went on for hours.

Arlette suffers from an illness where she will go through months of severe depression, and then she will have months where she is very high.

When she is feeling well she works as an Interior Decorator.

Rick and Arlette Kvam were married May 21, 1983. They have three children who were the following ages when I met Arlette: Jacques (22), Vanessa (20), and Chelsea (18).

When Chelsea was graduating from high school on May 26, 2007 I was invited to the graduation and the luncheon afterwards. At the time Arlette was undergoing depression, thus remained inside and did not come out to the meeting of the guests. When she heard that I was there she came outdoors where refreshments were being served, and joined me for the luncheon.

On another occasion Arlette and I were having a long visit at a drive-in. I mentioned that I was thinking about writing up my autobiography and told her about the retreat I had made at Glouchester, Massachusetts when I wrote 800 pages about my life.

Arlette found my life so interesting that she insisted I get a notebook and begin writing the story of my life. Her strong urging prompted me to do so, thus she is in some way responsible for this writing of my autobiography.

On February 14, 2007 Ricardo and Arlette Kvam and their daughter Chelsea had dinner at my home.

Chelsea was involved in a very serious serious auto accident on May 21, 2008 and was quite severely injured.

My friendship with Arlette has continued and she came to visit me in Preston where we had a long visit. She is a very interesting person.

(67)   Sr. Anna Maria Lionetti

I met Sr. Anna Maria Lionetti who is a Religious of the Sacred Heart of Mary while I was Spiritual Director of the North American College in Rome. She was with Sr. Brendan and the other Religious of her Community who I knew.

Sr. Anna Maria was one of the Sisters who made the retreat I gave at Marymount. I remember that I played tennis with her and a number of the Sisters when it became evident to me that they needed to relax and relieve the tension they were undergoing.

We became friends and the friendship continued by correspondence when she returned to the Bronx in New York.

Later she moved and worked in Mexico. My last address for her was: Sr. Anna Maria Lionetti, Communidad Corazon de Maria, APDO #5, Calle Franci Amacuzac, Morelos 62640, Mexico.

(68)   Peggy Lovrien

Peggy Lovrien was the Liturgist at the Diocese of Winona Pastoral Center. She was from Adrian, Minnesota. She was born April 22, 1952.

I came to know her and had a high regard for her. We invited her to come to Preston and advise us when we renovated St. Colomban Church.

A Priest friend of hers came and spent some days with me at Preston.

When a number of changes were made at the Pastoral Center, Peggy was let go, together with several others. She then was employed as Liturgist at the Archdiocese of Dubuque. Her address is: Peggy Lovrien, Archdiocese of Dubuque, 1229 Mt. Loretta Avenue, Dubuque, IA 52003.

We continue to have occasional contact by mail.

(69)   Novella Meisner

I came to know Novella Meisner through Arlette Kvam. I was asked to be in "Beauty and the Beast" at Spring Valley. Novella played the part of my favorite daughter in the play. She was an excellent actress.

Novella got a divorce from her husband and married Pete Stier.

I visited with Novella Meisner, Martha Sue della Brueve and Mary Engesser on November 7, 2004 and I saw her in the play "Victorian Christmas" at St. John's Church, Wykoff, Minnesota on December 5, 2004.

At the KC banquet on January 29, 2005 Novella provided the entertainment.

Preston celebrated its Sesquicentennial July 29-31, 2005. For the Ecumenical Service at 10 a.m. I had suggested that Novella sing "The Holy City" and that we would apply it to Preston rather than Jerusalem. It was a tremendous success. People were in tears. I have asked that she sing it at my funeral.

Fr. Francis Galles and Novella Meisner

(70)   Agnes Meium

Agnes Meium was Secretary-Bookkeeper at St. Columban Parish in Preston. She was married to Tom Meium and they had two children: Erika and Christopher.

They later moved to Wilmar, Minnesota.

(71)   Arneta Middendorf

Arneta Middendorf was from Adrian, Minnesota. She was a friend of my sister, Clara. I knew her back in the time when I was going with Delphine Voss.

Later Arneta lived in Owatonna and I continued to know her there. She also continued to be friends with Clara.

Later she moved to Hopkins, Minnesota.

(72)   Octavia Miles

Octavia was married to Kevin Miles and they later divorced. They had three children: Keaton, Samantha, and Benjamin. They lived in a rural area north of Mabel, Minnesota where they renovated an old house. At one time I gave them some money to help with the renovation.

The family seemed to be very religious. Keaton came and spent some time with me. They also corresponded with me.

After the divorce Octavia moved to Winona. Keaton moved with a friend to the Twin Cities. Benjamin and Samantha have both made independent moves. Kevin remarried a Catholic woman named Ann and they still reside at the renovated home in Mabel.

(73)   Sr. Placida Wrubel

I met Sr. Placida Wrubel shortly after I became Chaplain for the Franciscan Motherhouse at Assisi Heights in Rochester on September

23, 1971. Sr. Gretchen Berg assigned her to be the housekeeper at the Wilson home where I resided. Sr. Placida was, at that time, quite advanced in years but was whole heartedly dedicated to her work of caring for my living quarters.

I thought of her as being very humble, prayerful and holy. I think she also loved me greatly.

On one occasion Sr. Placida accidentally tipped over a very precious flower vase which I had received as a gift from Monika Kufferath, and it broke. Sister Placida was extremely distressed.

Fr. Bill Anderson was living with me at the Wilson home at that time. Sr. Placida showed him the broken vase and he, no doubt, saw how distressed she was. Being very handy at such things he simply glued the vase together so that you would never know it had been broken.

Still greatly upset, Sr. Placida explained to me what had happened. I think the vase is even more precious to me now because of Sr. Placida's concern about it.

Sr. Placida's love and care for me continued throughout the eight years I spent at Assisi Heights. Even after I left there, Sr. Placida continued to be very dear to me and I always looked forward to seeing her when I returned to Assisi Heights for a visit.

Sr. Placida died August 8, 2008. I feel that I still enjoy her love support from heaven.

(74)   Anne Phylis Muchiri

Anne Phylis Muchiri came to the United States from Africa. She was a student at Loras College in Dubuque. She visited me at Preston together with her mother, Mary Muchiri, and her daughter, Alisha Marie Kitutu on July 26-28, 2008.

Anne Phylis had two daughters: Alisha Marie Kitutu and Abigail.

Phylis later moved to Texas.

Anne Phylis Muchiri

(75)   Camellia Mukherjee

I came to know Camellia Mukherjee through a phone call she made when she was soliciting funds for Loras College. She later came to visit me. I helped her out financially.

We discussed the possibility of hiring her. She came to the United States from India. Her parents also came to visit me on one occasion.

Camellia later went to school out in the East and I lost contact with her.

Camellia Mukherjee

(76) Luna Nino

I came to know Luna Nina when she was living in Lanesboro. She later moved to Illinois and was with Expertz Rehab, Inc.

Luna visited me at Preston with a friend, Fred. She has a daughter, Gina.

(77) Carla Noack

Carla Noack was an actress at the Commonweal Theatre in Lanesboro. When I first knew her she was married to Dr. Michael Nemanich. She later divorced and married Chris Oden. That marriage also ended. She moved to Kansas City, Missouri, January 18, 1997. She returned to Lanesboro for a visit March 10, 1997.

I had dinner at Carla Noack's home on May 27, 1997.

(78) Fr. Robert Nogosek

Fr. Robert Nogosek was Rector of Holy Cross College in Rome, an Extension of Notre Dame University. I came to know him and persuaded him to make a Better World Retreat. He did and became very involved with the Better World Movement. He also got to know and became friends with Sr. Cuthbert (Later Monika Hellwig.)

Bob Nogosek and Monika Hellwig and I got together for a retreat. Father Nogosek suffered a nervous breakdown on May 30, 1966. On June 7, 1966 he returned to the United States.

Fr. Nogosek is now at Fatima House, Notre Dame, Indiana. His interest in Better World Retreats has continued.

(79) Gayle (Buse) O'Brian

Gayle Wagner from Iona, Minnesota married James Buse. They had six children: Mike, Patrick, Jim, Lisa, Tim and Danny. I had a very close relationship with Gayle. She was well educated.

I think James Buse wanted a farmer's wife, and though they lived on the farm Gayle was not a True Farmer's Wife. Consequently they divorced and later Gayle remarried and became Gayle O'Brian.

Gayle was born September 5, 1943 and died June 29, 2016 at the age of 73.

(80)   Jerome and Sharyol O'Conner

Jerome and Sharyol O'Connor were good neighbors and members of St. Columban Parish. They had six children.

Both Jerome and Sharyol were very helpful to me when I was Pastor at St. Columban Parish, and also after I retired. Both are good singers and both sing in the choir. They were especially helpful when I moved from my house to Traditions, which is Assisted Living.

On a number of occasions, Jerome and Sharyol have driven me to the Mayo Clinic. They have been true friends.

(81)   Mary Lou Ogle

Mary Lou Ogle is a sister to Fr. Bob Ogle who was very important in my life.

After I received news that Fr. Ogle had died, I sent a letter to Mary Lou at Fr. Bob's address and asked details about his last days and his death.

Mary Lou was very gracious and gave me a lot of information, and in ongoing correspondence she sent me many precious mementos of Fr. Bob. She sent me the book that was his Ph.D. dissertation: "The Faculties of Canadian Military Chaplains."

Mary Lou also sent the beautifully bound book "A Man of Letters" which was a compilation of all the letters Fr. Bob had sent to hundreds of family and friends discussing all that he experienced during the year he spent on sabbatical to India.

Another book Mary Lou sent me was a compilation of all the letters he wrote to his father during his years in Brazil. Sr. Teresa Sullivan of Gary, Indiana arranged these letters into chapters according to theme. (See the Bob Ogle entry for details.)

She also gave me a half-dozen DVD's that were the television programs Fr. Bob presented even after he was afflicted with cancer. He was like the Bishop Sheen of Canada.

One most special Momento was the beautiful notebook Mary Lou had given to her brother at Easter 1999, however he never did write in it. I also received a keychain of Fr. Bob, a vestment, newspaper clippings about Fr. Bob and a picture of herself.

Mary Lou came from Canada to visit me in 2001, and spent four days with me. We went to a play at Lanesboro and visited all the local sites.

(82)   Dan and Linda Ortmann

The Ortmann family, which was very large, were great supporters and friends of mine all the years I was Pastor at St. Francis Xavier Parish at Windom. Especially Dan and his wife Linda have continued to stay in contact with me even to the present day.

They were employed at the local grocery store. For a while they moved to Iowa, but returned to Windom.

Dan and Linda have two children: Rich and Kim.

Linda's birthday is March 25, 1949.

(83)   Colleen Ortmann

Colleen Ortmann was the Parish Organist and a good supporter of mine during the time I was Pastor at St. Francis Xavier Parish, Windom. She and her husband had seven children.

Her husband, Dick, died some years ago.

(84) Angelo and Julie Otero

Angelo was a Mayo Clinic Physician, and one of the first doctors to do knee replacements. He and his wife, Julie, were from Puerto Rico and intended to return there when Angelo completed all his education.

Angelo came to me one time and asked if I would direct him in a retreat. He made a retreat with me at Assisi Heights, and we became friends. This was May 4-6, 1973.

One time when I was visiting Angelo at his home his wife, Julie, overheard me speaking about death and the afterlife. This was July 5, 1973. She said she thought she should see me because she had concerns and fear about death. Julie came to visit me on July 11, 1973 and again on July 13, 1973 and also August 15, 1973. Thus I became friends with both of them.

Julie was at one time a ballet dancer. Julie promoted a ballet at Mayo High School, September 28-29, 1973.

Angelo and Julie had two children: Christina and Marta.

Later the family moved to Fort Worth, Texas. Clara and I visited with them in Texas at a later date. They had a very elaborate home with a swimming pool.

We have continued to be friends by mail and phone. Julie's parents also came to visit me at one time.

(85) Beverly Peterson

I became friends with Beverly Peterson in a strange way. One winter day I was driving back to the Rectory at St. Francis Xavier Church at Windom when I was Pastor there. The streets were somewhat icy. I was going downhill and though I applied the brakes a number of times I was sliding and could not stop when I came to a cross street. Beverly Peterson was driving on this cross street, and because I could not stop I ran into the passenger side of her car.

We both got out of our cars and it was quite evident to me that Beverly was very upset. I reached out to her but she did not respond. Her car was not a new car, but it was new for her and her husband, Wayne.

Beverly asked if we could go to her home which was on 17th Street, so that her husband could work out the insurance details.

Sometime later I saw Beverly in the local store and I went up to her and apologized for the inconvenience I had caused. She said it was okay. They got a good sum of money from my insurance.

Later Beverly came to the Rectory and was collecting money for some charitable cause. On that occasion we sat down and visited for a good long time. We talked about cooking and baking. She had just made some baklava. When she left she sent a piece of baklava to the Rectory so I could sample it. This, I thought, was very gracious. We had become friends in spite of our accident.

Shortly before I left Windom, Beverly came to the Rectory with another gift of food to say goodbye. We again had a very good visit.

I mentioned to Beverly that I was having a number of parishioners coming in to help me pack to get ready to move. Beverly, although she was not a Catholic, said she would be happy to come to help me pack.

Beverly came the next night to help me move, together with a rather large group of Catholics who arrived.

When each new Catholic came in I had to explain why Beverly Peterson, who was a Lutheran, was there, and how we had become friends through an automobile accident.

Each time I told the story Beverly would come and give me a hug. Because she was a very attractive woman, I told the story as often as I could.

We have continued to be friends by mail and email, and every time I am back in Windom I stop to see Beverly and Wayne. They have two children: Ingrid and Erik.

Beverly and Wayne travel quite a bit, and usually send me a postcard.

(86) Stephanie (Rea) and Nigel Pollard

I met Stephanie Rea and Maureen Burke, who were from England, while having a meeting at Rocca di Papa with Brother Saunders in regard to a Better World Retreat.

Stephanie and Maureen had left England with a Volkswagen and went to Germany where they thought they had a job teaching at a military base. The job had fallen through. Rather than facing the embarrassment of returning to England they decided to do some traveling. This is what brought them to Rome and to Rocca di Papa. We had lunch together. They were looking for a job to earn some money. I told them I might be able to help them out. They followed me into Rome.

Sr. Breda was able to get a job for Maureen, and Stephanie got a job taking care of a child of a prostitute.

Maureen and Stephanie stayed in Rome for more than a year. I then got to see them many times and showed them around the city. We became real friends.

Stephanie introduced me to Chancery Script beginning April 13, 1969 which thereafter had a considerable effect on my writing. Stephanie and Maureen left Rome November 14, 1969 but again Maureen came to visit me in Rome October 23-27, 1970.

After I returned to the United States in 1971, and I was taking a Better World Course at East Aurora, New York, Stephanie and Maureen stopped by for a visit. They were on their way to see Stephanie's sister who lived in Canada. They then planned to go to Minnesota and other places. They stopped at Iona and spent some time visiting my family. They wanted me to go along with them, but I felt I had to stay with the workshop I was attending.

Maureen later married and moved to Australia. Her husband died.

She came to visit me later and spent some time with me. She was frightened because of the weather when I drove her to the airport.

I was able to visit Stephanie at Bath, England at another time and she gave me, and Sr. Breda who was with me, a wonderful tour of the area. Stephanie later married Nigel Pollard.

The friendship has continued by mail and email, and Stephanie and Nigel came to visit me at Preston on May 12 and 13, 2017. We went to Spillville, IA, to see the Bily Clocks and Antonin Dvorak Museums.

(87)   Sr. Amata Schleich

Sr. Amata Schleich was my First and Second Grade teacher at St. Columba School in Iona. I liked her very much. You might say I had a real crush on her. I think she also liked me very much.

Sr. Amata made me the director of a percussion band which she organized. My dad made a baton that I was able to use in directing the band.

Sr. Amata was born Laverne Gertrude Schleich on August 29, 1910 in Spring Valley, Minnesota. She entered the Franciscan Congregation in 1930 from St. Ignatius Parish. Thus she was a Religious Sister only three years when she taught me in First Grade in 1933, and was only 23 years old.

She made her Profession of Vows in 1932 and began her teaching ministry at St. Mary Academy in Owatonna, Minnesota.

Besides Iona, Sr. Amata taught at various schools in Minnesota including Lake City, Currie, Winona, Wilmont, Austen, Albert Lee, St. James and Glencoe. She taught in Rochester at St. John's Parish from 1949-53 and at St. Francis Parish from 1977-1983. She also taught in Trenton and Portsmouth, Ohio, Watertown, South Dakota and Chicago, Illinois.

Sr. Amata retired to Assisi Heights in 1983 and celebrated her Diamond Jubilee in 1992.

Sr. Amata died May 28, 2000 at Assisi Heights. A Mass of Christian Burial was held on Wednesday, May 31, 2000 in the Chapel of our Lady of Lourdes, Assisi Heights. I was privileged to celebrate her Funeral Mass. She was buried in Calvary Cemetery, Rochester.

I continue to have fond memories of Sr. Amata.

(88)   Sr. Helen Rolfson

Sr. Helen Rolfson is a Franciscan Sister who came to Rome to further her research in regard to baptistries. I was able to introduce her to Rome. She arrived in Rome on January 14, 1970 and we went together to Subiaco and Tivoli on January 7, 1971, and she also accompanied me on trips to Assisi and Florence and Siena, December 19, 1968–January 1, 1969.

Our friendship continued when we both returned to the United States.

Sister Helen accompanied me to Glouchester, Massachusetts when I returned there for my second time in 1978.

(89)   Donna Schmidt

I do not remember how I first became acquainted with Donna Schmidt. Her daughters came to visit me at St. Columban, Preston.

When Donna's husband, Paul, died, at the funeral dinner there was a bag of popcorn at each place. Paul loved popcorn.

One of Donna's daughters, who was a very beautiful person, committed suicide. Donna was extraordinarily brave.

Donna and her husband and the whole family operated a wonderful bakery in St. James, Minnesota. It was known for miles around.

(90)   Msgr. Don Schmitz

Don Schmitz was a counselee of mine when I was Spiritual Director at Immaculate Heart of Mary Seminary in Winona, and again when I was Spiritual Director at the North American College in Rome. He was from a very good family in Caledonia and Sr. Shirley, a Franciscan, was his sister.

Don Schmitz was ordained a Priest at St. Peter's in Rome on December 16, 1964. I was his Assistant Priest at his First Mass at Clementine Altar in St. Peter's on December 17, 1964.

An Associate at Pax Christi in Rochester, he retired after 50 years.

He served at St. Mary's Parish, Winona, and Cotter High School, St. Francis of Assisi in Rochester, was Chaplain at Notre Dame Motherhouse, Mankato and taught at Good Counsel Academy in Mankato, was an Assistant at St. Mary's in Worthington, studied Canon Law at Catholic University, Washington D.C., was Chancellor of the Diocese of Winona for 15 years. He also was Spiritual Director at Immaculate Heart of Mary Seminary for four years and Pastor at Altura and Elba with four years at the Cathedral in Winona, also served in Harmony, Canton, Mabel, and Resurrection Church in Rochester.

I came to know Fr. Don again and appreciate him when he was Pastor at Harmony, Canton, and Mabel. We worked together very harmoniously and he was an inspiration and a great support to me.

(91)   Eddie and Jo Ann Schneider

Eddie and Jo Ann Schneider were good neighbors of mine when I was Pastor at St. Francis Xavier Church, Windom. They were very dear friends and supporters of mine when I was their Pastor .

They later moved to Fort Collins, Colorado, but we have continued to stay in contact.

(92)   Klaus and Karin Schneider

I met Klaus Schneider in St. Peter's Basilica in Rome when the Pope was celebrating the Mass. I had a good ticket for the event, but the Basilica was packed with people. When I arrived at the Tribune to which my ticket assigned me, Klaus saw that I was looking for a place to sit, and so he moved over and motioned me to come down and sit beside him.

We had a good discussion before the Mass began. He lived in Munich, Germany, but spoke English quite well.

At the end of Mass we exchanged addresses and email addresses. I invited Klaus to come and visit me at the North American College.

The next day I received a telephone call from Klaus and he asked if women could also visit the College. I assured him that they could, and he then told me there would be six people coming to visit me and see the College.

Klaus and his wife, Karin, came to the college. We visited for some time and then I gave them a tour of the college. Klaus usually had to translate because the others did not all speak English very well.

Sometime later Klaus called and asked if he and his wife could come and visit me in Rome. They came May 29-June 5, 1971, and I showed them around the city.

They invited me to visit them and I did visit while in Munich, September 24-26, 1982. Klaus was a very gracious guide.

I told Klaus that I would like to visit Auschwitz, the Concentration Camp. Though it must've been very hard for him to be there and show me what the Germans had done, especially to the Jews during the time of Hitler, we did go and see the Concentration Camp.

Although it was terrible to see, it was good that the Camp had been preserved so that many people can witness the inhumanity which individuals can show against one another.

After that very interesting visit with Klaus and Karin they have stayed in contact with me. Klaus calls several times a year.

When I was visiting Monica Kufferath in Switzerland, Klaus and Karin came to visit me. They had a car and gave me a good tour of Lenzburg, Switzerland, and the environs.

My friendship with Klaus and Karin is another instance as to how mysteriously God works in our lives.

The Schneiders have two daughters: Claudia and Irene.

(93)   Sr. Trudy Schomer

Sr. Trudy Schomer, who was born March 18, 1937 began work at St. Columban as Secretary-Bookkeeper on August 1, 1996.

She is a sister to Pat Capek and is a member of the Franciscan Sisters whose Motherhouse is at St. Cloud, Minnesota. She is presently back at the Motherhouse.

(94)   Sr. Seton Slater

Sr. Seton Slater from Wilmont, Minnesota, belongs to the Rochester Franciscan Community.

We have been close friends ever since I became Chaplain at the Franciscan Motherhouse. She worked with the elderly Sisters at their Motherhouse.

(95)   Mary Sotebeer

Mary Sotebeer was in high school when I was Chaplain at St. Francis Xavier Parish, Windom.

Once when she saw a picture of me she said "Oh I could draw his picture!" She did a large pencil drawing of me which is very good and I treasure it very much.

(96)   Ellen Speltz

Ellen Speltz is the daughter of John and MaryAnn Fuchsel of Winona.

Ellen was a Secretary at Immaculate Heart of Mary Seminary for a number of years.

One time when the priests of the Winona Area were meeting at the Seminary I arrived early and Ellen was there, and we got into a very good discussion and found we had a number of things in common. Her birthday is March 8, 1965. My birthday is also March 8, but 1927. She is married to a Speltz who is a Luxemburger.

I have enjoyed maintaining a low level contact with her ever since I met her. She lives at St. Charles, Minnesota.

(97)   Katherina Sveen

Katherina Sveen was in high school and a nearby neighbor when I was Pastor at St. Columban. Her parents were Catholic, but they joined an Evangelical church, and Catherine seems to be very taken up with her religion. She visited me quite frequently and I considered her a very good friend.

On one occasion when she visited me, she shared many of her pictures which I now have on my computer.

For a time she considered working on my autobiography and for a considerable time had the 800 pages I wrote when I made a retreat in Glouchester, Massachusetts in 1977.

We have lost contact with each other in recent years. She is presently living in St. Cloud.

Katherina Sveen

(98)   Arleen Tacke

Arlene Tacke was Housekeeper at the Our Lady of the Lake Church Rectory at Lake Oswego, Oregon when I spent a sabbatical there. Her husband was Andrew Tacke, but he was deceased. They had four children: Andrea, Teresa, Katie and John.

Arlene was very friendly and assisted me in many ways. She helped me make a big batch of cannelloni when we served a large number of people before my departure at the end of the sabbatical.

Arlene has continued to keep in touch with me ever since. She is presently living in Ontario, Oregon.

(99)   Monica Taylor

Monica Taylor was the Religious Education Coordinator at St. Patrick's Parish, Lanesboro, when I was Pastor there. Her husband is Lewis Taylor. Lewis and Monica married November 30, 1974. They have four children: Brenda, Marvin, Craig and Wendy.

Monica was an excellent Religious Education Coordinator and helped me out in many ways. I really considered her and her husband friends. Craig has stopped in to see me a number of times.

Monica and Lewis are now living in Rochester.

(100) Pamela Thompson

I am not sure how I came to know Pamela Thompson and her then husband, Daryl. He later became involved with another woman and Pamela and Daryl divorced. They lived in Rushford when I first knew them, and ran the P. J. Thompson Insurance Agency.

Pamela is very gifted musically. She played the big bass fiddle in the band to which she belonged. She later moved to Winona and in recent years taught herself to also play the guitar. She sings beautifully with her guitar and gives a number of concerts. She has given a couple of concerts at Traditions where I now live.

For a while Pamela worked at the Chancery in Winona, Minnesota. During that time once, when I was at St. Mary's Hospital in Rochester, she came to visit me. Her visit was the most significant of any of the visitors I had. She sang "Where the Bluebells Grow." It was very beautiful. Recently she came to see me again and sang for me. She now lives in Winona.

(101) Emily Torgrimson

I am not sure just how I became friends with Emily Torgrimson.

She is the founder of "Eat for Equity" which may explain how I came to know her.

I have enjoyed several of Emily's dinners when she served a large crowd. She emphasizes good nutritional food.

I have one of her aprons.

(102) Lawayn Trom

It was through a rather strange and chance meeting that I came to know and eventually share friendship with Lawayn Trom. We originally met at a Diocesan event, and when she discovered that I lived in Preston where she had been ministering at the jail, she asked me if I could also visit some of the inmates and bring Communion to the Catholic ones when she was not there. Thus we soon became longstanding friends.

Lawayn was a Lay Minister from Blooming Prairie who had been volunteering weekly at Fillmore County Jail for 15 years after one of her husband's co-workers was incarcerated there. She provided Christmas Eve, Easter Services and Weekly Bible Studies to jailmates for ten of those years. She especially considers her ten Christmas Eves "spent in jail" as some of the most memorable of her life.

I recall from our ministry that we were both visiting Joe Folkert on February 19, 2003.

Lawayn was born July 18, 1952 and thus she was 51 years old when I met her. A number of meetings with the family followed our first meeting and they have also visited me and stayed at my Preston Hermitage.

Lawayn has a B.A. in Sociology, a Minor in Librarianship, a Health Info Management 5th Year Certification, and a Masters of Ministry Degree in Spirituality, all of which have contributed to her goal of a well-rounded life. She has worked as a Retreat Presenter and Spiritual Director. She also works in Home Care and has training in Homeopathy and Natural Healing. By sharing all of this knowledge, she encourages individuals to live Wholistic and Integrative Lifestyles, and helps them to be knowledgeable of their own immune systems and natural health while living lives of Stillness and Spiritual Awareness.

Her husband was Douglas Trom. They had six children: Briana, Lawayn's daughter from a previous marriage, Ray and Jerry, two Korean adopted sons, and three home-schooled children: Marianne, Benjamin and Marie-Rose. For 33 years they lived on a farm at rural Blooming Prairie, Minnesota.

Recently Lawayn and Doug divorced. Her divorce from Douglas was a sad chapter in her life. Doug still resides at the farm while Lawayn lives in her Writer's Loft apartment in Owatonna, Minnesota.

Lawayn has long been fascinated and very interested in the story of my life. After she read some of the material I had written in preparation for my autobiography, Lawayn said that she would like to help me with its compilation. I gave her much of the material I had already written or collected. Thus she has taken all of my retreat notes and other materials and undertaken the task of writing up and editing my Life Story. As time went on she realized the task of doing my autobiography was bigger than she anticipated, however she has continued with the project.

I am deeply indebted to her for her friendship and the work she has done in writing my autobiography. She has told me that she feels honored to be a part of this writing experience.

Lawayn Trom

(103)   Marge (Kuisle) and Bill Urlich

I first met Marge Kuisle shortly after I arrived at Assisi Heights in Rochester as Chaplain in 1971. I know I had a meeting with her on December 7, 1971 at 4 p.m. I had visits with her again on January

18, 1972 at 5 p.m. and on January 24, 1973. She was very beautiful with bright red hair. A friendship developed.

At one point we discussed the possibility of her becoming my Secretary as I was making use of the Better World Movement in my assignment as Director of Spiritual Renewal in the Diocese of Winona.

On September 4, 1973 I had dinner at the Kuisle home.

Marge became acquainted with William Urlich and they married on June 8, 1974. Marge and Bill Urlich later moved to Pipestone, Minnesota. Our friendship continued and we were able to see each other on occasions, for example December 11, 1982.

Marge Kuisle was born December 8, 1950.

The Urlichs have two children: Maria and Larry.

(104)   Prathiba Varkey

Prathiba Varkey from India worked at the Mayo Clinic. At one time she was invited to be a speaker at Lanesboro. At the end of her presentation I spoke with her and she said she had never been to Lanesboro or the area and that she would like to get to know more about it. I offered to help her out in that regard. We exchanged email addresses and corresponded with each other and thus became friends.

She very much wanted to find a good man whom she might marry. At one time she was preparing for marriage when she discovered the man had deceived her and the relationship was broken off.

Shortly before Prathiba moved to Texas, her parents from India came to visit me.

We have continued a limited friendship through correspondence.

(105) Sr. Cabrini Walch

Sr. Cabrini Walch was one of the Franciscan Sisters at Assisi Heights who was very much attached to me. I thought of her as a most special person, and she was always very good to me.

Sr. Cabrini has since died and gone to heaven.

(106) Charlie and Karla Warner

I met Karla Warner when she worked at the restaurant in Canton, Minnesota. She was always very kind and helpful.

I officiated at the funeral of Karla's Father, Everett Fay, in September 1984. Karla and her husband, Charlie, and their daughter, Meagan, came to my home for a cannelloni dinner. Charlie works with a number of newspapers and Karla continues to work at the Canton Pub.

(107) Fr. Theodore Weber

Fr. Theodore Weber, born October 31, 1929 was Pastor at Our Lady of the Lake Church at Lake Oswego, Oregon when I spent a sabbatical there September 30, 1988–December 15, 1988.

He heard that I was having some difficulty in living with George Bell, and he offered that he would be glad to have me come and live at the Rectory. I accepted his offer and I enjoyed immensely my time in the parish and made quite a number of good friends.

Fr. Weber was always very good to me and gave me many opportunities to minister to people in the parish. I was able to make good use of my experience with the Better World Movement, Marriage Encounter and Teams of Our Lady.

I have continued to have a bit of contact with Fr. Weber even after returning to the Diocese of Winona.

I also became good friends with Deacon Jim Galluzzo who was living in the parish as an Associate.

I took courses at Marylhurst College while there.

(108)   Mary Whalen

I became acquainted with Mary Whalen, who had been married to Timothy Engesser, while offering Masses at Spring Valley. They had eight home-schooled children: Matthew, Monica, Andrew, Peter, James, John Michael, Thomas and Philip.

Both Mary and Timothy were very active in the parish. They later divorced and Timothy remarried.

(109)   Sr. Hildegundis Lang

Sr. Hildegundis was one of the three Dominican Sisters from Switzerland who worked in the kitchen at Immaculate Heart of Mary Seminary in Winona when I was Spiritual Director there for three years, 1959-1962. She was the youngest of the three and she was always very good to me.

I came to like her very much. I frequently offered Mss at the convent where they lived. I was later able to visit Ilanz, Switzerland, the place from where these Sisters came.

The other faculty members also appreciated the many years she had worked at the seminary and the very devoted service she gave.

Wanting to reward her for all she had done at the seminary the faculty decided they would pay her way to Rome so that she could go there and I would be able to show her around before I left Rome.

Sr. Hildegundis came to Rome May 9, 1971. I arranged a pensione where she could stay near the North American College. On May 13, 1971, I spent the whole day giving a tour of Rome to Sr. Hildegundis and her aunt, Monika. Among the places we visited was the Catacomb of St. Callistus. It was there I first met Monika Kufferath with whom I became a very close friend.

Sr. Hildegundis was in Rome from May 9 to May 16 and either I or Jim Buryska and Mike McDermott (Winona students at the North American College) gave her a great tour of Rome and the environs.

Sr. Hildegundis and the other Dominican Sisters later left the seminary in Winona and returned to Switzerland.

Sr. Hildegundis was always very special to me when I was Spiritual Director at Immaculate Heart of Mary for three years 1969-1971.

I have lost contact with Sr. Hildegundis since that time.

(110)   Ursala (Kufferath) and Klaus Wodsak

Ursula (Kufferath) is a sister to Monika Kufferath. Ursula came to visit Monika at the time I was also visiting her in Switzerland. Ursula's husband, Klaus Wodsak was also with us.

I had a very good discussion with Ursula.

Ursula also wrote to me when her sister, Monika, was seriously ill, and when she died.

(111)   Jean Anderson

Jean Anderson and her husband, Randy, were parishioners at St. Francis Xavier Parish when I was Pastor there. They had six children: Kari, Mindy, Nicole, Jay, Whitney, Briana.

Randy died at a very early age leaving Jean with the responsibility for the children. I felt a special need to help and support Jean. I always felt very close to her.

Jean Anderson and her daughters Kari, Mindy and Nicole came for supper on August 25, 1981. On September 14, 1981, we went for a hike in Kilen Woods State Park. I saw Jean again on September 22, 1981, and October 5, 1981. On November 22, 1981, I had dinner at Jean Anderson's home.

Jean later married Tom DeWall. They moved to Elk River, Minnesota, and then Zimmerman, Minnesota.

(112) Ludwig Behan

I met Ludwig Behan on July 22, 1950 on the train going to Munich. Trains were very crowded in Third Class and so I was standing in the aisle. Ludwig Behan was a young handsome man who got off the train at one of the stops and picked up an ice cream cone. When he got back on the train a small girl was sitting on her luggage with her mother in the aisle. She looked up at Ludwig with his ice cream cone, and he was moved with pity and gave it to her. I was impressed and engaged him in conversation.

When we arrived at Munich and the train stopped, I asked Ludwig if this was the place we should get off the train to take another train to Oberammergau where we were headed. He said it was, and he would show us. There were three of us students traveling together.

We had some time between trains and so we wanted to check our luggage. There was a long line waiting to check baggage. Rather than wait in the line Ludwig said he would like to take us to dinner.

When we were seated Ludwig went to make a phone call. When we told him we were going on to Oberammergau to see the Passion Play, but afterwards we would be returning to see Munich, he asked us to let him know of our Munich arrival, and he would meet us at the train station to give us a tour of Munich.

Francis Galles in Oberammergau in 1950

While he was gone to make the phone call, Bob Behan and Harry Butori and I discussed whether we could trust him and if we should let him know when we would be coming back to Munich. Harry Butori was quite sceptical as to whether we should tell him, but Bob Behan and I felt since there were three of us we had nothing to worry about. We told Ludwig the time of our return to Munich. We then went on to Oberammergau to see the Passion Play.

When we returned to Munich on July 25, Ludwig Behan was at the train station to meet us. He had taken off the afternoon from work and had come to Munich from Freising where he lived and worked, specifically to meet us.

Ludwig then took us to his mother's place. She lived in a Fourth Floor apartment and told us we could stay with her as long as we wanted. She did not speak English and we did not speak German, but we got along very well, often using gestures.

After we were settled in, Ludwig took us for a tour of the city with his car. He was an excellent guide and especially loved Rococo Architecture.

He never liked sad things but only churches, etc., that were joyful. He had been a prisoner of war in Russia during World War II.

That evening Ludwig took us to one of the finest restaurants in Munich.

Before leaving to return to Freising that evening, he gave us tickets so that we could go to the Opera the next evening.

He left us at his mother's apartment. There was a bed for one of us and a couch for another. One of us slept on the floor.

The next morning we went to Mass and Ludwig's mother accompanied us. I think she was proud to show off three American Seminarians who were preparing for the Priesthood.

After Mass she served us a lovely breakfast. We stayed three days. When we would return from sightseeing during the day she would have a lovely dinner ready for us.

The second night when we went to the Opera we had some of the finest seats in the house.

It was hard to leave Ludwig's mother; she had been so gracious. I felt that Ludwig did all of this for us to show that the German people who had engaged us in war were not all bad people

I continued to correspond with Ludwig, and the next two Christmases after our visit he sent a box of German cookies to us in Rome, and even sent a box of cookies to my parents in the United States.

Years later when I returned to Munich with my friend Klaus Schneider, I tried to locate Ludwig Behan, but without success. How I wish I still had contact with him. What an extraordinary person!

(113)   George Bell

I met George Bell in January, 1945 when I began studies at Loras College, Dubuque, Iowa. George was from Kentucky. He had polio in his younger years and was left with a slight handicap.

George had an excellent ear for music and was probably above all his professors in this regard. Because of the effects of polio he was somewhat limited as a pianist; however he had a tremendous appreciation of music and I was envious of him because he could be moved to tears when he heard a beautiful piece of music.

Together with Jim Murphy who was also quite good as a pianist, we became close friends of George Bell.

When I received the Basselin Scholarship to study at the Catholic University in Washington, D.C. 1946-49, I needed a reading knowledge of French or German for the Masters Degree. I had not had either.

George Bell came to my home in the summer of 1948, and spent a month with me to teach me French.

During George's visit we hitchhiked to Owensboro, Kentucky to visit his home.

I kept in touch with George Bell. After he got his Masters Degree in Music at St. Benedict's College in Atchison, Kansas, he taught music and was the Course Director at St. Charles, Missouri, and later moved to Portland, Oregon, where he continued teaching music.

When my Pastorate ended July 31, 1988 and I was given a sabbatical, I decided that I wanted to study piano and take some Philosophy or Theology courses. George Bell offered to teach me piano.

I went out to Portland, Oregon where George lived and moved in with him, and he began teaching me piano.

It soon became evident that with George's somewhat neurotic condition I would not be able to continue living with him or taking piano lessons from him.

Fortunately Fr. Theodore Weber offered to have me come and live at Our Lady of the Lake Rectory and help out at the parish. I then began taking piano lessons at Marylhurst College at Lake Oswego, Oregon.

I saw George Bell again on December 5, 1988. This was the last time I saw him. I understand that his psychological condition continued to increase.

George developed a friendship with Robert Wagner, 2813 Orchard Dr., Billings, MT 59102, who wrote to me and informed me of George's death. George, who was born April 24, 1923 died October 29, 1996 of a brain hemorrhage at age 73.

(114)   Mrs. Fay Benson

I met Mrs. Fay Benson at Lourdes on July 3, 1966. Fr. Al Giaquinto had visited me in Rome. I then accompanied him to Lourdes. He went on to Paris for a Sulpician meeting. My plane flight back to Rome was delayed for a considerable period of time. I was not feeling well and was not too eager to speak with anyone. However, at one point Mrs. Fay Benson and her sister, Evelyn Kidney, engaged me in conversation. They were from Cleveland, Ohio and they were also waiting for the plane flight to Rome.

Fay Benson was not a Catholic at the time. We apparently had a very significant discussion including talk about religion.

We exchanged addresses and I think I might have arranged for them to have an Audience with the Pope.

We carried on correspondence after that. December 9, 1966, some years later, Fay wrote to me and told me she was taking instructions and was going to enter the Catholic Church. Fay Benson was Baptized and became a Catholic on Christmas Eve, 1966. How mysteriously God works! Fay was Confirmed February 23, 1968.

Some years later, May 19-20, 1968 I visited Fay in Cleveland. We had become friends.

(115) Bishop Leo Binz

Bishop Leo Binz was the Bishop of Winona when I decided in 1945 to leave high school and begin preparation for the Priesthood.

After I spoke with Sr. Mary Clare and then Fr. Stephen Majerus, the Pastor at Iona, Fr. Majerus spoke to Bishop Binz about me.

Bishop Binz offered me three possibilities as to seminaries where I could begin my preparation to become a Priest: Crosier Seminary at Onamia, Minnesota, St. Mary's College in Winona, or Loras College in Dubuque. I got the impression that he preferred for me to attend Loras College. And so I sent an application there.

After a year at Loras College, Bishop Binz asked me to apply for the Theodore Basselin Scholarship. I did and I was granted that scholarship. This meant that all my expenses at the Catholic University in Washington, D.C. would be fully paid.

During my third year at the Catholic University, Bishop Binz came to Washington, D.C. for the Bishop's Annual Meeting. He asked to see all the students from the Diocese of Winona who were studying at the Catholic University. There were about five of us.

At the end of the meeting, Bishop Binz said he would like to see me. The other Seminarians all left.

When we were alone Bishop Binz asked if I ever thought about studying in Rome. I told him I did not feel I was a good enough student to do that. He said that was for him to decide.

He asked that I would think about it and prepare for it, but that I should not discuss it with anyone other than my parents and my Spiritual Director or Pastor .

You can imagine how the other Winona Diocesan Seminarians wondered what that meeting was all about, and I could not discuss it with them.

Later when I learned I would be going to Rome for Theology and I began to make inquiries about different ship companies, and pamphlets began to appear in my mail that was spread out on a table in the Reception Hall, the Winona Seminarians began to suspect I was being sent to Rome.

Shortly after I arrived in Rome Bishop Binz, together with Msgr. Dan Tierney, came to Rome and I got to see them when I had an Audience with Pope Pius XII.

I felt a real closeness to Bishop Binz, as with a friend.

Bishop Binz became the Coadjutor Archbishop of Dubuque, Iowa in 1954 and the Archbishop of Dubuque 1957-61. He was then named the Archbishop of Minneapolis and St. Paul 1962-75. He died October 9, 1979.

(116)   Vittorio Bonavenia

I came to know Vittorio Bonavenia when I became Spiritual Director at the North American College in Rome in 1962. Vittorio, who was from Sardinia, was one of the waiters at the college who served on the faculty table. He was always very friendly with me.

Vittorio was especially helpful when I went to the Island of Sardinia July 14-23, 1965. He made suggestions as to what I should see. I also visited his family in Sardinia and was treated very well.

I regret that I never saw him again after I left the College in 1971.

(117)   Jeanne Bonebrake

Jeanne Bonebrake was my sister Clara's oldest daughter. She married Richard Bonebrake and they had three children: Ann Marie, Scott and Noele.

When Jeanne went to high school with the Notre Dame Sisters in Mankato she thought seriously about becoming a Sister with the Notre Dame Order.

Jeanne's marriage to Richard Bonebrake ended in divorce. She later married Ron Hertzke and they lived in Saskatoon, Saskatchewan, Canada.

Clare and I visited them in Canada in 1983. Jeanne unfortunately had left the Catholic Church, but still seemed to be a very spiritual person.

Later when Jeanne had separated from her second husband and was back in Owatonna she became seriously ill.

I went to the hospital one evening to visit her and we had a long very serious discussion. When I was about to leave I got the impression that she wanted to return to the Catholic Church.

Jeanne died very shortly after that.

At her funeral I spoke of the visit I had with her so shortly before her death. I said that if our long visit in any way hastened her death I did not regret it because through our visit I think she had grown closer to Jesus again and wanted to return to the Church he had established.

Though I did not have much occasion to get to know her well, I felt we were friends.

(118)   Michael and Elizabeth Keane

Elizabeth Keane is Sr. Breda's sister. When I went to Ireland January 28-31, 2000 when Sr. Breda was seriously ill – (She died February 13, 2000) – I stayed at the home of Michael and Elizabeth and they showed me great hospitality.

They had two children: Erin and Heather.

Michael drove me to meet some of the family and see some of the sites. On January 30, 2000 all of the family gathered for the Mass I offered with Sr. Breda, and also celebrated the Sacrament of Anointing at the Milford Hospice where Sr. Breda was staying.

I felt especially close to Michael and Elizabeth.

(119)　Patrick and Kathleen Lyng

Patrick and Kathleen Lyng were the parents of my dear friend, Sr. Breda Lyng. Patrick and Kathleen had eight daughters.

I met Patrick and Kathleen when I visited Sr. Breda in Ireland and they were very welcoming to me and very gracious.

Patrick especially felt so honored that Mass was being offered in his home.

(120)　Sr. Margaret Mary Lyng

Sr. Margaret Mary Lyng was a sister to my friend Sr. Breda Lyng.

I met her when I visited the Lyng family in Ireland. She was stationed in France. Sr. Margaret Mary and Sr. Breda and I had dinner at Al Fico's in Rome March 26, 1967.

I saw her again when I went to Ireland shortly before Sr. Breda's death.

(121)　Br. Leonard Byankya

I met Br. Leonard Byankya in Uganda on July 31, 1969. Like Br. Majella Nsubuga, he was a member of the Brothers of Christian Instruction.

(122) Msgr. James Chambers

James Chambers was a classmate of mine when I was a student at the North American College in Rome. He was from Buffalo, New York.

He later became the Vice Rector at the North American College. I think he probably suggested to Archbishop O'Connor at the American College that I be invited to be the Spiritual Director there.

He was a good friend and very supportive of me.

Msgr. Chambers returned to the United States and died at a rather young age.

(123) Sr. Mary Clare Bofenkamp

Sr. Mary Clare from Adrian, Minnesota was one of my teachers in high school. She was a very good teacher and I liked her very much. She taught Latin.

Sr. Mary Clare was one of the first persons I spoke with about entering the seminary rather than going into the Navy during the Second World War. She was easy to talk with and did not try to force me in one direction; but simply gave me an opportunity to talk about my thoughts and feelings.

I kept in touch with her through the years. When I became Chaplain at Assisi Heights in Rochester, Sr. Mary Clare was in the Infirmary. I will never forget the joy and satisfaction she expressed when I celebrated my First Mass at Assisi Heights and took communion to her room in the Infirmary.

I continued to enjoy visits with Sr. Mary Clare in the Infirmary. She was born June 17, 1894 and died November 14, 1972. She is buried at Calvary Cemetary, Rochester, Minnesota.

(124) Countess Estelle Doheny

Countess Estelle Doheny was a good friend to Aunt Katie. She would often give clothes to Sr. Mary of St. Louis, who would then send them on to my family.

On June 14, 1944 Mother and I went to Los Angeles to see Sr. Mary of St. Louis, my aunt. One of the many wealthy friends and movie stars of Aunt Katie that we visited was Countess Estelle Doheny. She and her husband had become very wealthy in the oil business. They were somewhat involved in the Teapot Dome Scandal.

Mother and I visited Countess Estelle's elaborate home, and she also showed us some of the sites of Los Angeles.

(125) Maurice Mettler

I first met Maurice Mettler on September 27, 1988 when offering Mass at Our Lady of the Lake Church in Lake Oswego, Oregon. I was there on sabbatical. He came to daily Mass very regularly and we became friends.

His wife had died and he seemed quite lonely. He greatly appreciated the interest I showed him.

Morris had a daughter, Nancy, married to Frank Dowers. I also met them.

Even after I left Lake Oswego and returned to Minnesota, Maurice continued to write to me.

Maurice called me on March 21, 1991 and told me that he had lung cancer and was taking radiation. Maurice, after a period of illness, died on August 31, 1991.

(126) Frank and Nancy Dowers

Nancy Dowers was the daughter of Maurice Mettler who had become a good friend of mine while I was on sabbatical at Lake Oswego, Oregon, August to December 1988.

Nancy and her husband, Frank Dowers, came to visit me several times while I was at Lake Oswego.

(127) Rodella Schoo

Rodella Schoo was a classmate of mine in Grade and High School. I liked her very much and dated her a couple of times. She did not seem to show any great interest in me. On one occasion when we were together in the back seat of a car, and I put my arm around her shoulder, she very gracefully removed my arm.

Rodella married Bill Fahle and they had four children: Karen, Bill, Jim, and Vincent. They moved to San Diego, California.

I visited the family when I went to Summer School in San Francisco on August 3, 1970.

(128) Fr. Philip Farley

Fr. Philip Farley from Philadelphia came to the North American College as a Repetitor.

Fr. Farley was more conservative in his opinions than I was and we argued quite a bit, but I liked him very much. He was very intelligent and knowledgeable.

When he returned to the United States after completing his term of duty at the College I was surprised when I heard that he had married. Apparently he had become more liberal.

(129)   Fr. William Feree

Fr. William Feree was a Marionist. His address was Fr. William Feree, Marionist, via Latina 22, Roma 4, Italia. His phone number was: 760892 (or) 771892. While he entered into my life and played an important role while I was on the faculty at the North American College, 1962-1971, I do not have a strong memory as to how he influenced me. My failure to remember his interaction in my life indicates how important it is to write one's autobiography.

I do remember that there were a number of Marionist Priests or Seminarians on board ship one time when I crossed the ocean and I was very much impressed by them.

(130)   Msgr. William Forster

Msgr. William Forster from Boston was the Economo at the North American College while I was on the faculty. He was a very capable and likable person. Although he was quite liberal in his thinking, he was also very prudent.

Msgr. Forster became the Vice Chancellor of the Archdiocese of Boston on November 1, 1968.

I always admired how adept he was with the Italian language. All of the personnel at the College liked him very much.

(131)   Sr. Mary Francis

Sr. Mary Francis was a Good Shepherd Sister like my Aunt Katie. Thus I felt a special bond with her.

I remember especially a visit and good talk we had when I met her at St. Peter's Basilica, and we had dinner together.

We met later, on the Anniversary of her Religious Profession February 8, 1957. While I knew a number of Good Shepherd Sisters, Sr. Mary Francis always stood out.

One time when a number of her Sisters were going to the Holy Land, she could not go because she did not have enough money for the airfare. I gave her a fare sum of money that made it possible for her to visit the Holy Land also. She was extremely grateful.

I kept contact with her when she returned to Malaysia. She soon became ill and died at a very early age on June 7, 1970.

(132)   June Forrest

June Forrest was a girl from England whom I met when I was Spiritual Director at the North American College in Rome, and we became close friends.

June was especially helpful in 1970 when Monika Kufferath, whom I had recently met, wanted to return to Rome to celebrate Pentecost at the North American College, and could not find a place to stay. June said she had an extra room and that Monika could come and stay with her. And so she did.

June was with us for the Mass on Pentecost and for the whole day which we spent together.

June also became friends with Maureen Burke and Stephanie Rea, two other English girls whom I met March 27, 1969. They spent quite a bit of time together.

I also met June's mother when she came to Rome March 1- 4, 1971 and I gave her and June a tour of Rome. June helped me pack when I left Rome.

June became pregnant and unfortunately underwent an abortion and suffered psychologically a great deal. My friend Sr. Breda was able to help her considerably.

I eventually lost contact with June Forrest when I returned to the United States.

(133) Judith Theisen

Judith Theisen was my Secretary-Bookkeeper for a long time at St. Francis, Windom. She was very efficient and we were good friends.

Judith's husband was Leland and they had three children: Kenneth, Ryan and Stephen. They lived in the country.

(134) Gerald and Helen Galles

My brother, Gerald, was born October 7, 1925. He married Helen Hargrove. Helen became a Catholic and became very dear to me. She rendered the tremendous service to me of typing up in triplicate my Masters Degree Thesis.

Gerald and Helen never had any children. They later separated and Gerald married Jeanette October 23, 1970. They had two children: Gerald Jr. and Camilla.

Gerald was shot and killed May 18, 1974 by Carl Lee Morris. Because Carl Lee Morris was very wealthy my brother, Eugene, recommended that it would do no good to try to sue him. So he got off Scott Free. He also shot and killed his former wife.

Helen remarried after Gerald's death. Helen Bruning died February 20, 2002.

(135) Mary Ann Garland

Mary Ann Garland was born January 13 and baptized January 13; I did not record the year. I first knew Mary Ann Garland as Sr. Mary of the Cross. Sr. Mary of the Cross made her First Religious Profession October 20, 1957.

Sr. Mary of the Cross called Bishop Hickey, the Rector at the North American College, and indicated she would like to have a Confessor and Spiritual Director who could speak English. Bishop Hickey turned the request over to me.

Sr. Mary of the Cross lived at the Monastery of the Sisters of the Most Precious Blood. I went there to see her, but I could not see her and could only speak with her behind a grill.

Sr. Mary of the Cross said she would like me to come once a month for Spiritual Direction and Confession.

Thus I began going to the monastery once a month about 11 a.m. I would go into the confessional and Sr. Mary of the Cross would enter the penitent's side. I could not see her and she could not see me. My first visit was January 10, 1966.

Mr. Carol Garland and Mrs. Alice Seifert, the father and sister of Sr. Mary of the Cross, came to Rome on May 5, 1967.

Sr. Mary of the Cross began to be ill and her Superior did not really believe her. On February 23, 1968 Sr. Mary of the Cross was told that there was no cure for her illness.

On March 23, 1968 Sr. Mary of the Cross was told that she had multiple sclerosis.

On June 22, 1968 Sr. Mary the Cross gave me a relic of the True Cross of Jesus.

Sr. Mary of the Cross went to the hospital and I visited her there. This was the first time I actually saw her because she was always behind a screen or in the confessional before this visit on October 14, 1968.

I offered Mass at Sr. Mary of the Cross' hospital room on November 21, 1968, and at noon on December 4, I offered Mass at the Precious Blood Monastery with Sr. Mary of the Cross present.

At that time Sr. Mary of the Cross showed me the Instruments of Penance that she and all the Precious Blood Sisters used up until two years before that. The Discipline: there was a metal chain with which they beat their back for 10 minutes a day, a cincture that was a wire with piercing nodes which was used for an hour at midnight, and a bracelet with piercing nodes that was worn during Mass.

At my visit to Sister Mary of the Cross on December 18, 1968 she gave me her treasured Crucifix as a Christmas present. She said that Jesus had often spoken to her from this Crucifix. She also gave me the Instruments of Penance that she had shown me earlier.

I told Sr. Mary of the Cross about the 30-Day Retreat I had made in 1977 during which I had written up my whole life – 800 pages, and encouraged her to write her life and reflections.

She took my advice and began writing her life story. On January 16, 1969 she told me that she decided to name her writings "Heart Towards Heaven."

She continued to write her life story and years after gave her "book" to me.

Sr. Mary of the Cross' health continued to deteriorate, and on February 12, 1969 she spoke of her not eating for as much as a week at a time, and after that only a little soup.

I again visited with Sr. Mary of the Cross for counseling and Mass on February 26, 1969. The next day she left for the United States. I took her to the airport together with Sr. Anna Marie and Rita.

Sr. Mary of the Cross spoke of a whole new chapter of her life beginning; And so it was.

She now went to the Monastery of the Precious Blood at Manchester, New Hampshire. I was able to visit her there on September 11, 1970. I celebrated Mass there on September 12-13, 1970.

On August 19-20, 1974, I visited the former Sr. Mary of the Cross who had now left the Precious Blood Sisters and went back to her family name, Mary Ann Garland. She was living in an apartment at Manchester, New Hampshire. A gentleman, Andy Ray, who lived in an apartment above her helped her out a great deal. She seemed quite happy and content although her health was not too good. She seemed to be relieved to be away from the stresses of Religious Life.

Her sister and husband, Alice and Alfred Siefert, came to visit her. They had three children: John, Carol, and Caryn. Their address: Alice and Alfred Siefert, 33 Joann Drive, Westfield, MA 01085 (413) 568-3871

I visited MaryAnn on May 12-13, 1975. MaryAnn was able to join me for a swim at the Howard Johnson where I was staying. During my break, July 13, 1977, I again visited MaryAnn Garland. I have letters from MaryAnn dated for February 10, 1983, and January 18, 1984.

I had written a rather long letter to her which she apparently never received before her death. Her sister, Alice, read the letter and called me by phone September 29, 1997 and commented on the letter I had sent.

I regret that I did not keep in contact with Alice so I could have learned more about Mary Ann Garland's final days and death.

(136)   Sharon Ulrich

Not all of my many friendships have turned out well. My friendship with Sharon Ulrich is an example.

My acquaintance with Sharon began through Fr. Bill Anderson. After terminating his ministry at St. Adrian Parish, Adrian, Minnesota, Fr. Anderson came to live with me at Assisi Heights in Rochester on October 4, 1973. Needing rest and recuperation, Fr. Anderson resided with me until July 3, 1975.

Fr. Anderson knew Sharon Ulrich well, for she had been a teacher at St. Adrian School between the years 1965 and 1969.

Sharon used to call Fr. Anderson by telephone, and occasionally when he was out she would speak to me on the phone.

My first meeting with Sharon took place on Monday July 29, 1974 when she came to Assisi Heights to see Fr. Anderson.

Sharon was already one or two months pregnant at the time of her first visit. The father of her child was a married man from Worthington, Minnesota.

Sharon had come to know him through her work as an insurance salesperson, which she did between the years 1971 and 1978. According to statements given to me by Sharon, this man had promised to marry her.

Sharon and I had dinner together and when she came to depart she was quite evidently upset and shaking. I embraced her warmly for a minute.

Sharon's child was born in January, 1975 and she gave the child up for adoption.

Msgr. Stanley Hale played a considerable role in Sharon's life at that time. He had been Pastor at St. Mary's Parish in Worthington from 1943 to 1973, and even after his retirement continued a good friendship and counseling relationship with Sharon until his death on August 26, 1985.

Sharon worked at a number of different parishes, but usually for only a short period of time and her contract would not be renewed. She usually had conflicts with her employers who were men.

I think it was the winter or early spring of 1980 when Sharon and I shared our first physical intimacy. This was six years after our first meeting. Both Sharon and I knew this intimacy was not in keeping with the official teaching of the Church. Sharon had spent some years in a convent back in 1960-1963. She had been closely associated with church work for a number of years, and in more recent years she took courses in Theology that, perhaps, enabled her to be more updated on the current thinking and teaching of the Church than I was.

Sharon was 40 years old when I began to relate intimately with her. In a visit with Sharon on May 14, 1984 I shared with her the very personal notes I had written during the retreat. Out of the pages of very sacred and prayerful notes which I shared with Sharon the words she picked up were "my many loves."

She apparently was hoping for an exclusive relationship, and now realizing I had many good friends she became very angry, and our friendship went through a period of turmoil.

An opening for the position of Pastoral Worker occurred at St. Francis Xavier Parish, Windom, and St. Augustine Parish, Jeffers. Sharon was among those who applied for the position. She was interviewed for the position of Pastoral Worker on July 18, 1984 but was not accepted. The search committee was turned off by what they considered her arrogance.

Sharon thought I should have overruled the Search Committee's decision and hired her anyway. This I would not do.

Our relationship now continued to go downhill and Sharon threatened legal action.

On October 3, 1985 Sharon left a note at my back door indicating that she needed financial assistance because she had to receive more psychological help, and she said she believed I had an obligation and responsibility to assist her.

On October 21, 1985 Sharon informed her counselor, Fr. Ken Pierre, that she had contacted a lawyer.

Bishop Loras Waters wrote to me on November 8, 1985 informing me that Sharon was going to begin legal proceedings.

Sharon, through her lawyer, charged that I had used my counseling relationship with her to lead to an intimate relationship. She was suing both the Diocese of Winona and myself and asking for $100,000.

The case was eventually settled out of court. I did not pay anything to Sharon and I do not know if the Diocese gave her anything.

The last time I had any contact with Sharon was when she telephoned me twice and when I was not in, left a message. She stated in the message that she had forgiven me, but ended with words that indicated she was still bitter. I have often wondered what has become of her.

(137) Dave and Pat Hedelman

David and Pat Hedelman were hired July 14, 1984 as a couple to be Pastoral Workers at St. Francis Xavier Parish, Windom, and St. Augustine Parish, Jeffers. They had a son, Toby.

Dave and Pat did good work at the parishes and we became friends. However on June 7, 1985 they informed me that they would not renew their contract. The low pay we gave them (pay as to a single person) was probably the reason they felt they could not renew.

On July 28, 1985 I served a farewell dinner to the Hedelmans.

However in July, 1987 my sister, Clara, and I made an extensive trip by car to Oregon, Washington, California and Texas. On July 6, 1987 we visited the Hedelmans at Klamath Falls, Oregon. Abram Isaiah had now joined Toby as a member of their family.

Our only contact now is by mail.

(138) Most Reverend James Hickey

Bishop James Hickey was named Rector at the North American College in Rome on March 24, 1969 succeeding Bishop Reh, who had been appointed Ordinary of Saginaw. He had been appointed Auxiliary Bishop of Saginaw February 18, 1967.

I had written a letter to Cardinal Sheehan on January 20, 1969 suggesting the choice of a Rector that would enable the College to move into the future rather than being stalemated in the past.

On October 31, 1969 I had a good long discussion with Bishop Hickey about my future. He said that he would like to have me continue on at the College as the Spiritual Director for a time to create continuity on the faculty since there had been a considerable turnover. This I was quite willing to do.

Bishop Hickey was a good Rector, although I did have some differences with him, and especially over the famous homily I gave as celebrant of a Mass at the College on March 10, 1971 based on

Jeremiah 18:18-20 and Matthew 20:17-28. We had a good discussion about that and ended up not totally agreeing after a very frank discussion.

Bishop Hickey was Rector at the North American college for five years.

He then became Bishop of Cleveland, 1974-1980. He had a Doctorate in Canon Law and a Doctorate in Theology.

Bishop Hickey became the Archbishop of Washington from June 14, 1980 until the year 2000. He was elevated to the Cardinalate on June 28, 1988.

His Episcopal model was: Veritatem in Caritate – "Truth in Charity."

In January, 1988 Cardinal Hickey conducted the retreat for Pope John Paul II and his household.

The Washington Post in 1989 asked Cardinal Hickey how he would like to be remembered. Cardinal Hickey said, "First, I'd like them to say that he was always loyal to the Church, Second that he was a friend to Catholic Education, and Third, if they don't want to say the first two, at least they should chisel on the stone, "He served the poor."

After a rather long illness Cardinal Hickey died October 24, 2004. He was 84 years old.

The last time I saw Cardinal Hickey was at the North American College Alumni Convention in Washington, D.C. May 27-29, 1980.

(139)   Sr. Edmund Sullivan

I met Sr. Edmund Sullivan soon after I became Chaplain at Assisi Heights in Rochester on September 23, 1971.

Sr. Edmund's task at the time was to welcome guests who came to Assisi Heights and to make them feel at home. This she did, to a remarkable degree with regard to myself.

I cannot enumerate or measure the many ways and times she assisted me or gifted me. She made sure I was comfortable and had everything I needed at the Wilson house where I lived.

Sr. Edmund often received gifts of many kinds from people who were relatives or friends of the Franciscan Sisters. Thus I received a bicycle and a great amount of clothes and other things. She was for me a perfect example of someone who did not only preach Christianity but lived it. I felt a very warm friendship with her. This friendship continued even after I left Assisi Heights.

Sr. Edmund died December 24, 2000.

(140)   Marie Hoepner

Marie Hoepner worked at The Courier when I was Assistant Editor. She was always very friendly and helpful. I enjoyed her company.

Marie's husband died and in 1963 she married Andrew Owacke. I lost contact with her when I left The Courier and became the Spiritual Director at the North American College in Rome in 1962.

Marie's funeral was January 26, 1990.

(141)   Sister Ibone Belaustegigoitia

Sr. Ibone was born May 28, 1930, in Mexico. She made her Religious Profession with the Missionera Eucharistica on June 29.

I first met her in Rome when I was Spiritual Director at the North American College through a Better World Retreat. She was a very attractive and interesting person. In her younger years she won an international diving contest.

At one time she was in Paris, France and had a sister living in Spain.

I knew Sr. Ibone for a number of years and greatly enjoyed her.

Later Sr. Ibone left the Religious Community and married Luis Wickmann Munoz, a high ranking military person from Germany, December 2, 1972.

I lost all contact with her after that.

(142) Sr. Mary Jane Hefner

Sr. Mary Jane Hefner was a Rochester Franciscan Sister who taught many years at St. Columba School in Iona, Minnesota. She taught almost every member of my family except me. She was very well-liked, and a very down-to-earth person.

Although Sr. Mary Jane was never my teacher she always took a great interest in me, especially when I was preparing to become a priest and also after ordination. She was born December 18, 1900 and so she was 27 years older than I was, but she never seemed to really age. She had a sister whom I met who was born in 1908.

Sr. Mary Jane received the Habit in 1918, made First Vows in 1919 and Perpetual Vows in 1925. She celebrated her Silver Jubilee in 1944 and her Golden Jubilee on July 14, 1969 the Golden Anniversary of making Perpetual Vows.

I had a visit and supper with Sr. Mary Jane on August 16, 1970.

Sr. Mary Jane died August 20, 1975 at the age of 75.

Her funeral was at 10:30a.m. August 23, 1975.

(143)   Sr. Mary Julia

Sr. Mary Julia belonged to the same religious congregation as my good friend, Sr. Breda. Sr. Julia was very friendly and supportive of me during my years on the faculty of the North American College.

(144)   Donna M. (Kastning) Johnson

I remember Donna Kastning especially when she graduated from high school at Windom. At her graduation party I learned that she was going into the Army directly from high school. I thought at the time that she was such a young delicate and beautiful girl, that it seemed a shame that she would be going into the Army and would face all the challenges and changes that Army life would present.

My intuition was correct. Very shortly after enlisting in the Army she was arrested for a drug violation. I do not think she was guilty, but was framed by some of her companions.

[Recalled from my written notes is this info which related to her: donna johnson milbourne kastning, air force conspiracy to buy drugs. appelate; fought it. released 8 months, age 47; cyril iv, 20 2000, matthew 16 divorced, jt computer]

As a result she was sent to Military Prison for a couple of years. She wrote to me at the time and I tried to get her released by writing to someone Donna had suggested to me. I do not remember if she served her full-term.

I stayed in contact with her for some time after her release. She seems to have done very well. She married Cyril Johnson.

Donna Johnson's current address is: Donna Johnson, 3913 Benjamin Courts, Rocky Mount, NC 27803. Her telephone is: (252) 972-3927.

(145) Dr. Rudolph Klein

I met Dr. Rudolph Klein August 17, 1949 when I was about to board the SS Washington to sail to Le Havre, France, and then continue on to Rome to study Theology. He helped me with my luggage.

On board ship we had a good discussion on August 19, and a friendship developed.

At Paris I met Dr. Klein's friend, Irene Kraemer on August 24, 1949.

I again met Dr. Klein at the church Sacre Coeur and had dinner at the home of his friend, Irene Kraemer. The meal was a mini course French dinner with a change of wine with each course. Not accustomed to drinking so much wine I began to feel rather high by the end of the meal.

Though brief, my friendship with Dr. Rudolph Klein was quite significant at the time.

(146) Earl and Grace Krusemark

Earl and Grace Krusemark and their daughter, Julie, from Rochester, Minnesota, came to visit me in Rome April 6, 1969. Julie at the time was studying Art at Pisa, Italy.

I attended the funerals of both Earl and Grace at different times in Rochester when they died. Julie was living in Virginia at the time of her parents' death.

Earl and Grace had four children: Julie, Jean, Ruth and Ed.

Earl was born October 11, 1915, and died December 28, 2000. Grace was born in 1915 and died in 2002.

(147)   Michelle Walsh

Michelle Walsh was a postulant to the Franciscan Sisters when I became Chaplain at Assisi Heights. And so I probably saw her on a number of occasions.

On October 25, 1973 she came to visit me at the Wilson home where I lived. After a visit we had dinner together and became good friends. However I did not have much occasion to see her after that.

Michelle dropped out as a Franciscan postulant. She had been working at St. Mary's Hospital in Rochester.

Later Michelle moved to Columbus, Ohio and worked at the Westerville Pediatric Specialists, Inc., St. Anne's Medical Office Building, 495 Cooper Road, 3rd Floor, Westerville, OH 43081.

The last time I saw Michelle was at the funeral of Sr. Genevieve Speltz on November 24, 1999. She was with a friend of hers with whom she was living. My visit at that time was unfortunately very brief.

(148)   Fr. William Levada

I met Fr. William Levada when he returned to Rome for further studies 1967-1971. He went with me to to Fregene for a day's outing October 23, 1969. I again met Fr. William Levada when I was on sabbatical at Lake Oswego, Oregon, in 1988. While I was living at the Our Lady of the Lake Church Rectory he was an occasional visitor.

He was always very friendly and knowledgeable and interesting. Born June 15, 1936 he was about 52 years old at the time.

William Levada was ordained for the Archdiocese of Los Angeles December 20, 1961 in St. Peter's Basilica by Archbishop Martin J. O'Connor. Thus he would have been a student at the North American College in Rome from 1959 to 1962. He would have left the College just before I arrived in 1962. This was an additional reason for our bonding.

From 1962-1966 Fr. Levada served in parishes in the Archdiocese of Los Angeles. He went back to Rome for further studies in 1967-1961. I probably got acquainted with him during that time.

He was named the Auxiliary Bishop of Los Angeles March 25, 1983.

He was the Archbishop of Portland, Oregon 1986-1995 and was Archbishop of San Francisco 1995-2005. He was named a Cardinal March 24, 2006.

Cardinal Levada was Prefect of the Congregation for the Doctrine of the Faith under Pope Benedict XVI 2005-2012.

It is humbling to think that I was ever a friend to such an important person in the Church.

(149)   Fr. Edward Malatesta

Fr. Edward Malatesta was a Jesuit Priest very closely associated with the faculty and students at the North American College in Rome. He was like a Spiritual Director to me at several stages in my life when I had to make a major decision. He was especially helpful to me when I was nearing the end of my time at the North American College and I had to decide about my future.

I was thinking possibly of going on to get a Doctorate in Theology. He thought it would be better for me simply to use the special gifts and talents I had to guide and direct people spiritually.

In 1970, when I came back from Rome to attend a Summer School at San Francisco, I had a chance to visit with Fr. Malatesta who was at Sacred Heart Novitiate at Los Gatos, California. I also had a dinner with his parents.

I would love to get in contact with him again. He played an important role in my life for a short time.

(150) Sr. Carroll Saussy

On August 22, 1966 I left New York on the Independence to return to Rome. Three Sisters were among the passengers: Sr. Carroll Saussy, Sr. Patrice Geuting and Sr. Agnes Horrman.

I spent a considerable amount of time especially with Sr. Saussy, and it was through her that I later came to know Sr. Meg Canty.

Sr. Saussy was on her way to Rome to make a 30-Day Retreat in preparation for perpetual vows which she made on February 3, 1967.

After making her perpetual vows she returned to San Francisco, California, and later to St. Louis, Missouri, then Topeka, Kansas, and New Orleans, Louisiana, and St. Louis again.

Carroll Saussy later left religious life and married.

(151) Chris and Bernard Seidling

Chris Seidling was Secretary-Bookkeeper for me for a time when I was Pastor at Preston, Fountain and Lanesboro. She and her husband, Bernie, became good friends of mine.

Bernie was born April 8, 1951 and Chris was born June 9, 1951.

Chris and Bernie had four children: Vince, Neil, Angela and Luke. The children would at times join their mother when she came to work.

The family moved to Hudson, Wisconsin. Later Chris and Bernie moved to Florida and divorced. Bernie became involved in a complicated lawsuit.

(152) Carol (Cada) and Vernon Spitzer

Carol (Cada) Spitzer worked at The Courier office when I was Assistant Editor. The Cada family were all friends of mine and consequently Carol was also a special friend of mine.

Unfortunately I used Carol somewhat to spite Carol King who also worked at The Courier Office.

Carol Cada married Vernon Spitzer and they both continued to be friends of mine.

Carol and Vernon had five children: Bobby, Lori, Gwen, Patty Lynn and Ronnie.

Unfortunately Vernon died at a rather early adult age.

(153) Phyllis Strei (Mueller)

I met Phyllis Strei in 1972 when I was Chaplain at Assisi Heights. I think my first meeting was at a retreat I gave that she attended. She was living in Mankato, Minnesota.

Phyllis came to visit me on October 20, 1972 and a number of times after that. She seriously wanted to grow in holiness. Phyllis later married Warner Mueller and I lost contact with her. She and her husband lived in Faribault, Minnesota.

Phyllis died October 17, 1995.

(154) Alice Wills

Alice Wills and her husband Stephen lived at Mountain Lake, Minnesota and were parishioners at St. Francis Xavier Parish at Windom.

Their two children were Elizabeth and Matthew.

Alice came quite often for counseling and support. We became good friends.

Alice later moved to North Mankato, but we kept in contact by mail.

(155) Msgr. Roy Literski

Msgr. Roy Literski is probably my dearest priest friend. Although Roy is a year older than I am he was ordained a year after me. We were together as students for three years at the North American College in Rome, and during that time in the summers we traveled a good part of Europe together.

Roy was ordained as a priest in Rome on December 19, 1953. He had grown up on his father's farm in Rollingstone, Minnesota. He studied at St. Mary's College in Winona, Minnesota and then went to Rome where he studied Theology.

After ordination and his return to the United States he served as an Assistant Priest at St. Stanislaus Parish in Winona. The bishop then sent him back to Rome to earn a Doctorate in Philosophy.

Fr. Roy went on to serve as Chaplain and Professor at St. Mary's College in Winona, Rector at Immaculate Heart of Mary Seminary, and as the Bishop's right-hand man as Vicar General of the Diocese of Winona.

He was named a Monsignor and although Msgr. Literski served high offices in the diocese he always wanted to be a parish pastor. He got his wish when he was appointed Pastor at St. Stanislaus Parish in Winona for several years, and then went on to become Pastor at St. Francis Xavier Parish in Windom, Resurrection Parish in Rochester and then Rector at the Cathedral of the Sacred Heart in Winona.

Msgr. Literski owned his own home in Winona during his retirement and then moved on to St. Anne's Hospice where he continued to serve by offering Mass, Anointing the Sick and performing funerals.

Together with Fr. Leland Smith he has traveled a good part of the world. He had one sister, Eileen, who lives in Colorado.

Our friendship has continued and deepened all through the years.

(156)   Leland Smith

I first came to know and become friends with Leland Smith during the year and a half I spent at Loras College in Dubuque, Iowa. Our paths separated when I received the Basselin Scholarship and went on to study Philosophy at the Catholic University in Washington, D.C.

Later when we were both priests our friendship continued through the years. I enjoyed a number of cruises with him in his houseboat on the Mississippi River.

Though Fr. Smith later discontinued ministry as a priest our friendship has continued. He has been a wonderful host at his home in Winona.

(157)   Msgr. James Habiger

James Habiger from Owatonna was in Theology at the Catholic University when I was a Basselin student studying Philosophy. A friendship began that lasted and grew many years.

James Habiger was born February 6, 1927. He was ordained a Priest at Sacred Heart Church, Owatonna on May 19, 1951. His father had died when he was only two years old. His mother then moved from Harvey, North Dakota to Owatonna, Minnesota with Jim and his two siblings, Joe and Jean.

As a pastor Fr. Habiger served parishes in Austin, Winona and Rochester. He was my Pastor and I was his Assistant at St. John's Parish for three years, 1959-1962.

From 1960-1976, Msgr. Habiger was the Superintendent of Education for the Winona Diocese.

Msgr. Habiger moved to St. Paul in 1982 to become the Lobbyist for the Minnesota Catholic Conference, and continued in this position until 1995. He was an advocate on behalf of the poor on healthcare and education. While in St. Paul Msgr. Habiger also worked at several

Twin Cities parishes and at the University of St. Thomas where he
lived, and as Chaplain in the Legislature.

He was known for his great full laugh and he was quick to share
a joke.

Among his survivors is his sister, Jean (Habiger) Matthews of
Owatonna.

Msgr. Habiger died at the age of 85 on October 9, 2012.

He was a true friend and I think he cared a great deal for me.

MSGR. JAMES D. HABIGER

FEBRUARY 6, 1929 - OCTOBER 9, 2012

(158)   Msgr. Daniel Tierney

I first met Fr. Daniel Tierney when he came to Rome with Bishop
Leo Binz in 1959. I had just begun my studies at the North American
College in Rome. He was Editor of The Courier at the time.

Four years later my first assignment as a Priest was as Assistant Editor of The Courier and Assistant at St. John's Parish in Winona where Msgr. Tierney was the Pastor.

He was very good to me and helpful to introduce me to parish ministry as a priest and also to learn the operation of a newspaper. He actually let me do much of the parish work.

Unfortunately as time went on because of my immaturity and jealousy, friction developed during the six years I was with him in the parish and the nine years I was Assistant Editor of The Courier. After my six years with him in the parish Msgr. Tierney was transferred as Pastor, but he continued on as Editor of The Courier even after I became Spiritual Director at Immaculate Heart of Mary Seminary in Winona, and then returned to Rome as Spiritual Director at the North American College there.

Unfortunately Msgr. Tierney became addicted to alcohol in his later years. He died December 28, 1982. His funeral was January 3, 1983.

(159)   Helen Chase

My friendship with Helen Chase was unique and interesting. Fr. Vince Bertolini and I joined the Loyola University Tour Group that went to Leningrad, Moscow, Warsaw, Czestochowa and Budapest April 9, 1968-April 20, 1968.

On April 15 we were traveling by bus from Moscow to Warsaw. Fr. Jim Rausch from St. Cloud sat next to me.

At one point in the journey Helen Chase, who was with the Loyola University students, came back and asked when we would arrive at our destination. An extended conversation ensued.

Helen was standing in the aisle and I invited her to take my place and I would stand. Although her conversation went on for as much as an hour she continued to stand.

While I don't remember all we talked about it must have been very interesting. Fr. Rausch did not join in the conversation, but commented later that listening to our conversation was the highlight of the whole trip for him.

When Helen got off the bus at Warsaw she waited for me and gave me a warm hug before we went into the hotel where we stayed.

I saw Helen again the next day and possibly a number of times during the rest of our journey. We exchanged addresses and corresponded for some time even after she finished at Loyola and returned to her home in New York.

On August 9, 1968 I went to St. Cloud to visit Bishop Speltz. On that occasion I also saw Fr. Jim Rausch again and he commented on how impressed he had been by overhearing the conversation that Helen Chase and I had on the bus.

Helen sent me the book Siddhartha on January 2, 1969.

At sometime later Helen wrote and asked if I would take some friends of hers on a tour of Rome, however I was now back in the United States and that was impossible.

I only regret that I did not keep up the contact with Helen Chase. I wonder what became of her.

(160) Matthew Kelly

Matthew Kelly grew up in Australia. During his college years he underwent a profound conversion.

Matthew moved to the United States and after some time he began what has become known as "Dynamic Catholic."

Matthew was concerned that so many Catholics leave the church after Confirmation. He realized this was because most Catholics have never had the genius of Catholicism presented to them in a way that is inspiring, compelling, and relevant to their daily lives.

I first heard Matthew Kelly speak at an area Priests meeting some years ago, and I was very impressed. A couple of years later I heard him speak at the Cathedral in Winona, the church packed with people.

I joined The Ambassadors Club which seeks to support and spread the work which Matthew Kelly does through his program known as "Dynamic Catholic." I donate $100 a month to this work.

Recently I heard Matthew speak again to a packed church at Stewartville, Minnesota.

In 2014 Dynamic Catholic released DECISION POINT which is now the most used Confirmation program in America. Dynamic Catholic launched Best Lent Ever and Best Advent Ever in 2015, and nearly half a million people have experienced those free email programs.

Next year Dynamic Catholic will release Blessed First Reconciliation and Blessed First Communion as well as Better Together, Our Marriage Preparation Experience. They are also in the research phase of creating the most effective RCIA program in the world. Future planned programs are SUNDAY MASS, DAILY PRAYER, BIRTH AND BAPTISM, and DEATH AND DYING.

I am proud to support Matthew Kelly and his work, and I consider him a friend.

Matthew's wife is Maggie and they have four beautiful children: Walter, Isabel, Harry and Ralph.

(161) Br. Majella Nsubuga

I do not remember precisely the date when I first met Brother Majella Nsubuga but I think it was probably in July 1963 that he came to the Villa Caterina at Castel Gondolfo and asked if I would be his Spiritual Director. He was with the Christian Brothers of Uganda. He asked if he might see me about once a month.

I was the Spiritual Director at the North American College in Rome at the time. When we moved back into the city, Br. Majella would come to my apartment once a month regularly for Spiritual Direction. I would usually spend an hour or more time with him each month. A real friendship began to develop.

The nature of this friendship is quite evident, I think, by a letter Br. Majella wrote to me from Spain September 28, 1944. His letter was as follows:

Noviciado de San Jose,
Nanclares de la Oca,
Alaba, Spain.

September 28, 1964.
The Very Reverend Msgr. Francis Galles,
North American College,
Vatican City.

Very Reverend Father,

It is nearly three months since we parted and we have not heard from each other. I am sure you have had a very good time in United States and you are able to meet your folk and enjoy the good family affection that one expects after a year or two of absence. I guess you are back now in good shape, and already set at your work.

The 4th of October will be St. Francis Day, and that is one more reason why I have written to you, Father, to wish you in advance "Happy Feast Day." I shall certainly be united with you in prayer to pray the good Saint Francis to inflame your heart with that charity and love of souls with which his heart burned as long as he trode this wretched earth of ours. This will be one little way by which I will try to pay you back for the spiritual encouragement you have given me since divine Providence put you on my way. Indeed, since a few months I have taken the habit of remembering you in Daily Mass, but 4th of October will be special: it will be the feast of a father for a son, and being a poor religious, I will have no dollar to give but that.

Father, things did not turn out as I had expected. I had a hard time to get my passport renewed from Uganda, for I had hung on to a British passport beyond the time accorded by my new masters. I ought to have surrendered the old British passport soon after we had thrown off the colonial yoke, and demanded a new passport bearing the seal of the new regime. For my lack of allegiance I had to receive my passport nearly two months after it had been issued. And even then had it not been due to the intercession of the Viker General of my diocese I would never have received it in time to be able to come to Spain.

Thus it happened, Father, that I missed the liturgical session in Paris, which took place in July, and I was only able to leave Castel Gondolfo August 31, for Spain. Nevertheless, Providence was very good. I had ample time to work at my thesis, to help an old Brother wash the dishes and thus relieved him of our work while he cooked for half a dozen Brothers who had remained at home during the holidays, and make a good retreat preached by a warm-hearted, Italian Franciscan Friar, who told us much about the Holy Ghost and His gifts, charity-love, etc. There was certainly much food for my soul, and I took as much as I could digest at the moment.

I am here at the Novitiate trying to pick up some information from an experienced novice-master. After having heard from my superiors, it is most probable I might be given that job on my return to Uganda. So I have to be prepared, Father.

Tomorrow, the 29 September, I will be 42 years old. I have thought more seriously than ever on those 42 years of my existence on earth. I have tried to weigh it in the light of Faith. Ah, Father, it weighs very little! I have sometimes contrasted myself against these mountains here of Castile, rocky and dense as they are, volume for volume, and I have found myself a real speck of dust. Yet in this little spec there is God's image. That's the riddle, Father. I have thought of this, Father, more than I have ever thought of it before.

Then there was a time when I thought I knew something, and when I really thought I was worth something. But when a black man finds himself in the sea of white intelligences, as I actually find myself in Europe, with so much to learn and so little time at one's disposal; and when one thinks of so many people in Africa, hungry for knowledge because of its power, expecting us to come back to them with lots of it – Father, I am overwhelmed with confusion. In value of knowledge, those 42 years are worth almost nothing in contrast with what you people know, can learn and give back to your people during the same span of life. Yes, Father, I am 42; no, the skull is 42, but the brain is only of an I.Q. of an European or an American boy of 15 years of age. So, Father, I have to work, and work very hard to bridge the gap as far as it is humanly possible. And if ever you fall on some article in your readings of those unfortunate people who have started to learn at a late age, kindly lend it to me to encourage me along. Who knows, perhaps, God will give me a few more years to live, and if I am not idle, during those years, I may catch up.

But above all, Father, the 42 years appear little consoling to me, and probably that is more reason why God has kept me ignorant of so many useful things, because of sin. If I had loved and served God for my very youth like so many children here, surely I would have had more light, and greater chances would have fallen in my way. My experience of sin is that it makes the future obscure, it unsettles one in his plans, and where one's human efforts are not rewarded with tangible success, one is soon led to discouragement and even despair, in less one is sustained by the devil. Here, I not theological, but I am just telling you why I have felt, and what often passes into my head when I try to anylize the causes of my ignorance during those 42 years. I might be wrong; still I am persuaded that sin had something to do with it.

Am I ungrateful, Father? No I thank God very often for the gift of life, of my Baptism, of His mercy when I had sinned, of my vocation, and many favours besides. But sometimes, I feel afraid of Him; sometimes, I suspect that He has not forgiven us all, or that He must certainly take me to task for the sins of others, though for the latter's I also asked Him pardon. Still, who can know God's heart? Father, kindly pray for me that God may forgive us all, and that He may give me the grace to make up for the honour and glory I have not given Him during the last 42 years of my life.

Thank you, Reverend Father, for everything you have done for my poor soul during the time you have adopted me as your spiritual son.

I am, Reverend Father,
Very gratefully yours in Our Lord.
Br. Majella Nsubuga

Br. Majella Nsubuga greatly surprised me on November 4, 1964 when he gave me a gift of a beautiful black onyx crucifix from Uganda that is about a foot high. It must have cost him a great deal of money. To this day I proudly display it in my room and treasure it. This crucifix is displayed on the cover of this book.

I wrote to Br. Majella to thank him for this very precious and beautiful gift.

Br. Majella replied to my letter with a very significant and important letter on November 19, 1964. His comments about white and black people are so interesting that I reproduce his entire lengthy letter.

Instituto San Giuseppe,
Villa Ercolano 7,
Castel Gondolfo – Roma.

November 19, 1964.

The Very Reverend Msgr. F. Galles,
North American College,
Via del Giancolo 14,
Roma.

Very Reverend Father,

Your letter was as much a surprise as my gift was to you. I have really been surprised! Anyhow, I thank you very sincerely for the letter and for your kind appreciation of my token of gratitude to you, Father.

I am grateful, too, for the prayers, and for your spiritual direction. It has done me a lot of good. Besides, the sympathy and kindness with which you have always received me and listened to my spiritual problems have taught me more than you can imagine. I have learnt to listen to others patiently so as to learn from them, and be able to help them the better. When I will be given direction of souls in my Congregation, your good example will stand me in good stead.

You say, Reverend Father, that you have learnt something from my conversation with you. Perhaps, yes! If I am the first African that you have known intimately, then, my contact with you, Father, has revealed to you something of the interior of an African soul, his heart and his response to love and esteem of his person. Although I would not call myself one of the best specimen of an African soul, yet, if you have been able to cause to shine the bit of goodness that God put in me, it is because you have, from the very beginning, shown me love, sympathy, understanding and respect.

Father, don't find it funny that I talk to you like that. Since you are now my spiritual father, let me tell you something.

I think White Priests have an urgent mission to fulfill towards the colored people, and to us black men. It is a difficult job, I know. The white man has to descend from the pedestal of his superiority to where the coloured man is, take him up by the hand, and climb back with him to where God has destined both of them to be. This is not an easy job. To the White man, who has for ages been used to domineer over others, this descent means humility, patience and self-forgetfulness, and a real love-in-faith. For the coloured man, it demands courage and a will to accept to be helped, a hope in the possibility of his salvation, a break with his unhappy history which fills his heart with prejudice and with his white brother, Rancour against those sincere Whites who have a mind to go the long way to help him out of his social, economic and spiritual miseries. In other words the black man must laugh away the beclouded past and cheerfully undertake. with his white brother, the march into the future of promise. When both of them will have been able to march hand in hand as real brothers, each respecting and sincerely loving one another, then the most painful problems of colour will be solved. The White Priest, as a minister of God and the personal representative of the Good Samaritan, must pave the way.

Dear Father, you will forgive the expression, but you certainly came down from your pedestal to meet a stranger, for I was a stranger to you. You received me with love and sympathy, and kindness; and not being satisfied with that put me into a lift – what you, Americans, prefer to call an elevator – and with you, I was elevated, if I may say so, into your very office, where you have always made me feel at home. That was enough to convert me, and it would have converted any coloured man who has not been used to such receptions. Father, that is the answer to the change of heart of any coloured man: love, sympathy, understanding, and respect of his person. You have shown me all, Father, and I thank you and congratulate you: and believe me, Reverend Father, you have certainly merited more than the Ebony crucifix, which is today, and tomorrow is no more. I will give you that in love and prayer that you may be a holy minister of God, and a zealous apostle near those young men whom Divine Providence has confided to your care.

I will pray for the Seminarists who will be ordained soon. I have put your letter under the statue of St. Joseph, Patron of vocations, and to whom I have a great devotion that he take those 61 young men under his care, and prepare them to receive the Holy Orders in a saintly manner; and once they have received them, to persevere, in spite, the odds, in God's service. P.T.O.

Thanking you once again for your beautiful letter, for the spiritual encouragement you have given me up to now, and for your kind prayers,

I remain, Very Reverend Monsignor,

Very respectfully and gratefully your in Christ,
Br. Majella Nsubuga

Br. Majella and I talked one time about the possibility of the two of us going on Mission to Africa. With my suggestion and encouragement Br. Majella had made a retreat at the Better World Center at Rocca Di Papa. He was greatly inspired.

We thought that in working in the Missions in Africa I could supply the Theology and Br. Majella would know the culture. With something of this in mind Br. Majella arranged that I would be able to make a trip to Uganda for four weeks: July 24, 1969-August 27, 1969.

Br. Majella had arranged that I would be able to spend most of my time while in Uganda at the Katigonda National Major Seminary.

I was in Uganda when Pope Paul VI came for the Canonization of the Uganda Martyrs and he also ordained 12 African Bishops at Kulola Park, Uganda.

Br. Majella either took me sightseeing himself throughout Uganda or arranged for other brothers of his Order to take me on tour. I was able to see elephants, buffalos, hippos, waterbuck, antelope, warthogs and 20 lions.

After four interesting weeks in Uganda I went on to Nairobi, Kenya, where Sr. Monica Muthani, whom I knew from Rome, took me to meet her family and numerous other places in Kenya.

I returned to Rome on September 4, 1969.

After I returned to the United States from Rome in 1971 I lost contact with Br. Majella. I tried to locate him again but failed. I wonder if perhaps he was martyred in another revolution that took place in Uganda.

Br. Majella Nsubuga

(162)   Shirley Doris Gordon

My friendship with Shirley Doris Gordon was very unusual. It began with more than an hour meeting.

I flew from Rome to Cairo, Egypt on September 10, 1963, and then on September 12 I flew to Beirut, Lebanon where I met the Pilgrimage Group with which I would tour the Holy Land. That evening someone pointed out to me that there was an American with the group. I met Shirley Gordon very briefly that night.

The next day our Pilgrimage Group traveled on to Baalbek. When we got out of the vans with which we were traveling I met Shirley Gordon again.

Because the guide for our Franciscan Pilgrimage Group spoke Italian and Shirley did not, she arranged for a guide who spoke English to take her through the marvelous old Roman ruins. Her regard for the dignity of each person became evident to me when she told me the name of her guide. It was evident that she saw him as a person worthy of respect as she called him by his name.

As she walked through the ruins – interesting as they were – we seemed more interested in each other, and shared a great deal about ourselves.

Shirley was with the Malaysian Sociological Institute in Malaysia. She would be staying for a time in Baalbek, and thus she would no longer be with our Pilgrimage group. We exchanged email addresses so that we could keep in touch.

When we came out of the ruins there was a whole bunch of children waiting for us and expecting candy and other gifts. One could tend to ignore them but Shirley spoke to them in Arabic and it was evident the children were impressed because someone had regard for them. This made a deep impression on me.

We continued on our Pilgrimage and I regretted Shirley would no longer be with us.

We did, however, correspond and a real friendship developed.

On April 21-24, 1964 Shirley and her mother, Erna Kruder, came to Rome. I arranged for them to have an Audience with the Pope.

We had a dinner together at an outdoor café. I was greatly impressed to learn more about Shirley's work with the Malaysian Sociological Research Institute. This organization, which Shirley helped found, did research on the origin and influence of Islam in Malaysia. This was a way to help people have a greater regard for their background and identity.

When Shirley, who was born March 29, 1929 was about 17 or 18 years old she was going through a crisis in her life. She then saw the Catholic Church with its rules and regulations as a path that might bring more order and direction into her life. She joined the Catholic Church at that time. However with her work in Malaysia she became very interested in Buddhism, and embraced much of its teaching, and no longer practiced her Catholic faith.

After some time in Malaysia Shirley's mother became very eager to return to the United States. Shirley who was in a wheelchair due to an accident tried to hasten the work she was doing on a book she was writing and worked day and night, so she could accompany her mother back to the States.

The people who lived in Erna Kruder Gordon's home failed to move out and Erna was in a very unhappy situation for some time. Thus on March 1, 1966 she committed suicide. Shirley later described her mother's suicide as "spitting at life."

Shirley called me from the States and said she would be passing through Rome on the way to Malaysia and would like to see me. I met her at the airport at Rome and tried to give her the support she needed at the time.

It was during that visit when I took a picture of Shirley at my apartment. I gave the film to one of the students at the American College to develop. When he brought an enlarged photo of Shirley to me I realized it was quite a remarkable image. I asked the student to make another copy of the picture so that I could send it to Shirley in Malaysia. Shirley had the photo on display and some photographer who saw it commented that it must have been taken by some famous European photographer. I continue to treasure that picture.

After I returned to the United States Shirley and a friend of hers, Fatimah Haran from Malaysia, came to visit me in Rochester.

At the time a demonstration was planned in Rochester to promote the return of American Servicemen's bodies to the States. When she heard about it Shirley wanted to join in the demonstration. I joined her in the only political demonstration in which I have ever participated.

Because of her identification with the Arabic culture and Buddhism Shirley changed her name to Alijah. On July 9, 2003 Alijah sent me a copy of the book "On Becoming Alijah" which she had written. In this 400 page book, Part I: From the American Revolutionary War through Burma, March 1957, is a story of Alijah's life. It is the story of the person who did a tremendous amount of work to help the people of Malaysia to come to a better understanding of their culture and the influence of Islam upon it.

I do not know if Alijah ever got around to writing Part 2 of her life. However through the years of our friendship Alijah sent me more than a half-dozen books that she either wrote or edited. It almost seems impossible that one person could have done so much in the course of her life. Each of the books is a treasury of knowledge and experience.

Alijah was also responsible for the publication of "Intisari" which was a monthly newsletter.

Alijah was involved in a political demonstration in the Philippine Islands at one time. As a result a Court Order was brought against her that would not permit her to re-enter Malaysia. At her request I wrote a letter at the time defending her and seeking a reversal of the Order so that she would be able to return to Malaysia. Eventually the suit against her was lifted and she was able to return there.

Alijah returned to the United States for a visit October 1-30, 1986.

Alijah died November 18, 2003 at the age of 74.

(163)   Fay Benson

My relationship with Fay Benson was rather brief but significant.

I met her at Lourdes on July 2, 1966 when I went there with Fr. Al Giaquinto. I was not feeling very well at the time. Fr. Giaquinto had left and gone on to Paris. I was waiting for my flight back to Rome.

Because I was not feeling well I was not interested in visiting with anyone. However Mrs. Fay Benson from Cleveland, Ohio and her traveling companion, Evelyn Kidney, engaged me in conversation. Fay was not Catholic at the time. We had a considerable period of conversation and exchanged addresses.

In Rome we met again and I arranged an Audience with the Pope for them. I am not sure if there was a connection, but on December 9, 1966 I received a letter from Fay Benson in which she told me that she would be baptized and enter the Catholic Church on Christmas Eve.

(164)   Fr. John Marshall

Fr. John Marshall was appointed as Economo or Business Manager at the North American College in Rome on September 5, 1969 to replace Fr. Magaldi.

Fr. Marshall was always very friendly and supportive. He tended not to take sides in controversies.

(165)   Bishop Francis Reh

Bp. Reh became the Rector at the North American College on September 5, 1964 succeeding Archbishop Martin J O'Connor. He continued in that position until 1968 when he became Bishop of Saginaw, Michigan. I was a Spiritual Director at the College from 1962-1971, thus our terms of office overlapped.

Bp. Reh was quite progressive in his leadership, but at times we had some rather strong discussions and differences. After one of these very heated discussions in the Dining Room, Bp. Reh returned to the Faculty Room and said to the faculty members present, "Frank is a saint." He was referring to the way I had borne up under his very heated disagreement with my stance and position. I probably tended to favor the position the students held.

One of these times of disagreement occurred at a Faculty and Student Council Meeting that took place in the Recreation Hall. At one point in the discussion Bishop Reh said that he is not going to invite priests to leave a position in the States and become members on the faculty where they would have less to say then the students have.

I spoke up and said that I agreed with the Bishop, especially in regard to rules in the rulebook that were totally ignored by the students and were thus quite meaningless. Bishop Reh asked what I was referring to, and I pointed out that the rule of silence in the rulebook was totally ignored by the students. The Bishop said that rule is no longer in the book, and the students all chimed in and said it is. It was then that a committee of faculty and students was set up to rewrite the rulebook.

I liked Bishop Reh in spite of our disagreements at times. He went on to become the Bishop of Saginaw, Michigan in 1968 until he resigned April 29, 1980.

Bishop Reh died in Saginaw November 14, 1994. He was 83 years old.

(166)   Ann Patterson

Ann Patterson was one of those persons who was sent to me by someone so that I might show them around Rome. Thus I met Ann Patterson and a friend of hers, and became friends with them. They were studying in Ireland at the time.

Ann lost the buckle on her shoe, and I took one of the buckles from my Msgr. shoes and gave it to her. She was quite proud to be able to sport shoes with a Msgr. Buckle.

Ann Patterson and Kathy Hansen visited with me in my apartment at the North American College on December 25, 1967. The next day we made a tour of the Catacombs, St. Paul Outside the Walls, Castel Gondolfo, St. Peter in Chains and St. Mary Major. We also did some bowling at the College, and had supper in my room. Brian Turner from Toronto, Ontario, Canada was also with us. He later gave me a picture book of Canada.

Back in the United States, I had a visit and pizza with Ann Patterson and Tom Gibson on August 1, 1968.

Ann Patterson and Thomas Gibson married on August 1, 1969.

(167)   Sr. Muriel Gag

Sr. Muriel Gag became my Secretary-Bookkeeper on October 29, 1971.

Sr. Gretchen Berg, as Head of the Franciscan Community of Sisters, made the appointment. I got the impression that Sr. Muriel did not really want to take on this job, but I liked her very much and she did very well in this work.

Later Sr. Muriel left the Franciscan Community. She died February 16, 2008.

(168) Lori Erding

Lori Erding was a neighbor when I became Pastor at St. Columban Church in Preston.

On November 13, 2002 I had my right hip replaced at Methodist Hospital by Dr. Robert T. Trousdale. I returned home on November 18, 2002.

Lori Ecker came and rendered invaluable service during the time of my recovery at home.

Lori and Gregg Erding married April 28, 2001.

(169) Marlene Vos

Marlene Vos was a close neighbor of mine when I was Pastor of St. Francis Xavier Parish at Windom. Her husband, Chuck, was also a good friend of mine. They had two children: John and Tammy.

For a time Marlene, although she was not a Catholic, served as Bookkeeper for the parish. I always felt a close friendship with her and with Chuck.

Chuck died at a rather early age and Marlene moved to Mesa, Arizona for a time. She is living in Rochester, Minnesota but still enjoys returning to Mesa, Arizona to see friends.

Our friendship has continued and I again received Marlene's Christmas card and letter in 2016.

(170) Genevieve Vedder

I am deeply indebted to my Aunt Katie (Sr. Mary of St. Louis) for the deep and important friendship that I developed with Genevieve Vedder and to her husband Milton W. Vedder.

Genevieve Vedder was one of the many friends that Sr. Mary of St. Louis had developed in Los Angeles, California. Some of them had considerable wealth and some were movie stars like Irene Dunne, for example.

When I was a Senior in High School, Genevieve Vedder learned through my aunt that I was planning to study to become a priest. My aunt knew, of course, that my family did not have a great deal of money. Aunt Katie, who had already helped my family in many ways, made known to Genevieve by aspirations and need. Genevieve offered to pay all my education expenses if I studied to be a priest.

In June 1944 mother and I went to Los Angeles, California, to see Aunt Katie. At that time I probably also saw Genevieve Vedder, but I don't have any clear memory of meeting Genevieve at that time. I do seem, however, to remember her ranch and the orange trees there.

When I left high school in the middle of my senior year and began studies at Loras College in Dubuque, Genevieve began to help me out financially.

When I received the Theodore Basselin Scholarship to study at the Catholic University in Washington, D.C., for three years all of my education expenses were paid by the scholarship. However Genevieve sent me money to pay for my clothes and personal expenses.

Then when I studied Theology in Rome for four years, the Diocese of Winona paid my tuition at the North American College, but Genevieve sent me considerable money for my personal expenses and to be able to travel throughout Europe during our summer vacations.

Genevieve paid for the beautiful chalice I had made in Rome. It cost over $200, but would be worth much more today.

Genevieve was not able to attend my ordination on December 20, 1952, but she gave $400 to the fund that was raised to enable my parents to make the trip to Rome and to attend my ordination.

When I studied at the University of San Francisco in the summer of 1970 I made a trip to Los Angeles July 30-August 4. During that time I had a dinner with Genevieve Vedder, Michael and Patricia Rye and Phil Johnson.

I still have the many letters Genevieve Vedder wrote to me all during the years I knew her.

My last visit with Mrs. Vedder was on July 7, 1980.

Milton Vedder died May 4, 1961 and Genevieve died April 23, 1985.

(171)   Sr. Bernice Jirik

Sr. Bernice Jirik came to me for counseling at Assisi Heights, and we became good friends.

Born September 17, 1935 Sr. Bernice was eight years younger than I. She died September 14, 2011.

(172)   Fr. Leroy Eikens

Fr. Leroy Eikens was born November 4, 1920.

After I was invited to be the Spiritual Director at the North American College in Rome, Bishop Fitzgerald asked me to conduct a retreat for a number of persons preparing to receive Holy Orders. Leroy Eikens was among the persons who made that retreat. That was my first meeting with him.

Later as a Priest Fr. Leroy and I tended to have a similar viewpoint in regard to many things pertaining to the Church. Thus we enjoyed a close relationship.

I visited him a number of times during his convalescence prior to his death.

I was asked to deliver the homily at his funeral. Like myself, Fr. Eikens felt that the Church was somewhat backtracking after the Second Vatican Council. I received numerous accolades in regard to this homily which I gave at Fr. Leroy's funeral.

(173)   Archbishop Martin J. O'Connor

Bishop O'Connor was the Rector at the North American College in Rome when I was a student there from 1949-53.

I greatly admired the work Bishop O'Connor did in starting up the college again after the Second World War and then building the new North American College on the Gianicolo Hill. The students had many stories about him because of his somewhat reclusive nature. We spoke of him having so much dignity that he could form a one-man procession.

I felt greatly honored in 1962 when I received a letter from Bishop O'Connor inviting me to become the Spiritual Director at the North American College. I served under him until November 5, 1964 when Bishop Reh succeeded him as Rector. Bishop O'Connor was elevated to Archbishop on September 5, 1963. During those years I could only admire him more for his ability and dedication.

The conflict between Archbishop O'Connor and Cardinal Spellman was quite generally recognized. I saw the great ability of Archbishop O'Connor when he welcomed President John F. Kennedy and Jacqueline to the North American College on July 2, 1963.

After the Second Vatican Council Archbishop O'Connor carried on the tasks of the Council by the work which he did with the Communications Commission that had been set up by that Council.

I remember the event that Archbishop O'Connor told about when he was waiting for a meeting he was to have with Pope John XXIII. When the Pope arrived late and got out of his car he kept repeating

"Bugie, Bugie, Bugie" – ("Lies! Lies! Lies!") That apparently was the response he had to a meeting that he had just attended with some high Vatican official.

Archbishop O'Connor died on December 1, 1986 at the age of 86.

(174)   Mary Ann Burnell

MaryAnn Burnell visited at Assisi Heights quite often when I was Chaplain there. Thus I came to know her early in my years there. I invited her to dinner at the Wilson home on November 20, 1972.

I visited with her again on June 18, 1973. By that time we had already become very good friends. On July 14, 1983 I had supper at Chippewa Falls, Wisconsin at 10:30pm with Mary Ann.

On July 18, 1985 I had lunch with Mary Ann and Sr. Geraldine. At that time Mary Ann was thinking very seriously of joining a Religious Community. That was the reason she was with Sr. Geraldine. This was the last time I saw Mary Ann and I have often wondered what became of her.

(175)   Phyllis Strei

Sr. Phyllis Strei came to Assisi Heights while I was Chaplain there. I know I had a visit with her on April 13-14, 1973. She came for Spiritual Direction and we became friends.

We met again on May 28, 1973, June 9-10, 1973 and again on December 29-30, 1973.

Sr. Phyllis Strei left the Franciscan Community and married Mr. Muller.

(176)   Sr. Thaedeen Jirik

Sr. Thaedeen Jirik first came to me at Assisi Heights for counseling on June 21, 1973. Through the many times she came to see me, we became friends. Checking my appointment book Sr. Thaedeen came to me over 27 times in the course of the years.

Later on Sr. Thaedeen went back to her Baptismal Name of Bernice. Sr. Bernice died September 14, 2011.

(177)   Sr. Mary Teresa Carroll

Shortly before I completed my time as Spiritual Director at the North American College in Rome I was invited to accompany a group of Sisters to Assisi, Italy and to conduct a retreat for them. During our time at Assisi I got to speak with and to get to know all of the Sisters in the group except Sr. Mary Teresa Carroll who seemed to be quite distant and uncommunicative.

Fortunately as we were about to return to Rome by bus on July 14, 1969 I happened to get the seat next to Sister Mary Teresa Carroll. We had a wonderful discussion all the way back to Rome. So much that I arranged to meet sister Mary Teresa at the Sisters Convent after the retreat. She shared with me some of the material we had discussed on our bus ride. I visited with Sr. Mary Teresa in Boston on August 15, 1970.

Through ongoing correspondence a friendship began to develop. When I made a 30-day Retreat at Glouchester, Massachusetts in 1977, Sr. Mary Teresa came on our free day July 25, 1977 and spent the day with me. We had dinner together and our friendship greatly deepened.

The following year when I made another 30-day Retreat I was hoping that Sr. Mary Teresa would again come and spend the day off with me but she did not call back and we did not get together.

In spite of the disappointment our relationship continued by correspondence. I wrote to her before Christmas and sent a donation of money. You can imagine my shock and horror when one of the Sisters in her Community wrote to inform me that Sr. Mary Teresa had been killed in an auto accident on December 22, 2004.

At my request a Sister of her Community sent me a picture of Sr. Mary Teresa. This has helped to keep alive the memory of the friendship that had begun in a rather mysterious way and continued to grow.

Sr. Mary Teresa Carroll

(178)   Bernice Bertrand

Bernice Bertrand, born August 9, 1926 was a year ahead of me in Grade School and High School. I was attracted to her, but thought of her as being out of my class since her family was quite wealthy.

I used to envy her when each day at lunch she would have an orange or some other fruit.

We corresponded when I went to Loras College to begin studying for the Priesthood. However after a time I wrote to her and said I thought we should not continue the correspondence, lest it might lead me away from my vocation toward the Priesthood. To this day I continue to regret having written that letter.

Bernice graduated from St. Catherine College in St. Paul, Minnesota on June June 7, 1948. She also attended the University of Minnesota. She later worked as a Registered Nurse at St. Joseph's Hospital in St. Paul and also taught Student Nurses at the Worthington Minnesota Hospital.

She never married.

Bernice came to visit me at Assisi Heights on May 9-10, 1975.

She later developed an illness that considerably distorted her features. One time when I was at home in Iona I failed to recognize Bernice and she remarked that I did not ever recognize her.

Bernice died April 17, 1987. Her funeral was on April 23, 1987. She was 60 years old.

(179) Kathy Attwood

Kathy Attwood began work as my Secretary-Bookkeeper on August 15, 1991. Before her marriage to James Attwood she was Kathleen Wherley. James and Kathy had two children: Jessica and Emily.

Kathy was born November 15, 1957 and James was born September 16, 1956.

I used to enjoy very much the discussions Kathy and I had over coffee in the mornings.

Kathy left a note for me that she was resigning effective August 15. She apparently was angry in regard to something I had done. She had applied for and was expecting to be hired for another job. When this other job fell through she wanted her job back.

We had in the meantime interviewed another person for the job as Secretary-Bookkeeper. Kathy thought I could have intervened and kept her on if I had wanted to do so. Kathy's last day at work was October 4, 1993.

I enjoyed an Italian dinner with Jim and Kathy on March 30, 2001.

(180)   Lisa O'Connor

Lisa O'Connor began as Religious Education Coordinator at St. Columban and St. Patrick's on August 15, 1991. Lisa held this position for only a brief time. She remarried and moved to Owatonna, Minnesota.

At Jerome O'Connor's suggestion I gave my Yamaha piano to Lisa, for which I had paid $1,478.70.

(181)   Mr. and Mrs. John Rouen

Mr. and Mrs. John Rouen were among the many wealthy friends that my aunt, Sr. Mary of St. Louis had. The Rouens were also very supportive and generous to me.

Mother and I went to Los Angeles in June, 1944 to see Sr. Mary of St. Louis (Mother's sister) and among Sr. Mary of St. Louis's many friends we also saw Agnes and John Rouen.

Agnes took us to Bell Air and Good Shepherd Church.

We also met Rouen's sons John and Pat. A daughter, Peggy, was married.

(182)   Irene Dunne

Irene Dunne, the famous movie star, was one of Sr. Mary of St. Louis's many friends. Sr. Mary of St. Louis spoke to Irene Dunne about me. I have three letters that Irene Dunne wrote to me.

While I was a student at the North American College in Rome, I received a letter from Irene informing me that she would be in Rome and would be happy to meet me.

I spent quite a time getting permission from Msgr. Richard Burns, the Vice Rector at the College, to be able to visit a woman at a hotel.

On May 11, 1950 I went to the Excelsior Hotel where Irene was staying and had a nice visit with her. She was very gracious and down-to-earth. I also met her husband, Dr. Francis Griffin, and their teenage daughter, Mary Frances.

(183)   Lucille Herrick

Lucille Herrick was among the 56 participants who made the Christian Community Retreat which I gave at Winona July 24-29, 1966. She was so impressed with my work that she gave $1000 for the retreat and said that she would raise $1800 more.

I continued to correspond and stay in contact with Lucille for some time.

(184)   Kathleen (Kathy Horvath) Moriarty

Kathy Moriarty was born November 5, 1949.

Kathy was a Pastoral Worker at St. Pius Parish, Rochester, when I first met her. I think our first meeting was October 10, 1976. We became friends and she came a number of times to visit me when I was Chaplain at Assisi Heights. Because of her education and background she was very helpful to me. Later, Kathy became Religious Education Coordinator.

Kathy came to see me about once a month for five years. She was very creative and knowledgeable and thus I enjoyed her company very much. We became very good friends.

I became Associate Pastor at St. Pius X in 1977-78 when they needed extra help. Thus I also had more contact with Kathy.

After I moved from Assisi Heights and became Pastor at Windom and Jeffers, we still saw each other a number of times.

Kathy met Jim Moriarity and became very attracted to him and they married. They later moved to Florissant, Colorado where I visited them on one occasion.

Kathy (Horvath) Moriarty

(185) Jesus Christ

My last and very best friend is Jesus Christ. Though I have never seen him in the flesh, touched him and felt the warmth of his hand, I have come to know him and love him with every fiber of my being.

Even before I began school I heard his name and began to be enthralled by the stories I heard about him. He seemed so distant and yet so very close.

When I was told I would receive him into my heart with my First Communion, I hardly knew what to expect.

As time went on the stories about Jesus became more engaging. While I was growing in knowledge and love of Jesus, I was also becoming aware that I could disappoint and offend him by sin, and yet sin became a part of my life.

From a rather early age, probably when I was in the Seventh or Eighth Grade, I began to feel that I might be invited to be a special friend of Jesus by becoming a priest. This urge may have been drowned out at times as I began to be attracted to women.

Nevertheless the desire to do something meaningful with my life persisted and in my late High School years, I began to feel that I wanted to be united with Jesus as a friend by becoming a priest.

The growth of that friendship with ups and downs continued throughout my seminary years.

On December 20, 1952 when I was ordained as a priest, the realization that I was now a special friend of Jesus came without a great deal of feeling.

Through 64 years as a priest I felt ups and downs about my friendship with Jesus.

Many friendships which I have described, have entered into my life. In and through these friendships, I often experienced real love.

Now in my old age I see more and more that Jesus gave these many friendships to me so that I might grow in my ability to love and give myself away in true friendship.

Thus I have come to see that my friendship with Jesus is the origin and basis for all my many friendships. And so I have come to realize that my friendship with Jesus is the most important of all my relationships. I want to spend my remaining hours of my life nurturing and cherishing this greatest friendship for which I was created and toward which my whole life is moving and expanding.

Yes, without a doubt, my friendship with Jesus is the last and greatest of all my friendships.

185 of My Many Friendships

Dr. Maureen Burke (253)
Patricia Capek (253)
Shirley Carter (254)
Don Claseman (254)
James & Mary Cook (255)
Dharmini Cropper (255)
Mike & Sue Curley (255)
Glen & Mary Ann Davis (256)
Jean (Anderson) DeWall (256)
Hank & Mary Clare Doran (256)
Phil & Heidi Dybing (257)
Sylvia Gail (Galles) Ellsworth (257)
Sr. Agnes Fleming (258)
Jeanette Fortier (258)
Joy Fox (259)
Carolyn Freese (259)
James & Jerrie Gabriel (259)
Leola & Viola Ehleringer (260)
Leo & Joanne Hansen & Kathy (260)
Fatimah Herran (261)
Blanch (Hargrove) Jarrett (261)
Don & Elsa Hofmeister (262)
Msgr. Warren Holleran (262)
Sr. Cynthia Howe (263)
James & Katherine Hust (264)
Rose Ann Hamm (265)
Michael & Elizabeth Keane (266)
Francis Kelly (266)
Sr. Mary Elizabeth Keyser (267)
Fr. Tony Kilroy (267)
Carol King (267)
The Obritsch Family (269)
Arlette Kvam (269)
Sr. Anna Marie Lionetti (271)
Peggy Lovrien (271)
Novella Meisner (272)
Agnes Meium (273)

Arneta Middendorf (273)
Octavia Miles (273)
Sr. Placida Wrubel (273)
Anne Phylis Muchiri (274)
Camellia Mukherjee (275)
Luna Nino (276)
Carla Noack (276)
Fr. Robert Nogosek (276)
Gayle (Buse) O'Brian (276)
Jerome & Sharyol O'Connor (277)
Mary Lou Ogle (277)
Dan & Linda Ortmann (278)
Colleen Ortmann (278)
Angelo & Julie Otero (279)
Beverly Peterson (279)
Stephanie (Rea) & Nigel Pollard (281)
Sr. Amata Schleich (282)
Sr. Helen Rolfson (283)
Donna Schmidt (283)
Msgr. Don Schmitz (284)
Eddie & JoAnn Schneider (284)
Klaus & Karin Schneider (285)
Sr. Trudy Schomer (286)
Sr. Seton Slater (286)
Mary Sotebeer (286)
Ellen Speltz (287)
Katherine Sveen (287)
Arleen Tacke (288)
Monica Tayler (288)
Pamela Thompson (289)
Emily Torgrimson (289)
Lawayne Trom (289)
Marge (Kuisle) & Bill Urlick (291)
Prathiba Varkey (292)
Sr. Cabrini Walch (293)
Charlie & Karla Warner (293)
Fr. Theodore Weber (293)

Mary Whalen (294)
Sr. Hildegundis Lang (294)
Klaus & Ursula Wodsak (295)
Jean Anderson (295)
Ludwig Behan (296)
George Bell (299)
Mrs. Fay Benson (300)
Bishop Leo Binz (301)
Vittorio Bonavenia (302)
Jeanne Bonebrake (302)
Michael & Elizabeth Keane (303)
Patrick & Kathleen Lyng (304)
Sr. Margaret Mary Lyng (304)
Br. Leonard Byanka (304)
Msgr James Chambers (305)
Sr. Mary Clare (305)
Countess Estelle Doheny (306)
Maurice Mettler (306)
Frank & Nancy Dowers (307)
Rodella (Schoo) & Bill Fahle (307)
Fr. Philip Farley (307)
Fr. William Feree (308)
Msgr. William Forster (308)
Sr. Mary Francis (308)
June Forrest (309)
Judith Theisen (310)
Gerald and Helen Galles (310)
Mary Ann Garland (310)
Sharon Ulrick (313)
Dave & Pat Hedelmann (316)
Most Rev. James Hickey (316)
Sr. Edmund Sullivan (317)
Marie (Hoeppner) & Andrew Owecke (318)
Sr. Amaya Belaustegigoitia (318)
Sr. Mary Jane Hefner (319)
Sr. Mary Julia (320)
Donna M. Kastning (320)

Dr. Rudolph Klein (321)
Earl & Grace Krusemark (321)
Michelle Walsh (322)
Rev. William Levada (322)
Fr. Edward Malatesta (323)
Sr. Saussy Carroll (324)
Chris & Bernard Seidling (324)
Carol (Cada) and Vernon Spitzer (324)
Phyllis (Strei) Muller (325)
Alice Wills (325)
Msgr Roy Literski (326)
Leland Smith (327)
Msgr James Habiger (327)
Msgr Dan Tierney (328)
Helen Chase (329)
Matthew Kelly (330)
Br. Majella Nusabuga (331)
Shirle Gordon (339)
Fay Benson (342)
Fr. John Marshall (343)
Bp. Francis Reh (343)
Ann Patterson (344)
Sr. Murial Gag (344)
Lori Erding (345)
Marlene Vos (345)
Genevieve Vedder (346)
Sr. Bernice Jirik (347)
Fr. Leroy Eikens (347)
Archbishop Martin J. O'Connor (348)
Mary Ann Burnell (349)
Phyllis Strei (349)
Sr. Thaedeen (349)
Sr. Mary Teresa Carroll (350)
Bernice Bertrand (351)
Kathy Attwood (352)
Lisa O'Connor (353)
Mr. & Mrs. John Rauen (353)